ROBERT SMALLS:
TALES
OF THE
TALENTED
TENTH

WORDS AND PICTURES
JOEL CHRISTIAN GILL

CHICAGO
REVIEW
PRESS

First edition

Published by Chicago Review Press Incorporated
814 North Franklin Street
Chicago, Illinois 60610
ISBN 978-1-68275-066-7

Library of Congress Control Number: 2021932774

Cover design: Joel Christian Gill
Cover illustration: Joel Christian Gill

Printed in the United States of America.

5 4 3 2 1

Contents

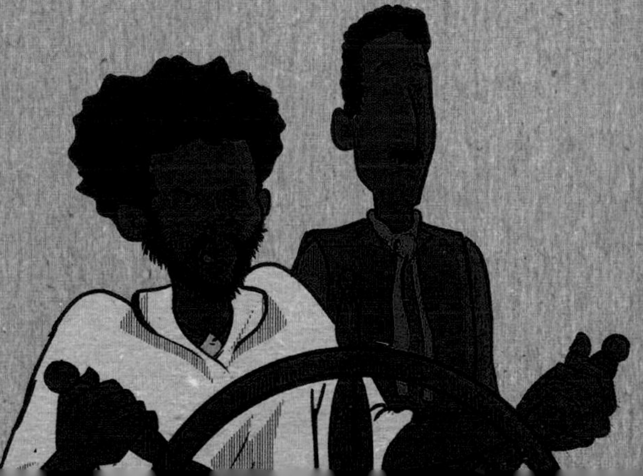

Foreword

Comic books are no stranger to men and women who know how to make themselves invisible. Cloaked in disguise and aided by special powers or gadgets, these alter egos often seek justice through clandestine means for a greater good. It would be easy to cast Robert Smalls in this light. At only 23 years of age, the enslaved African American deckhand from South Carolina dared to emancipate himself during the Civil War by seizing a Confederate ammunitions transport ship, and imitating the White captain long enough to sail the vessel out of Charleston harbor. He risked his life and that of 15 others, including his wife, Hannah, and their children, to navigate through the fog in hopes of finding refuge with the Union Navy.

Eyewitness accounts supply us with the sights and sounds of a daring adventure: the captain's floppy straw hat pulled low over a brown-skinned face; the Confederate battle flag hoisted high alongside the state's white palmetto tree and crescent moon; and the special signal that Smalls knew the checkpoint guards would be waiting to hear — two long whistles and one short. Writing in 1947, historian Carter G. Woodson describes how Smalls, camouflaged in a gold-trimmed jacket, folded his arms and leaned against the windowsill of the pilothouse to approximate the casual stance of the captain. Then, with Fort Sumter behind him, Smalls steered in the direction of the Union blockade, knowing that if the US sailors couldn't see the white bedsheet now flying from the Rebel ship's mast, the fugitives would be blown out of the water. Only caped crusaders would put themselves in so much danger!

Yet we need not analogize Smalls as a superhero (or a super human) to prove that he was worthy of freedom and fully capable of claiming it. Neither praise nor the rhetoric of battle that the Civil War setting so readily provides is necessary to argue that his cause was just. His portrait doesn't have to be larger than life for us to understand why he would be willing to sacrifice everything to make that life better.

Joel Christian Gill shows that we can also honor the Lowcountry freedman by seeing him, first and foremost, as a person. Through word and image, this volume of Tales of the Talented Tenth places Smalls's humanity at the heart of his undeniable heroism. We see the resolve born of the hurt and indignity he suffered as an adolescent and later, as a father denied the chance to buy his own family out of bondage. We see his intelligence in action and track his deliberations among a courageous community, using the knowledge he obtained as an enslaved laborer to plan their escape. And with each illustration, we recognize Smalls, not by the stamped copper slave tag around his neck, but by the determined gleam in his eye.

The early morning heist on May 13, 1862, was only the beginning of his days in freedom. There is so much more to learn about the man who would go on to become a soldier, a businessman, and a US congressman with enough resources to buy the very property on which he was born enslaved. For those who may be discovering Robert Smalls and the origins of his secret identity for the first time, the riveting pages of this comic are a perfect place to start.

Dr. Qiana Whitted
Professor of English and African American Studies
at the University of South Carolina.
Author of the Eisner Award-winning book,
EC Comics: Race, Shock, and Social Protest

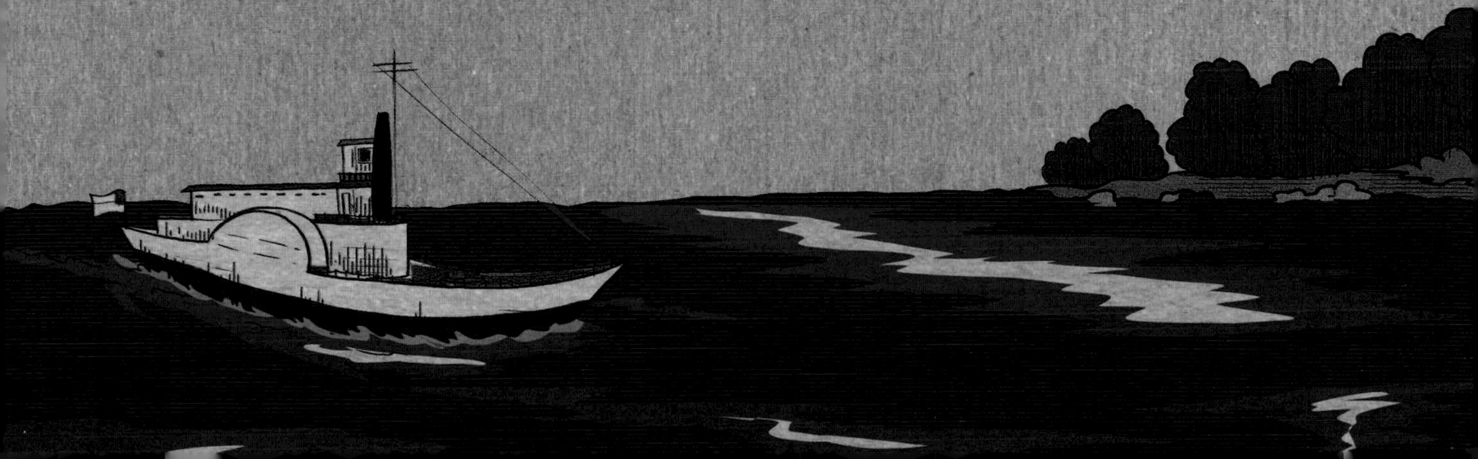

Introduction

When I came up with the name "Tales of the Talented Tenth," it was after reading an essay from W. E. B. Du Bois about how Black people need a "talented tenth" to rise up and lead them to the fabled better place. I write this in the summer of 2020, the summer of our continued discontent with the dehumanization of Black people, and it's clear to me that the talented tenth are following the 90% who are standing up and telling us that it's the forgotten majority whose stories deserve to be told.

That doesn't negate the premise of what the series Tales of The Talented Tenth is about. It does, however, shift its meaning a bit. The talented tenth are a group of people who have been ignored by history to the extent that when we hear about them, we often say, "I can't believe that I have never heard of them." These extraordinary people are examples of how biases embedded in society and culture have ignored the remarkable stories of Black people.

The stories of Black people's accomplishments in the realms of art, politics, science, society, and culture belie the common (and conceived) notion that Black people are inferior. When I write and draw stories immortalizing Black people performing brave, heroic, or ingenious feats, I'm striking out at that narrative and saying that society has portrayed Black people disingeniously. The cunning lawman outwitting villains in the Old West, or the adventurous Black woman riding her motorcycle all around the world don't fit the narrative of Black people being something wholly different and inferior to White people. The courageous enslaved African trying to win his freedom at all cost is the the same shiftless, lazy, and stupid individual who we see portrayed in media and pop culture for most of the 20th century. It is a false narrative. The 90% object loudly to that narrative.

Tales of The Talented Tenth is for the 90%. These stories are what the 90% have longed for; stories that deserve to be told about people who look like them. These stories are also for people who want to expand their ideas and knowledge base. Black people make up 13% of the population in the United States, but how much of American culture is dominated by what Black people have created? The 90% know how much we have contributed [a lot] and cry out for their stories to be heard.

The Tales of the Talented Tenth started out as stories about those talented few, but as my research has shown, more than a few have been ignored, and the people, all the people, want to be seen.

Joel Christian Gill
#28daysarenotenough

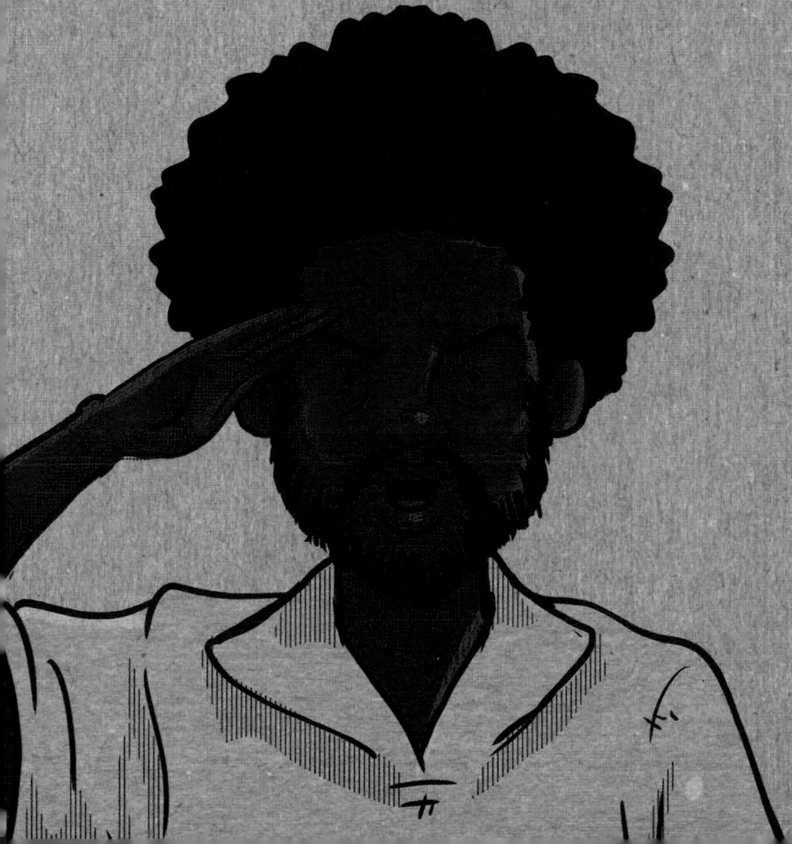

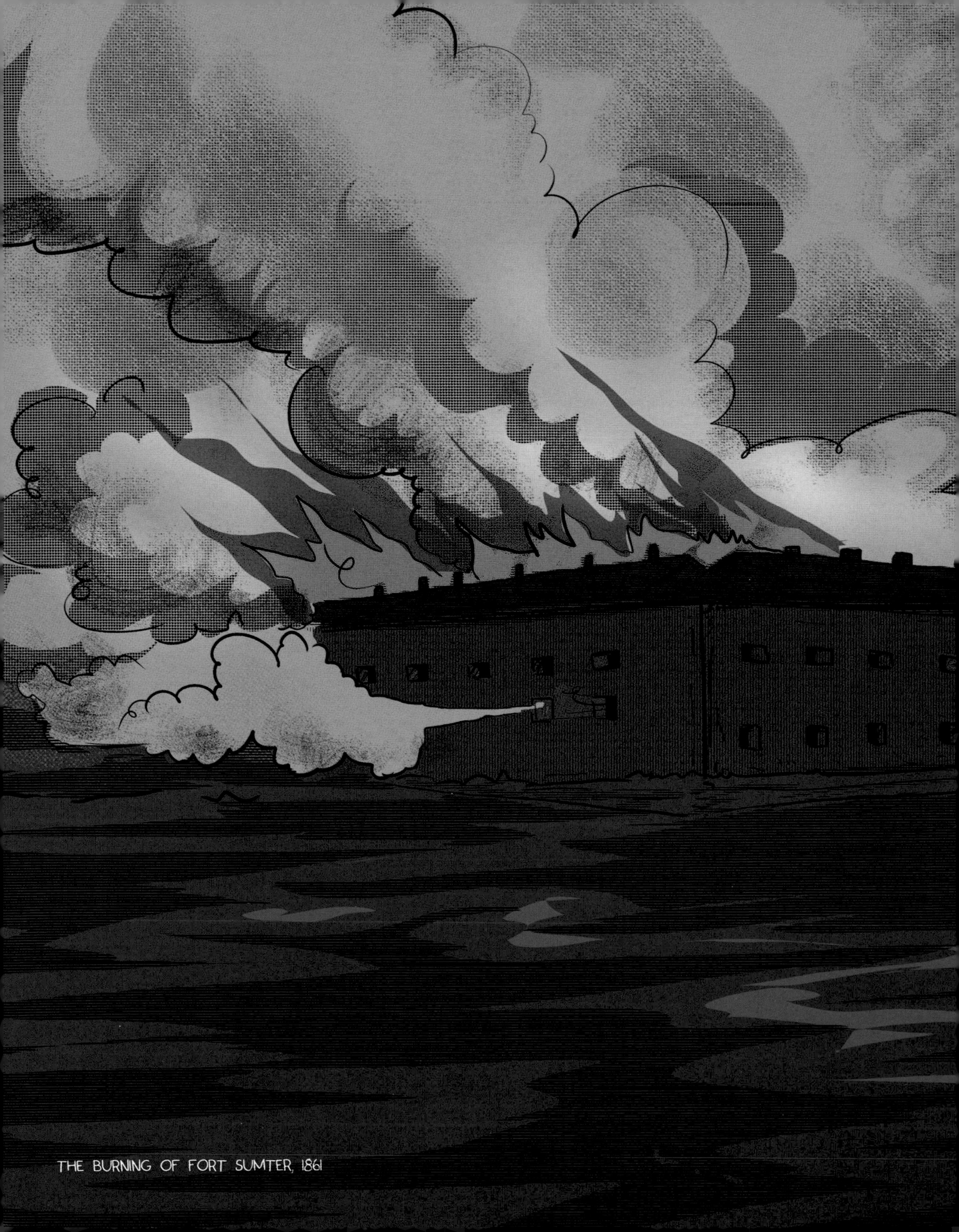

THE BURNING OF FORT SUMTER, 1861

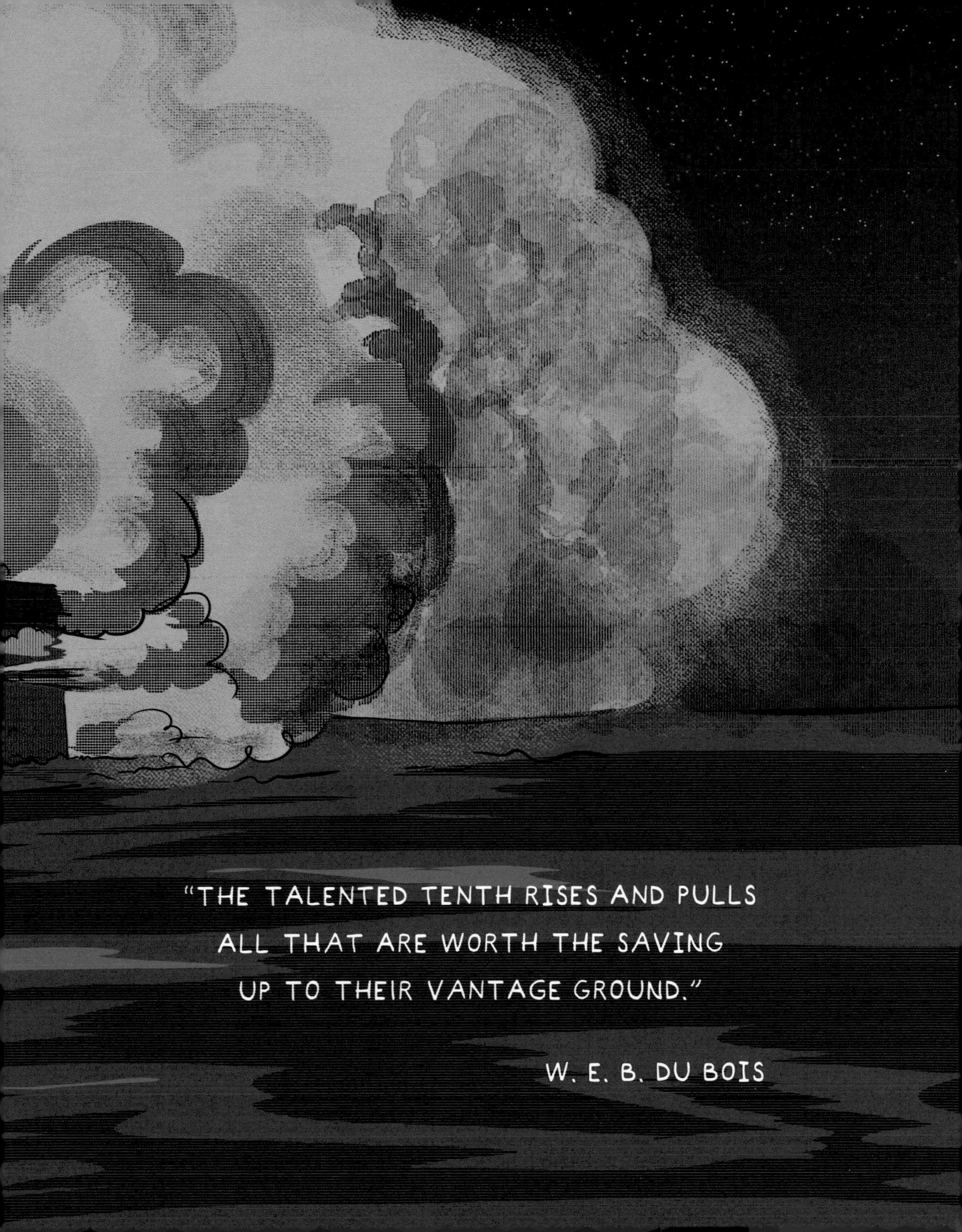
"THE TALENTED TENTH RISES AND PULLS
ALL THAT ARE WORTH THE SAVING
UP TO THEIR VANTAGE GROUND."
W. E. B. DU BOIS

PROLOGUE

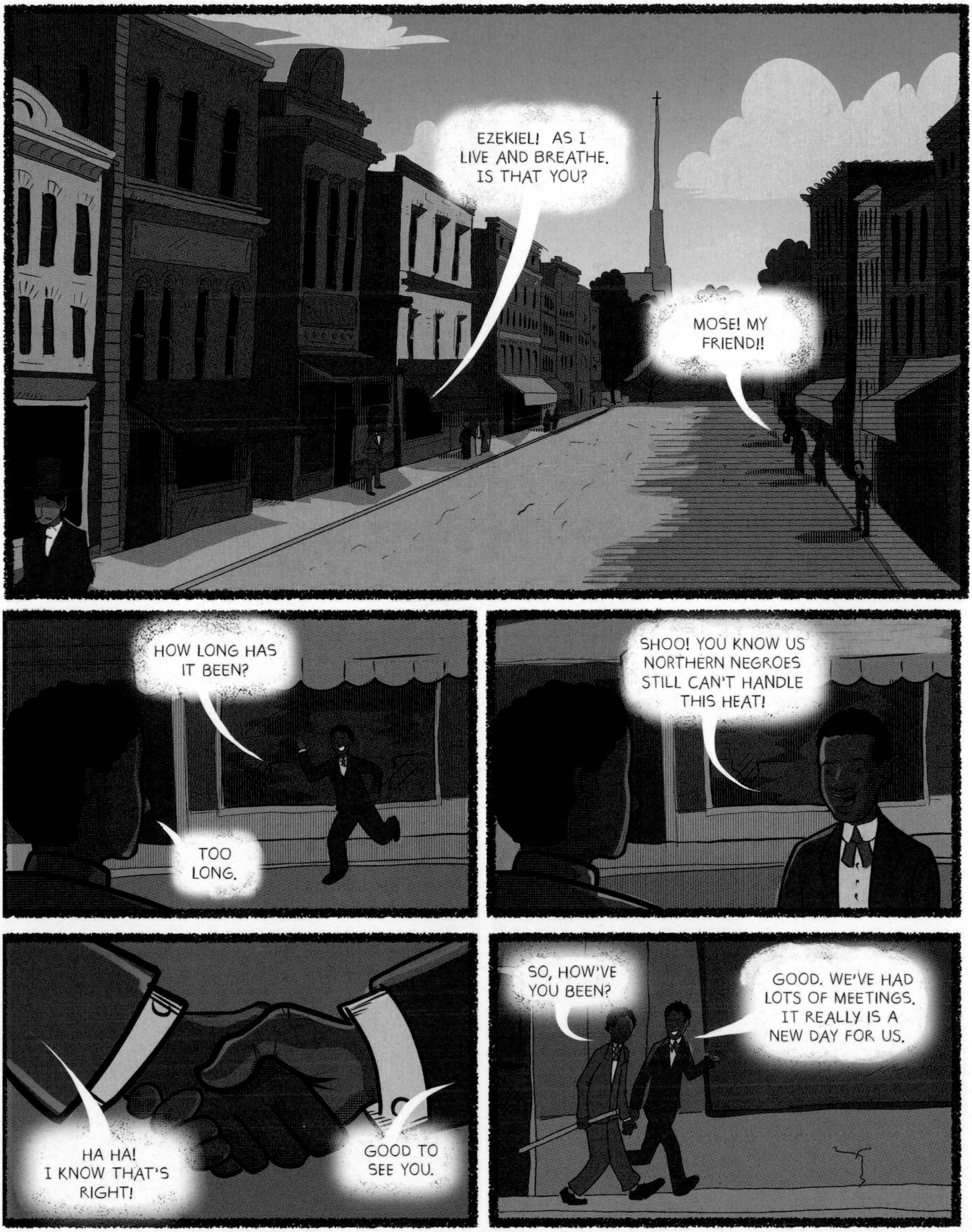
EZEKIEL! AS I LIVE AND BREATHE. IS THAT YOU?
MOSE! MY FRIEND!!
HOW LONG HAS IT BEEN?
TOO LONG.
SHOO! YOU KNOW US NORTHERN NEGROES STILL CAN'T HANDLE THIS HEAT!
HA HA! I KNOW THAT'S RIGHT!
GOOD TO SEE YOU.
SO, HOW'VE YOU BEEN?
GOOD. WE'VE HAD LOTS OF MEETINGS. IT REALLY IS A NEW DAY FOR US.

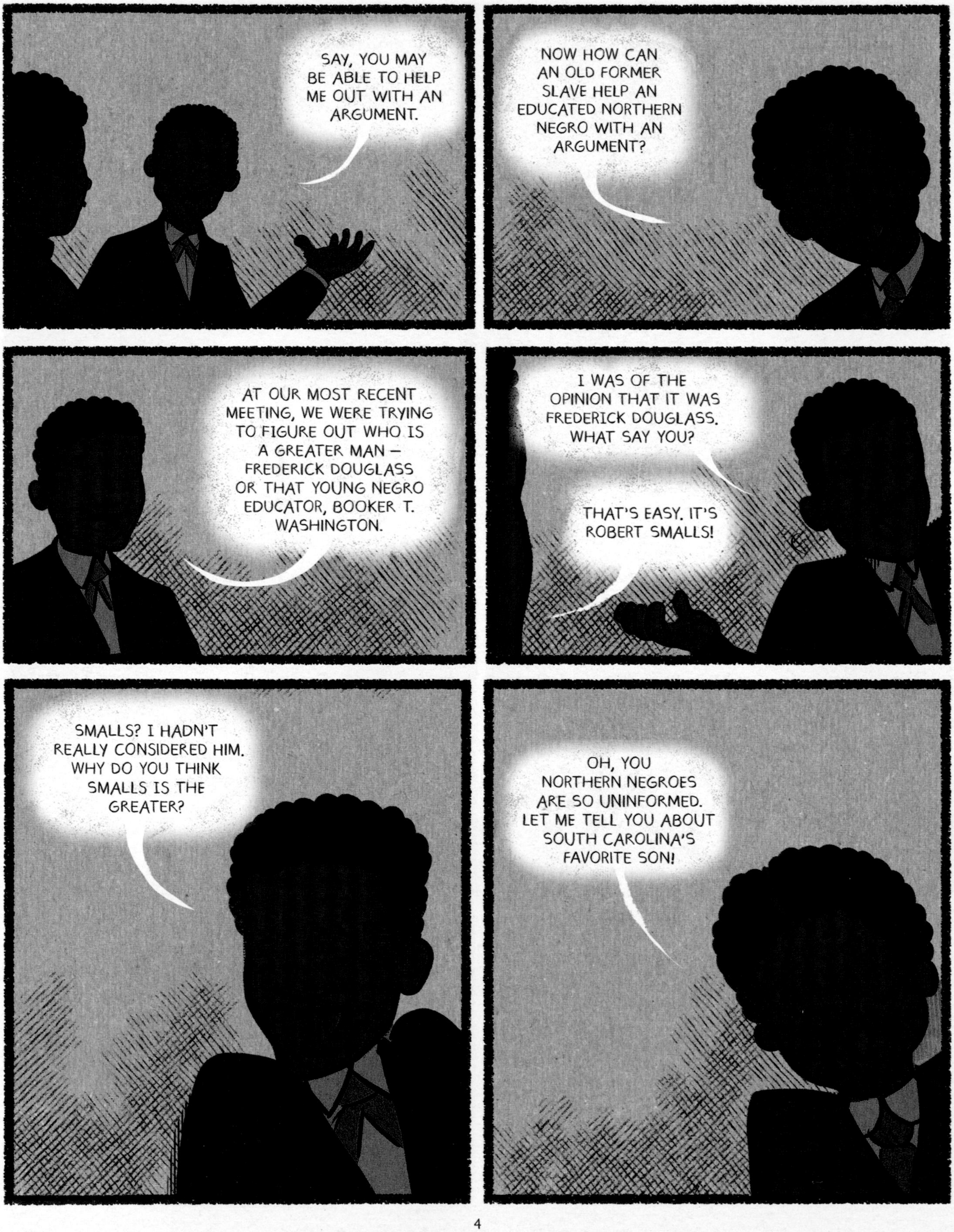
SAY, YOU MAY BE ABLE TO HELP ME OUT WITH AN ARGUMENT.
NOW HOW CAN AN OLD FORMER SLAVE HELP AN EDUCATED NORTHERN NEGRO WITH AN ARGUMENT?
AT OUR MOST RECENT MEETING, WE WERE TRYING TO FIGURE OUT WHO IS A GREATER MAN — FREDERICK DOUGLASS OR THAT YOUNG NEGRO EDUCATOR, BOOKER T. WASHINGTON.
I WAS OF THE OPINION THAT IT WAS FREDERICK DOUGLASS. WHAT SAY YOU?
THAT'S EASY. IT'S ROBERT SMALLS!
SMALLS? I HADN'T REALLY CONSIDERED HIM. WHY DO YOU THINK SMALLS IS THE GREATER?
OH, YOU NORTHERN NEGROES ARE SO UNINFORMED. LET ME TELL YOU ABOUT SOUTH CAROLINA'S FAVORITE SON!

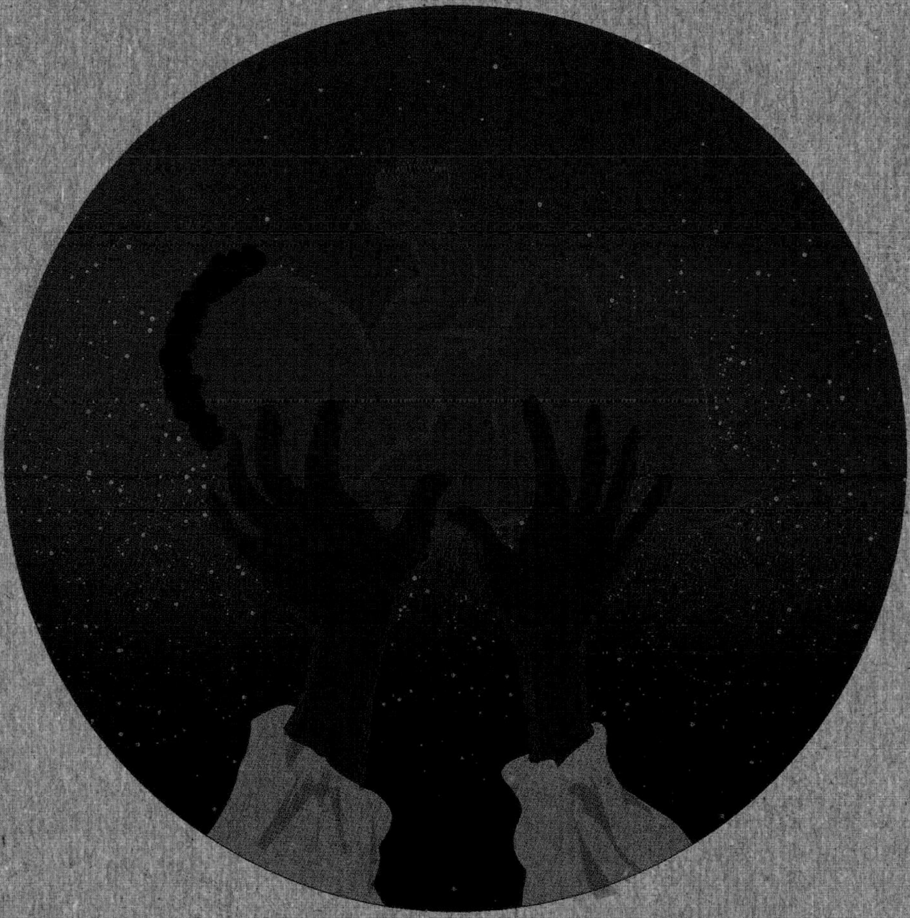

CHAPTER ONE

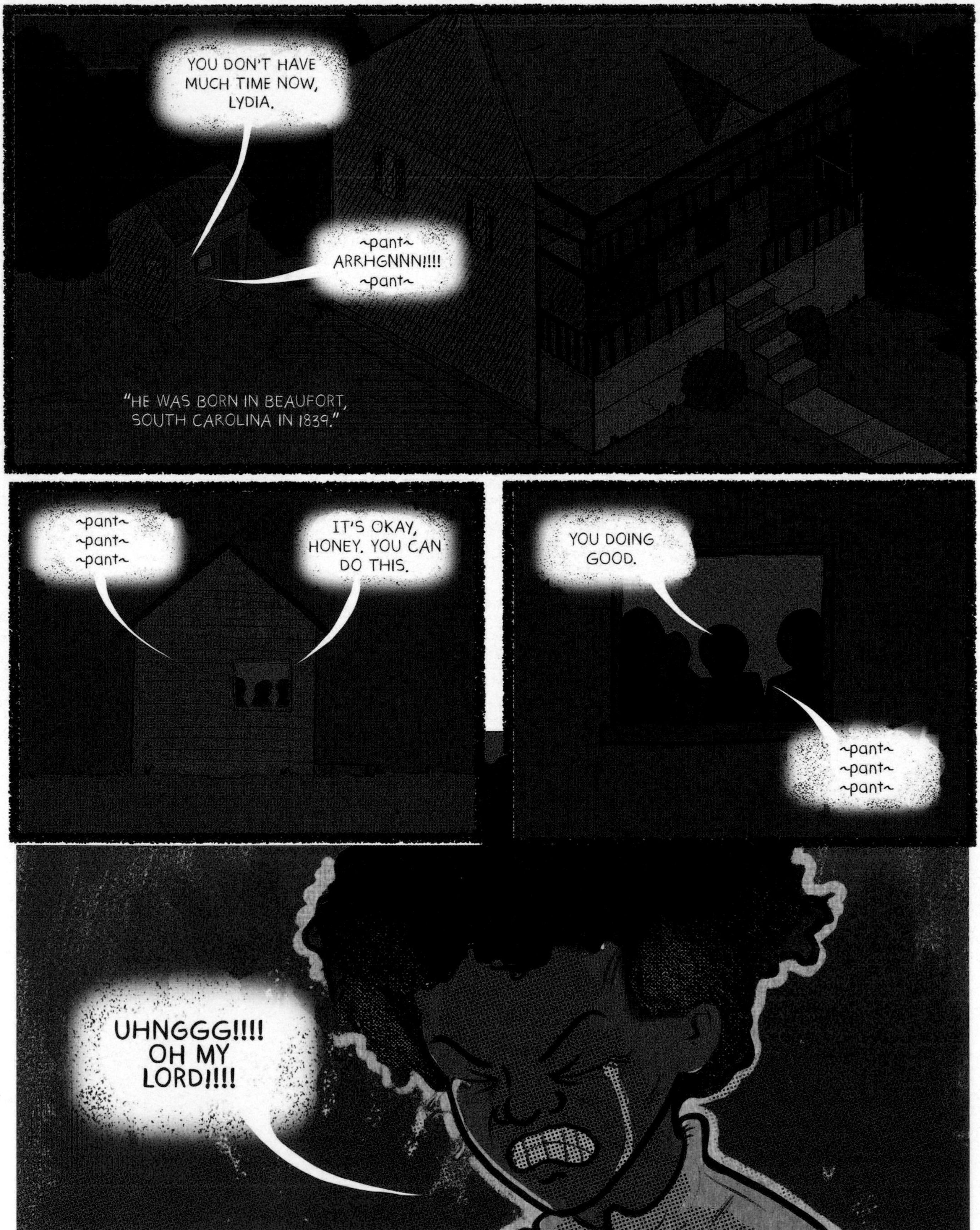
YOU DON'T HAVE MUCH TIME NOW, LYDIA.
~pant~ ARRHGNNN!!!! ~pant~
"HE WAS BORN IN BEAUFORT, SOUTH CAROLINA IN 1839."
~pant~ ~pant~ ~pant~
IT'S OKAY, HONEY. YOU CAN DO THIS.
YOU DOING GOOD.
~pant~ ~pant~ ~pant~
UHNGGG!!!! OH MY LORD!!!!

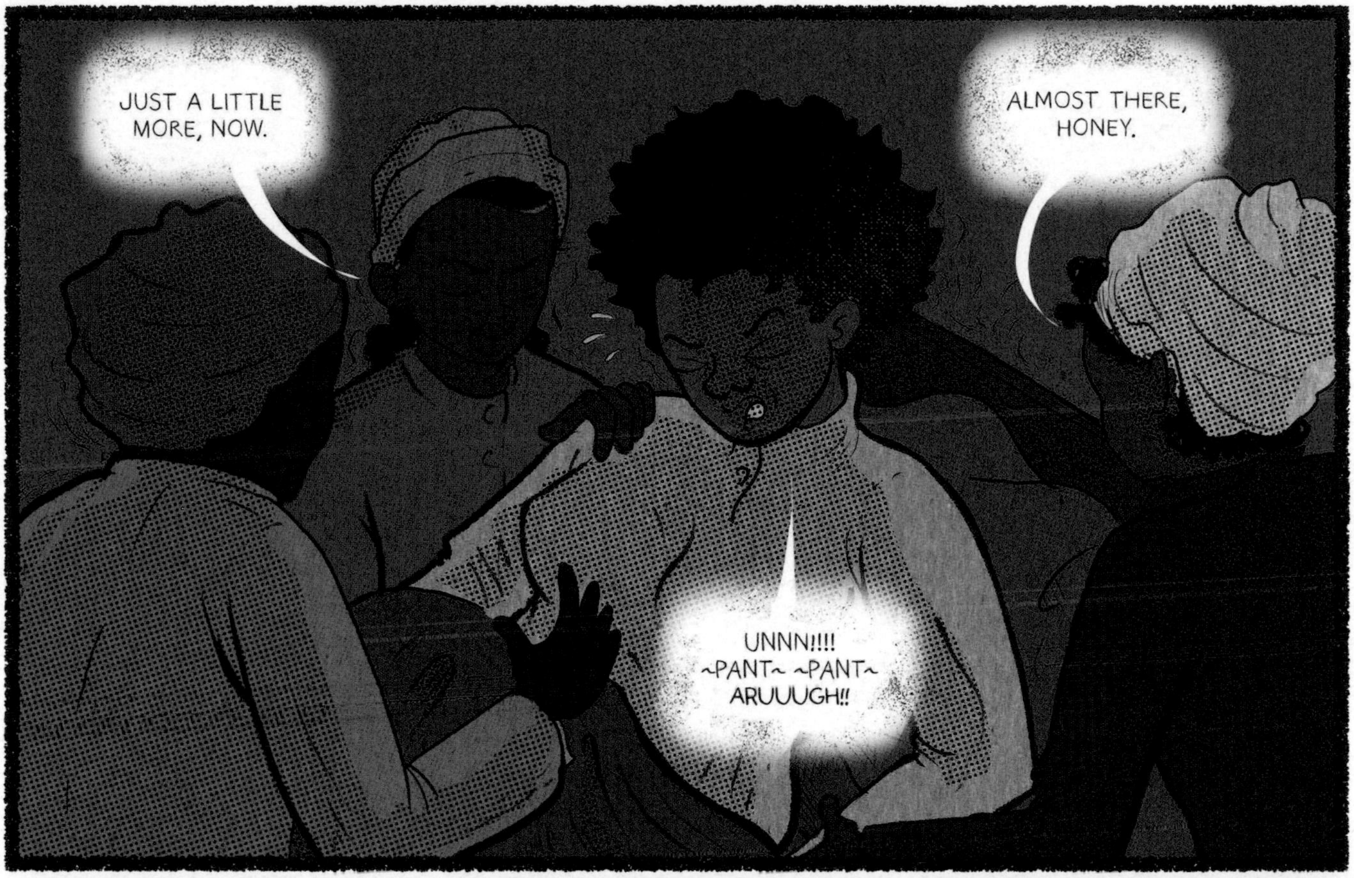

JUST A LITTLE MORE, NOW.
ALMOST THERE, HONEY.
UNNN!!!! ~PANT~ ~PANT~ ARUUUGH!!

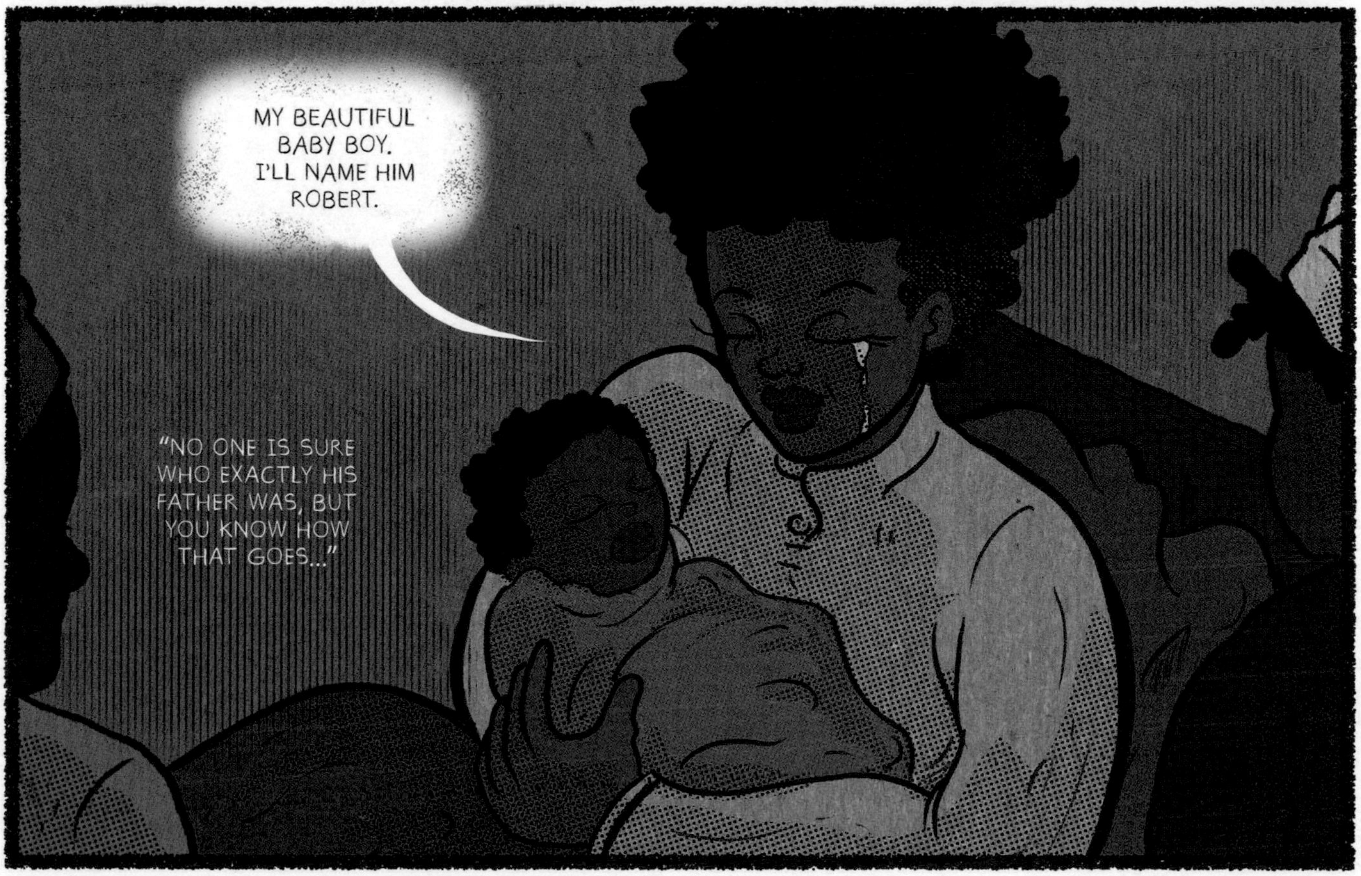

MY BEAUTIFUL BABY BOY. I'LL NAME HIM ROBERT.
"NO ONE IS SURE WHO EXACTLY HIS FATHER WAS, BUT YOU KNOW HOW THAT GOES..."

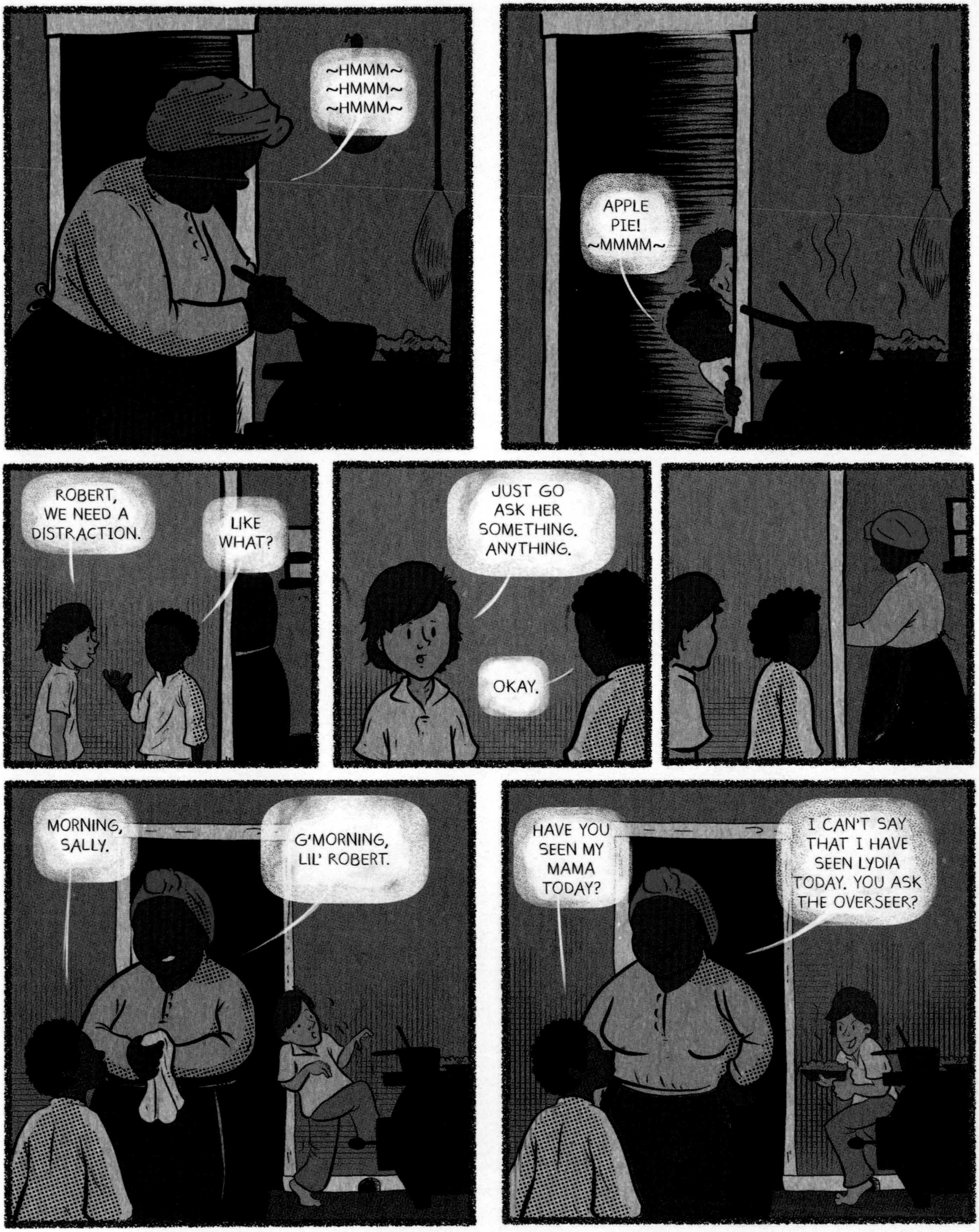
~HMMM~ ~HMMM~ ~HMMM~
APPLE PIE! ~MMMM~
ROBERT, WE NEED A DISTRACTION.
LIKE WHAT?
JUST GO ASK HER SOMETHING. ANYTHING.
OKAY.
MORNING, SALLY.
G'MORNING, LIL' ROBERT.
HAVE YOU SEEN MY MAMA TODAY?
I CAN'T SAY THAT I HAVE SEEN LYDIA TODAY. YOU ASK THE OVERSEER?

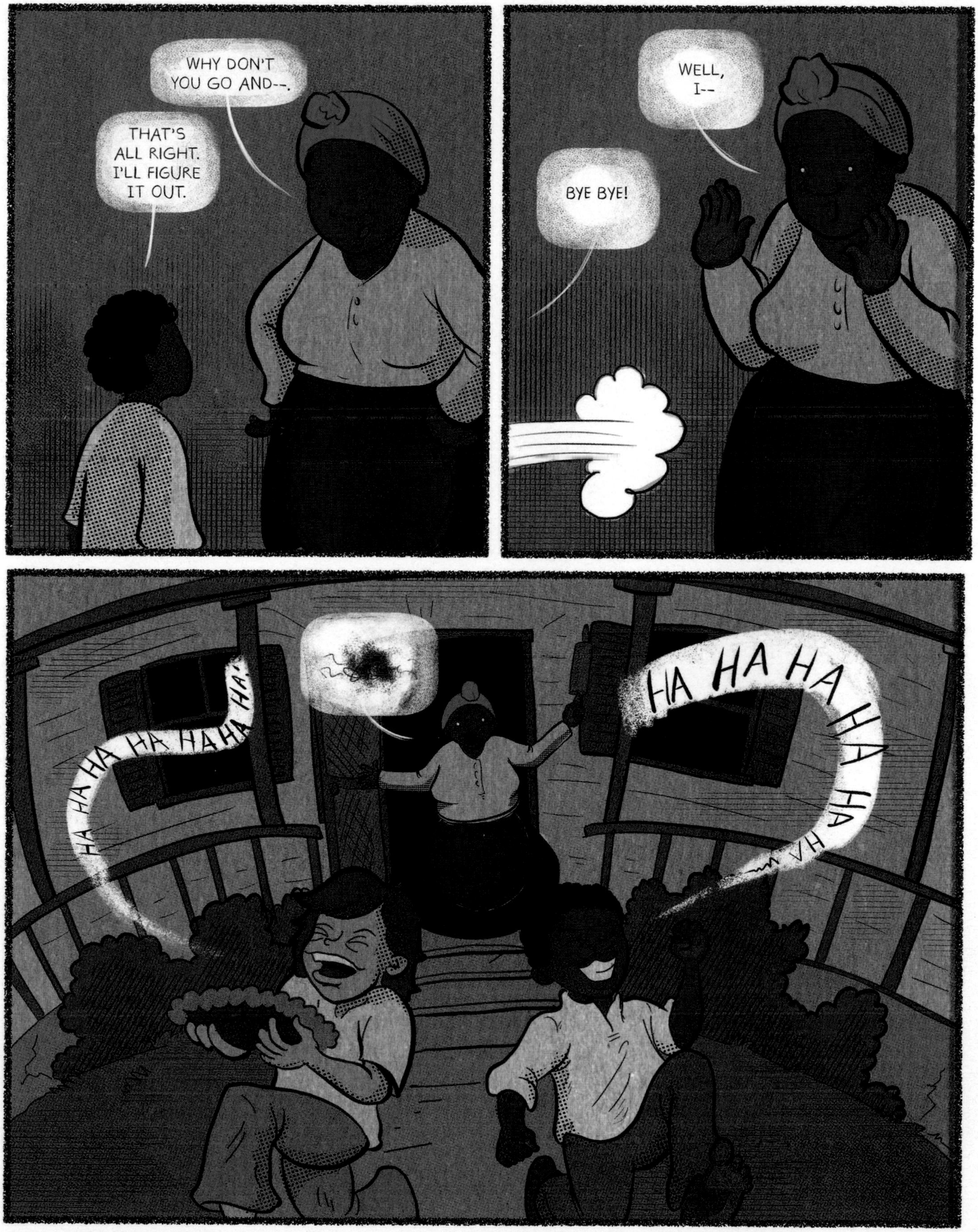
WHY DON'T YOU GO AND--.
THAT'S ALL RIGHT. I'LL FIGURE IT OUT.
WELL, I--
BYE BYE!
HA HA HA HA HA HA HA!
HA HA HA HA HA HA HA

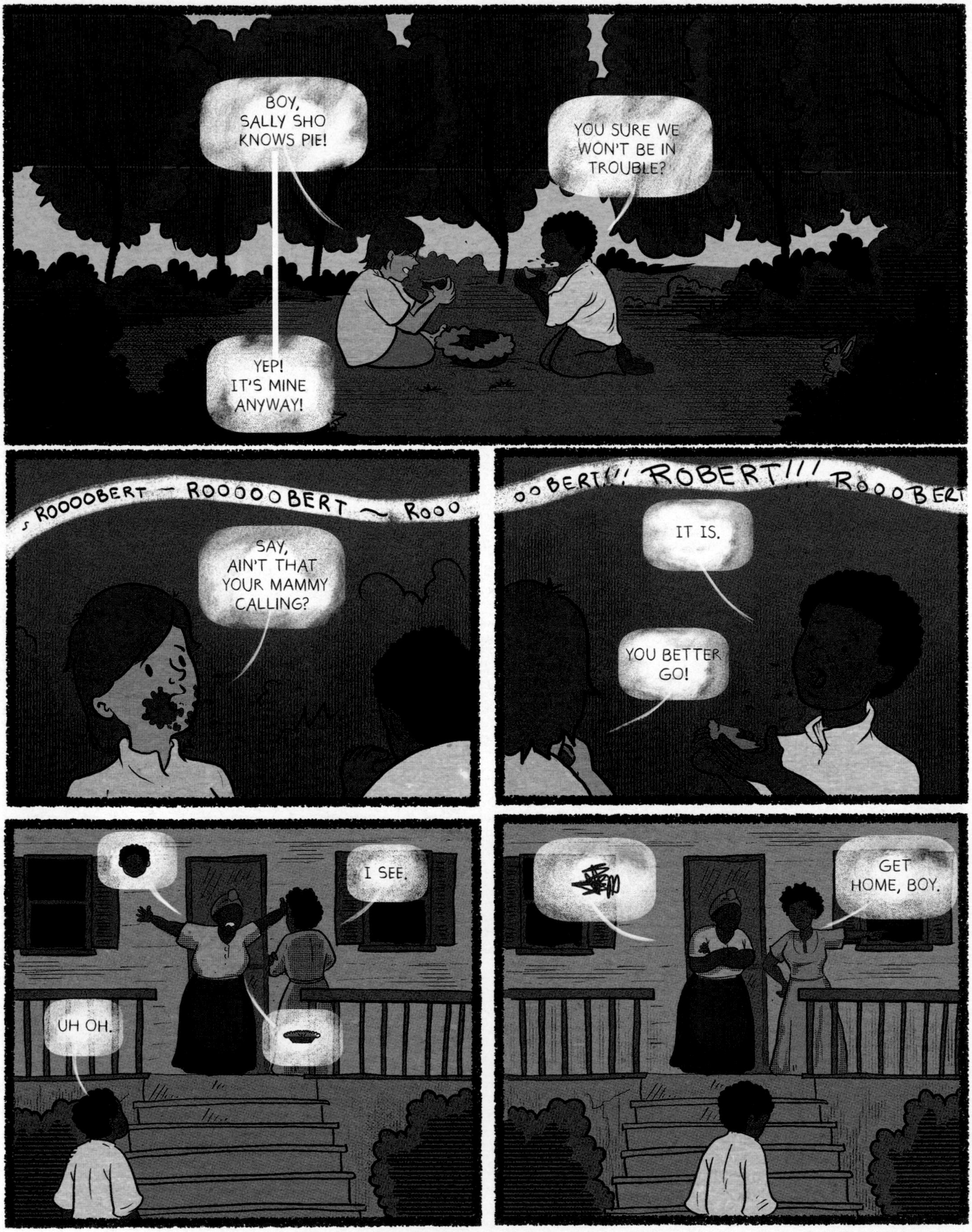
BOY, SALLY SHO KNOWS PIE!
YOU SURE WE WON'T BE IN TROUBLE?
YEP! IT'S MINE ANYWAY!
ROOOOBERT ~ ROOOOOBERT ~ ROOO
SAY, AIN'T THAT YOUR MAMMY CALLING?
OOBERT!!! ROBERT!!! ROOOBERT
IT IS.
YOU BETTER GO!
I SEE.
UH OH.
GET HOME, BOY.

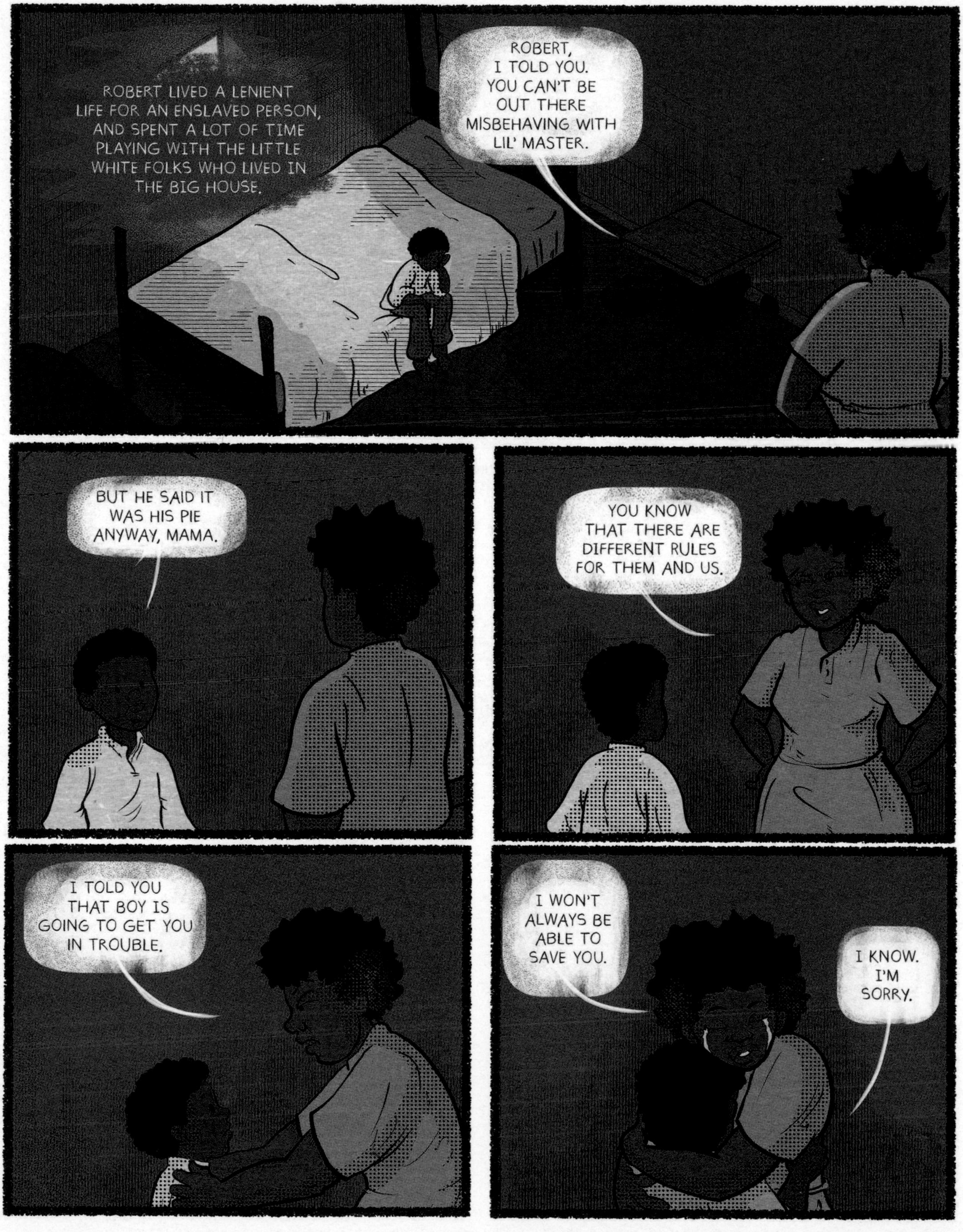
ROBERT LIVED A LENIENT LIFE FOR AN ENSLAVED PERSON, AND SPENT A LOT OF TIME PLAYING WITH THE LITTLE WHITE FOLKS WHO LIVED IN THE BIG HOUSE.
ROBERT, I TOLD YOU. YOU CAN'T BE OUT THERE MISBEHAVING WITH LIL' MASTER.
BUT HE SAID IT WAS HIS PIE ANYWAY, MAMA.
YOU KNOW THAT THERE ARE DIFFERENT RULES FOR THEM AND US.
I TOLD YOU THAT BOY IS GOING TO GET YOU IN TROUBLE.
I WON'T ALWAYS BE ABLE TO SAVE YOU.
I KNOW. I'M SORRY.

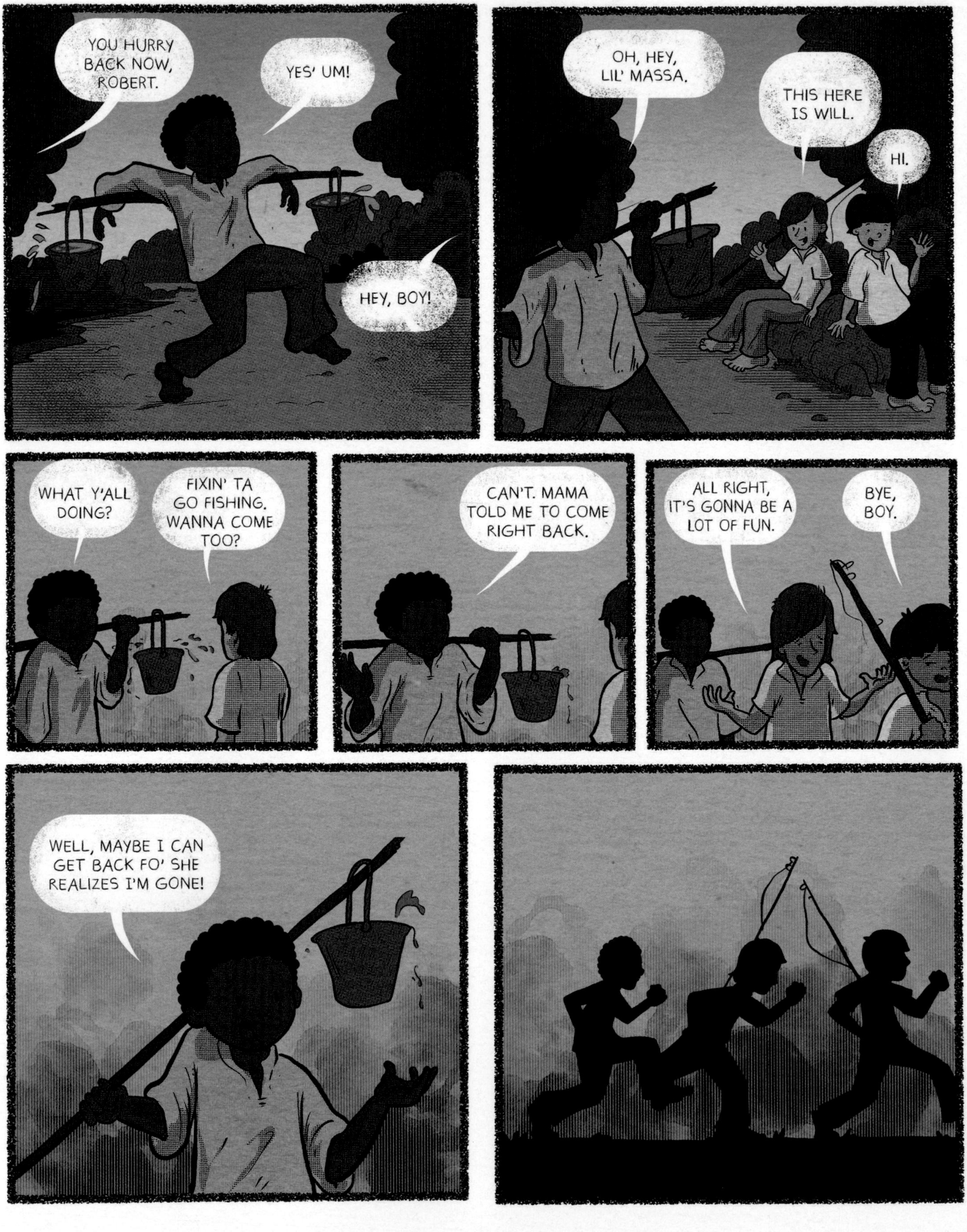
YOU HURRY BACK NOW, ROBERT.
YES' UM!
HEY, BOY!
OH, HEY, LIL' MASSA.
THIS HERE IS WILL.
HI.
WHAT Y'ALL DOING?
FIXIN' TA GO FISHING. WANNA COME TOO?
CAN'T. MAMA TOLD ME TO COME RIGHT BACK.
ALL RIGHT, IT'S GONNA BE A LOT OF FUN.
BYE, BOY.
WELL, MAYBE I CAN GET BACK FO' SHE REALIZES I'M GONE!

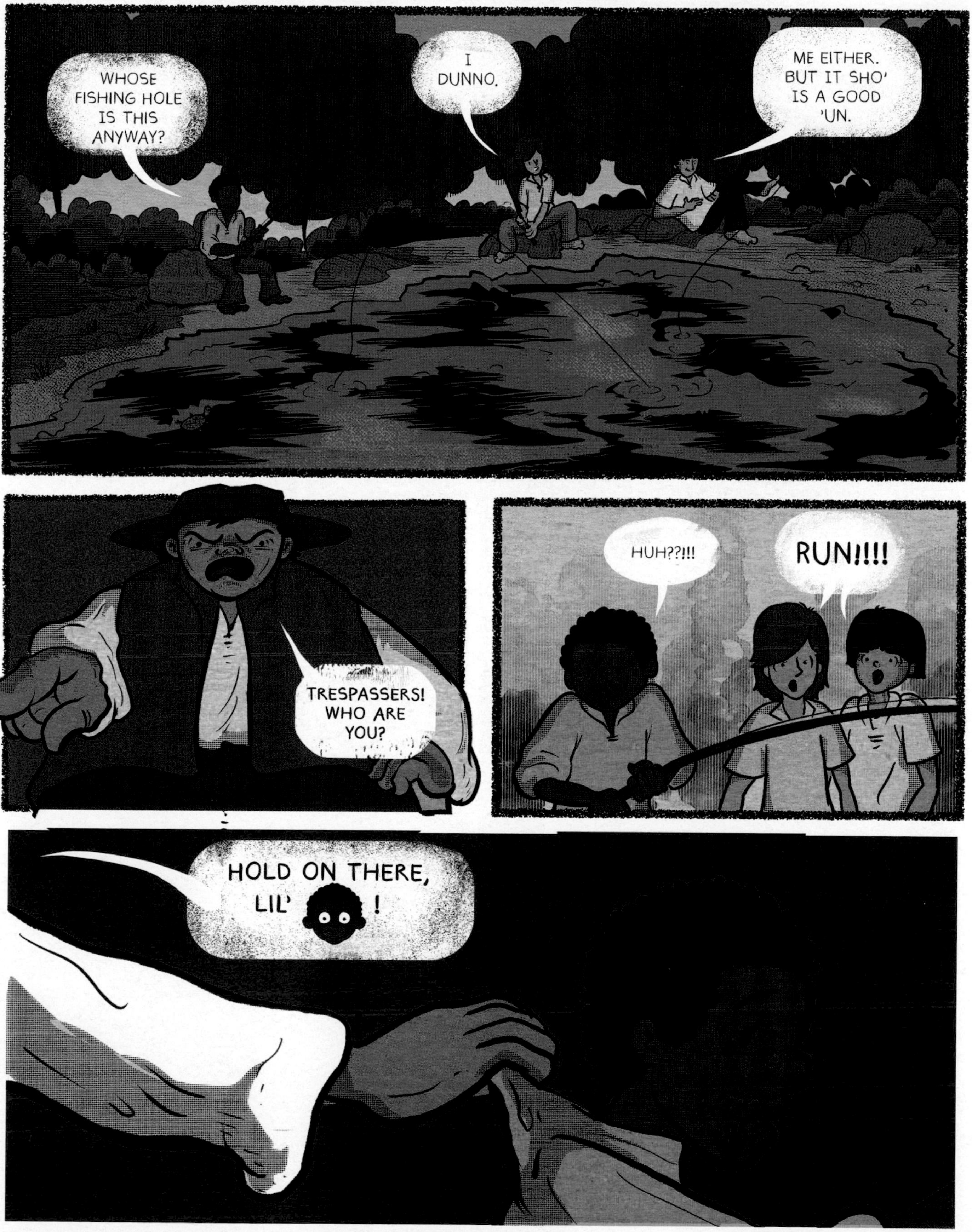
WHOSE FISHING HOLE IS THIS ANYWAY?
I DUNNO.
ME EITHER. BUT IT SHO' IS A GOOD 'UN.
TRESPASSERS! WHO ARE YOU?
HUH??!!!
RUN!!!!
HOLD ON THERE, LIL' !

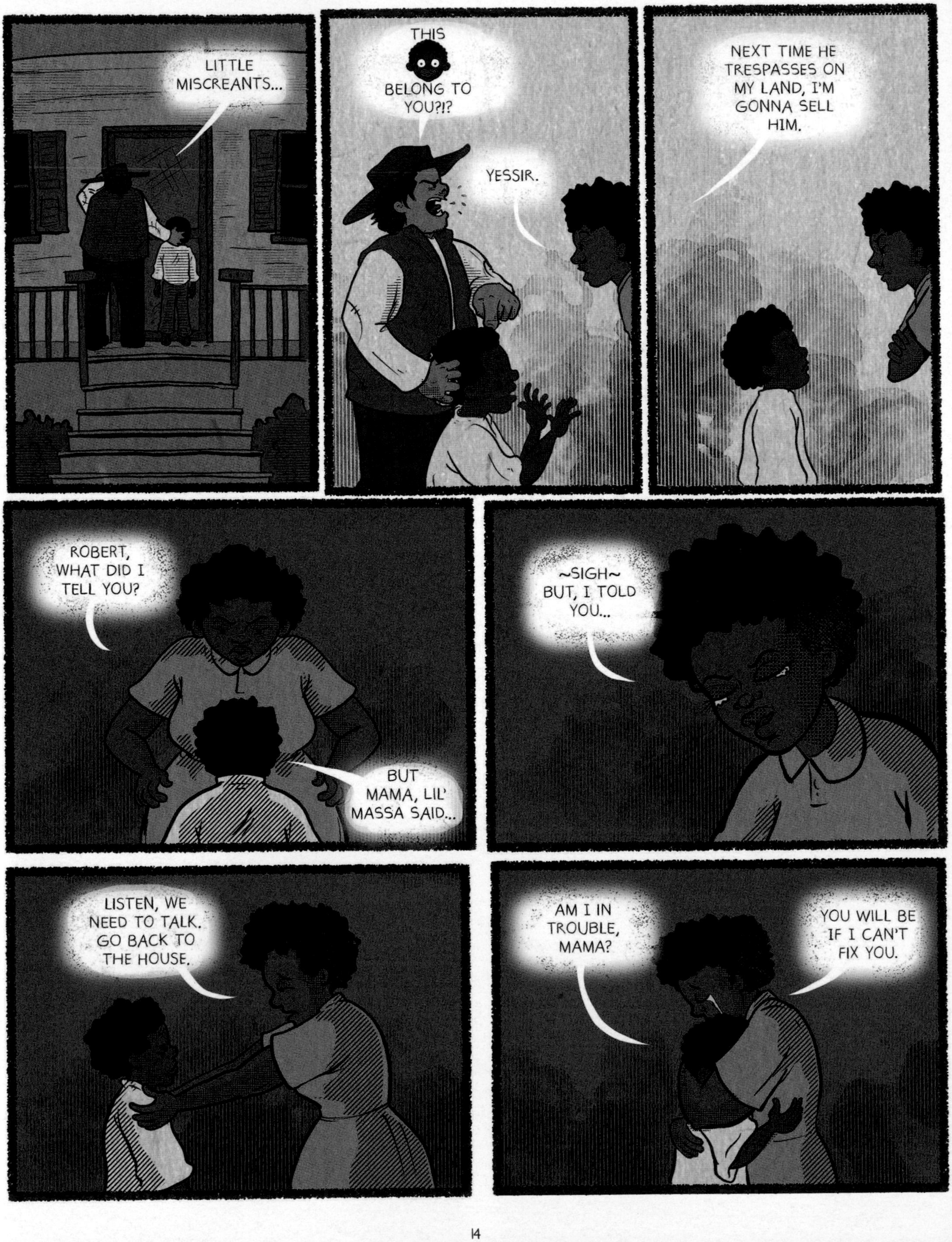
LITTLE MISCREANTS...
THIS BELONG TO YOU?!?
YESSIR.
NEXT TIME HE TRESPASSES ON MY LAND, I'M GONNA SELL HIM.
ROBERT, WHAT DID I TELL YOU?
BUT MAMA, LIL' MASSA SAID...
~SIGH~ BUT, I TOLD YOU...
LISTEN, WE NEED TO TALK. GO BACK TO THE HOUSE.
AM I IN TROUBLE, MAMA?
YOU WILL BE IF I CAN'T FIX YOU.

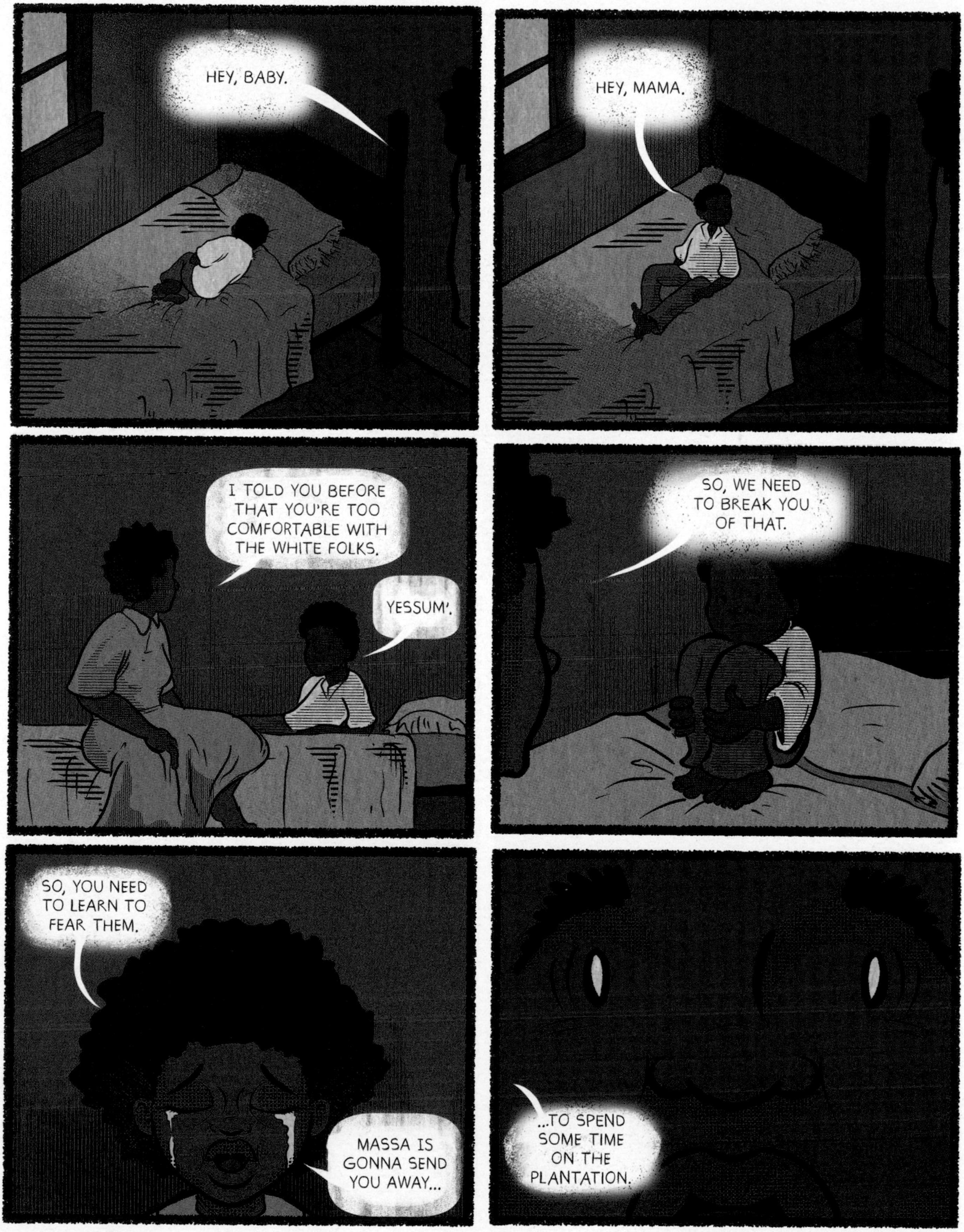
HEY, BABY.
HEY, MAMA.
I TOLD YOU BEFORE THAT YOU'RE TOO COMFORTABLE WITH THE WHITE FOLKS.
YESSUM'.
SO, WE NEED TO BREAK YOU OF THAT.
SO, YOU NEED TO LEARN TO FEAR THEM.
MASSA IS GONNA SEND YOU AWAY...
...TO SPEND SOME TIME ON THE PLANTATION.

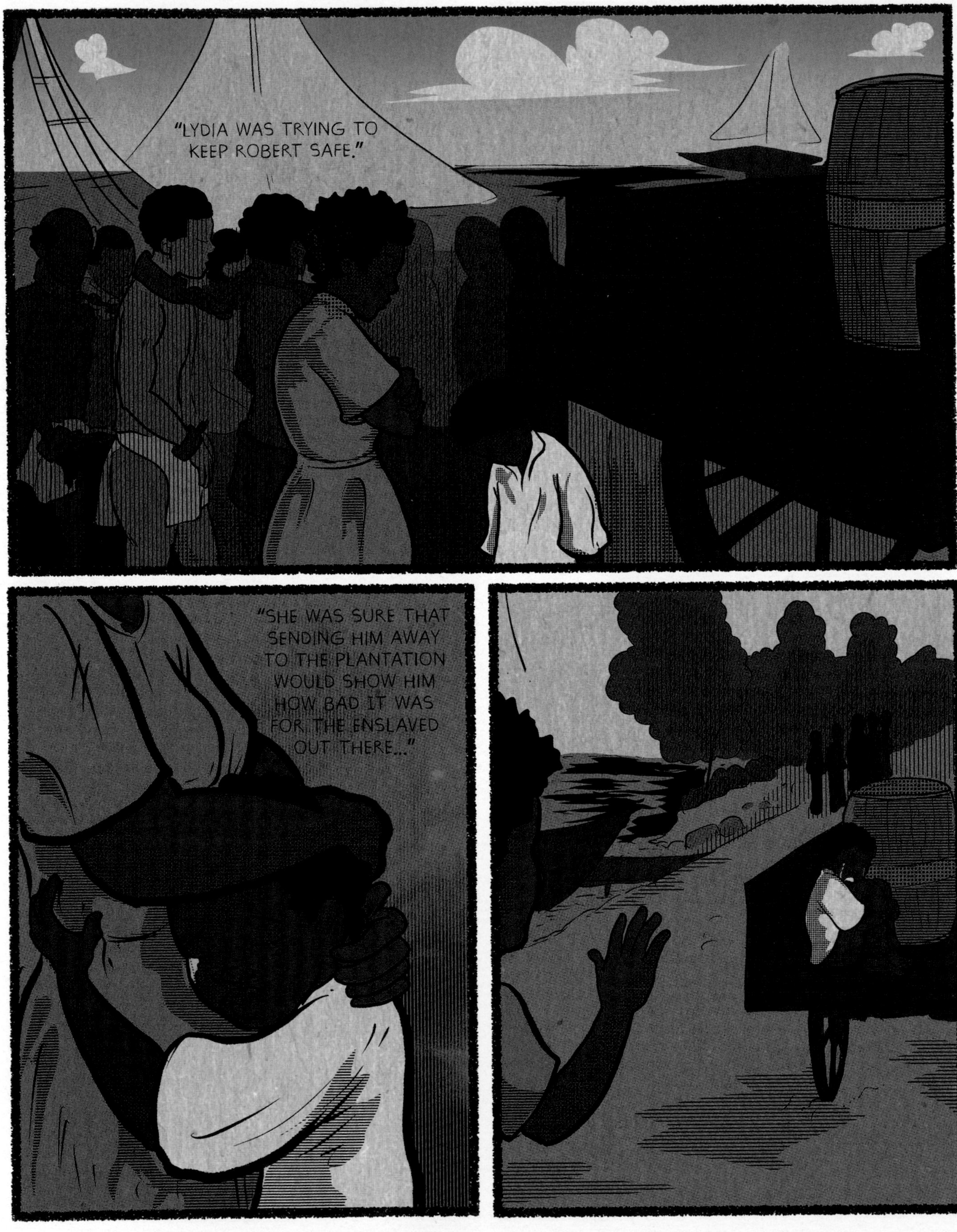
"LYDIA WAS TRYING TO KEEP ROBERT SAFE."
"SHE WAS SURE THAT SENDING HIM AWAY TO THE PLANTATION WOULD SHOW HIM HOW BAD IT WAS FOR THE ENSLAVED OUT THERE..."

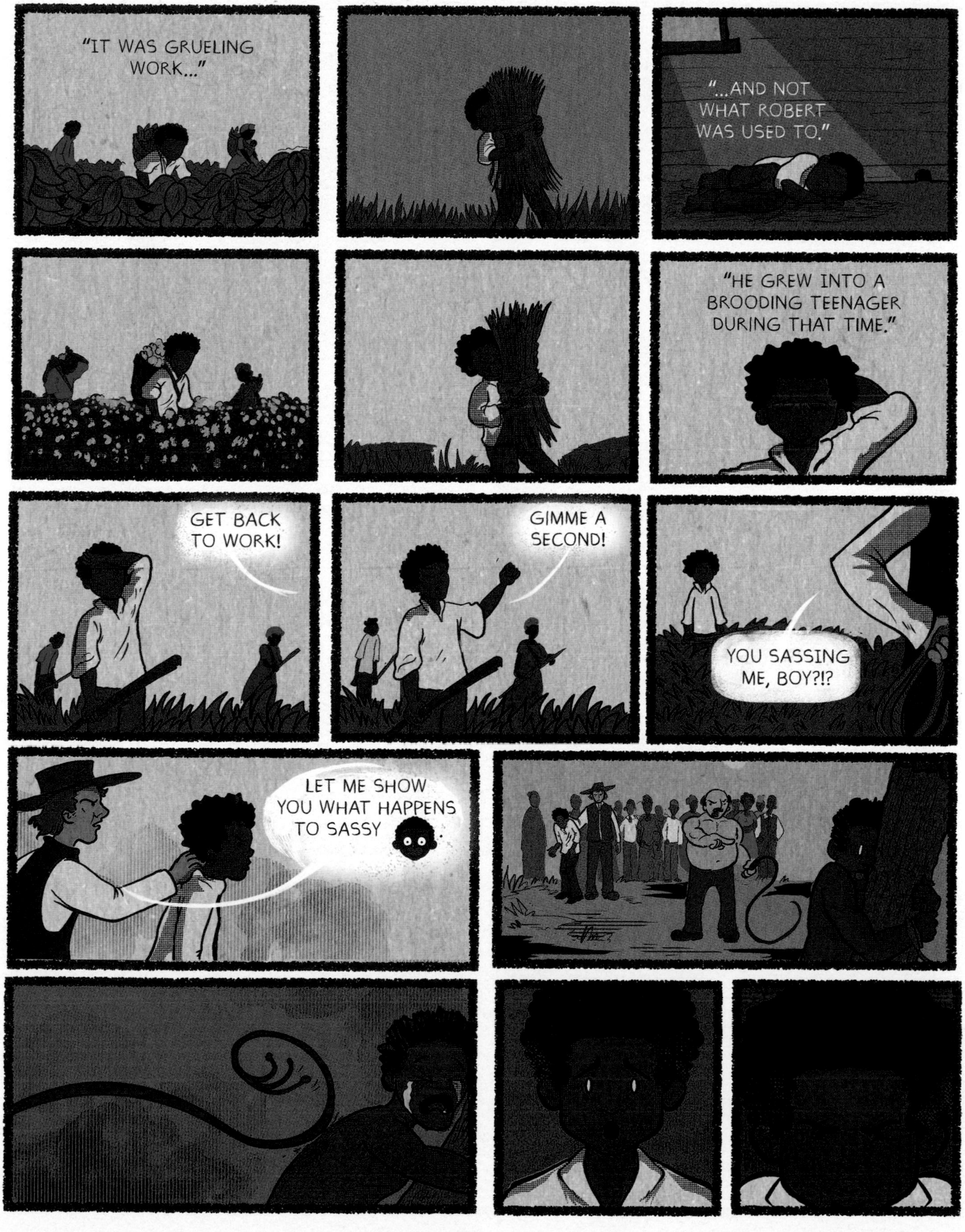
"IT WAS GRUELING WORK..."
"...AND NOT WHAT ROBERT WAS USED TO."
"HE GREW INTO A BROODING TEENAGER DURING THAT TIME."
GET BACK TO WORK!
GIMME A SECOND!
YOU SASSING ME, BOY?!?
LET ME SHOW YOU WHAT HAPPENS TO SASSY

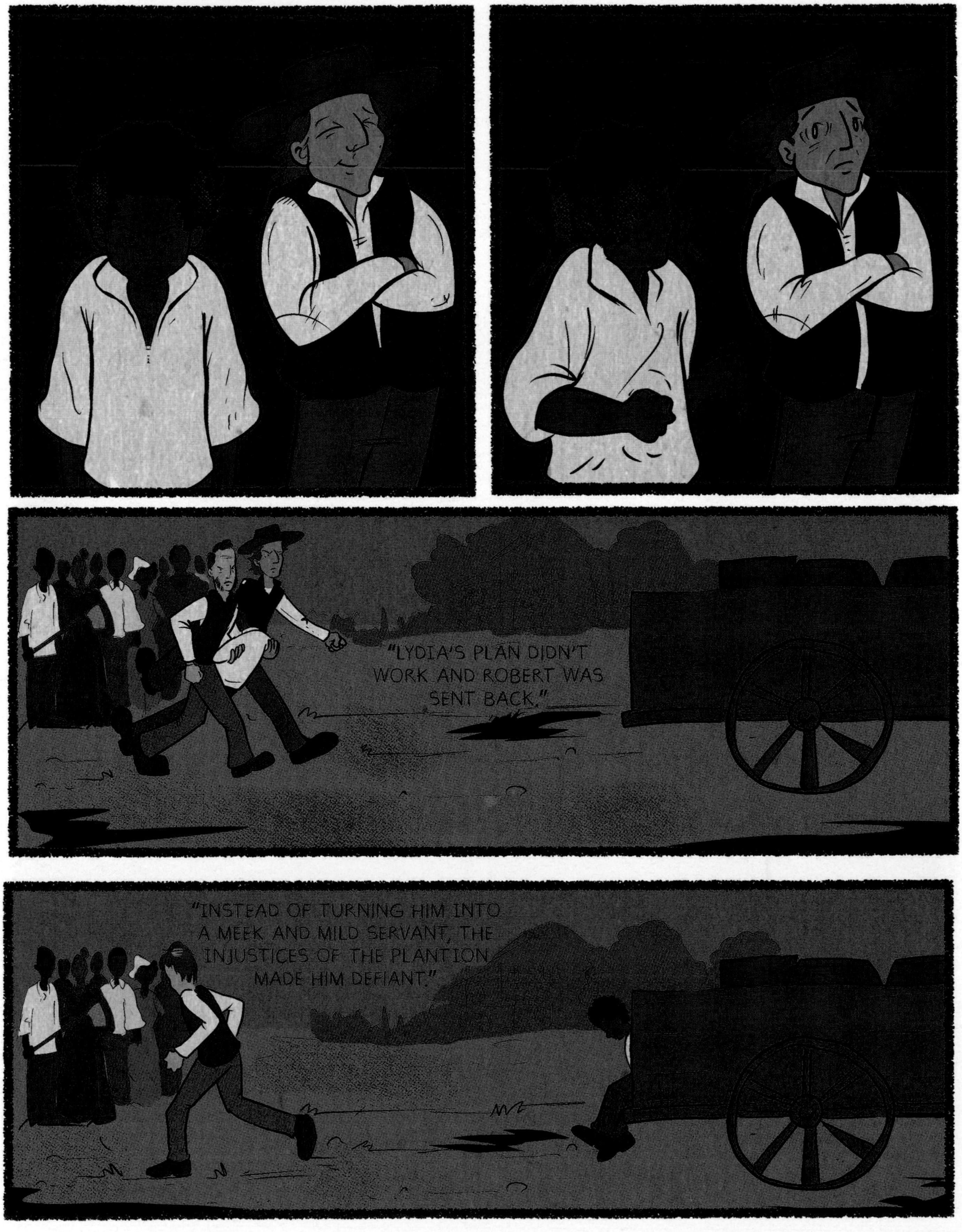
"LYDIA'S PLAN DIDN'T WORK AND ROBERT WAS SENT BACK."
"INSTEAD OF TURNING HIM INTO A MEEK AND MILD SERVANT, THE INJUSTICES OF THE PLANTION MADE HIM DEFIANT."

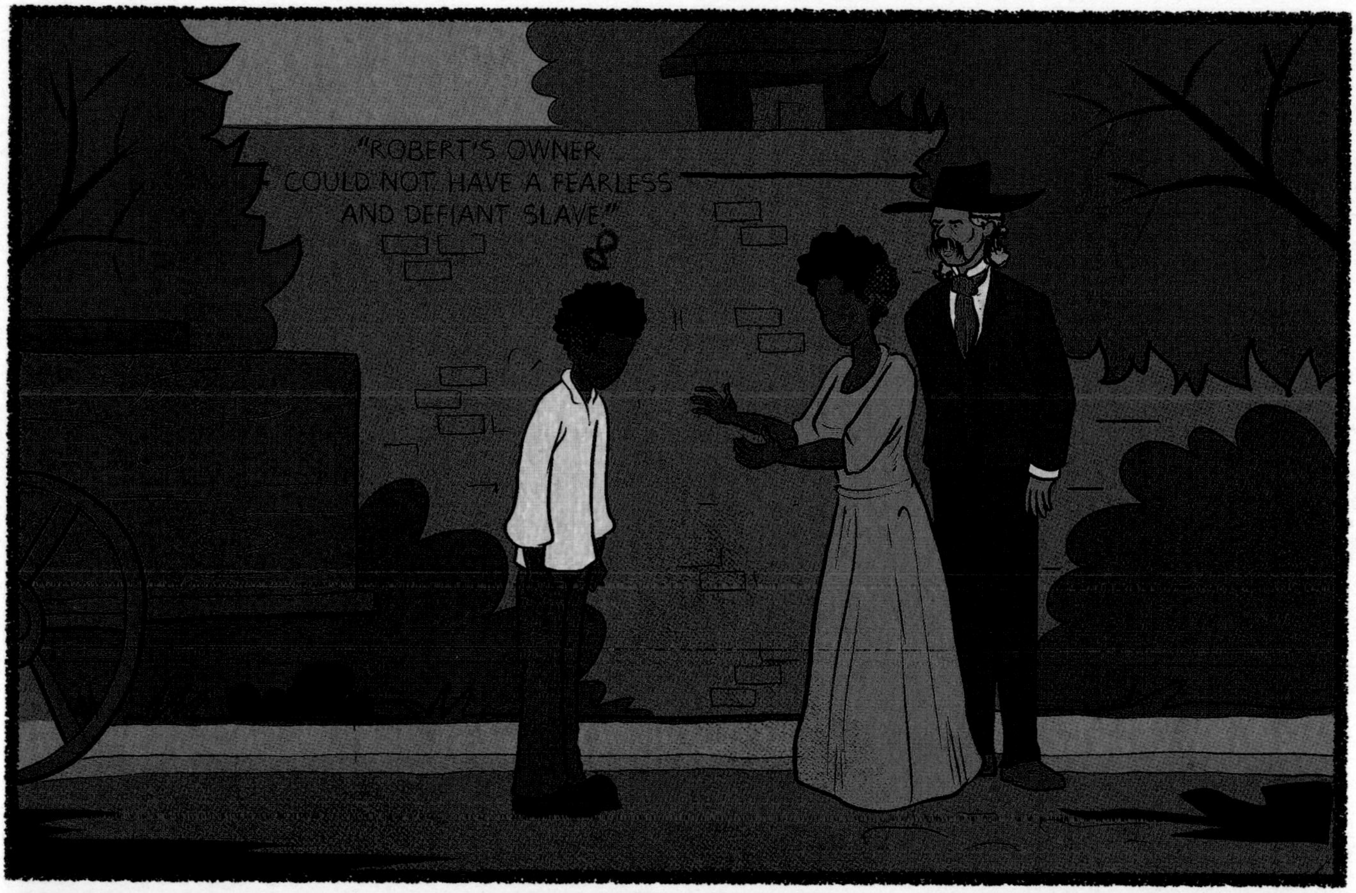
"ROBERT'S OWNER COULD NOT HAVE A FEARLESS AND DEFIANT SLAVE."

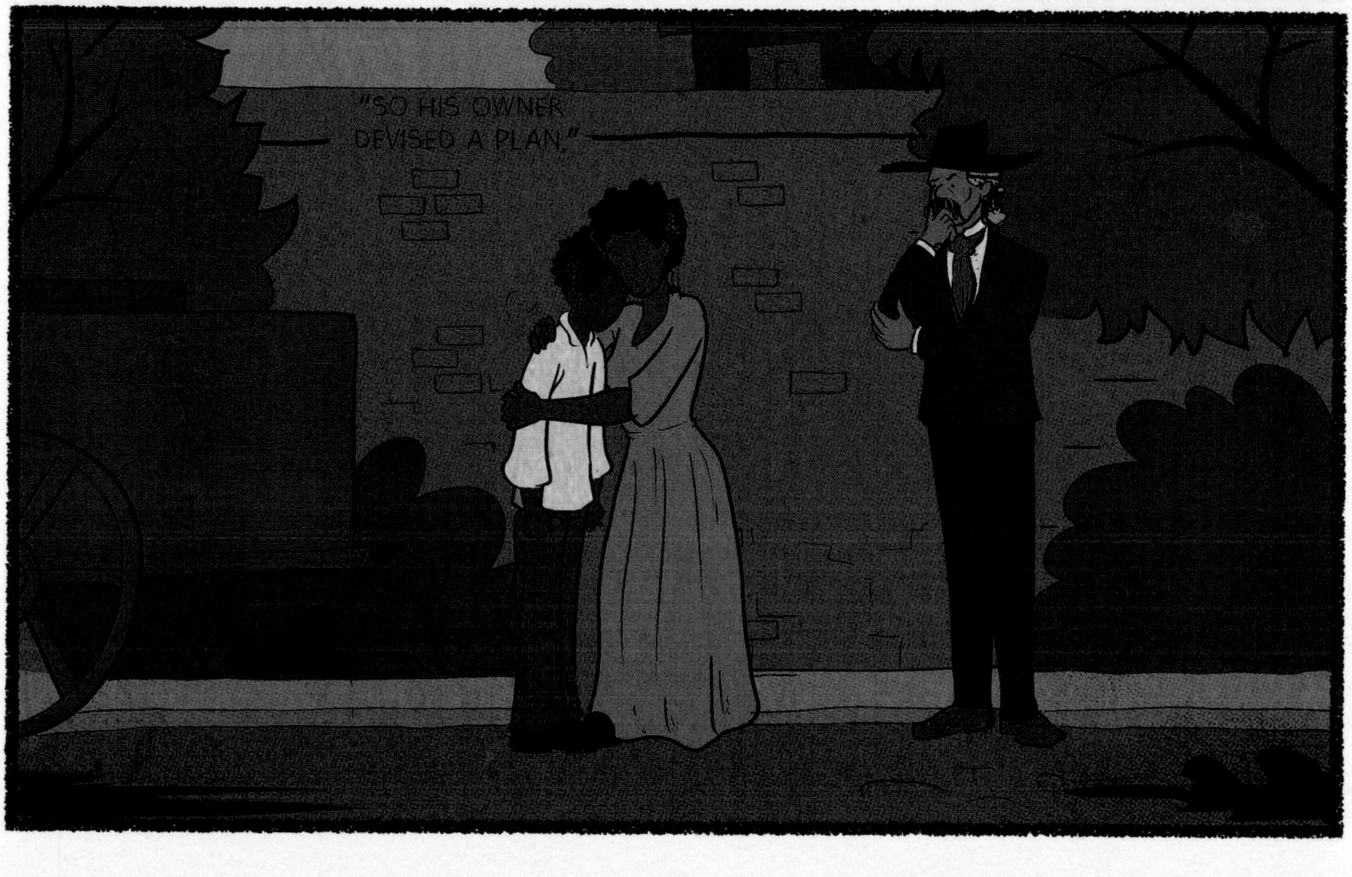
"SO HIS OWNER DEVISED A PLAN."

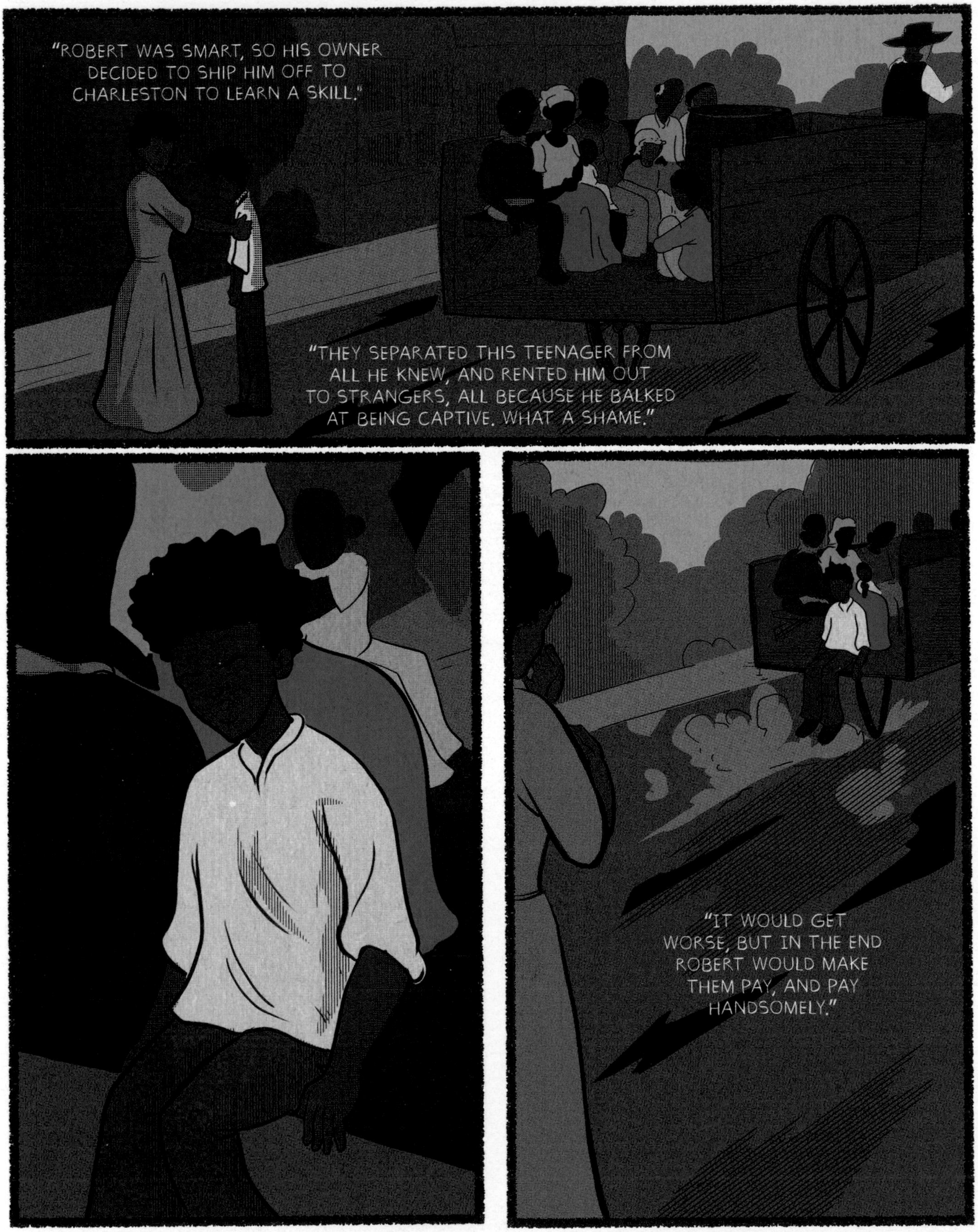
"ROBERT WAS SMART, SO HIS OWNER DECIDED TO SHIP HIM OFF TO CHARLESTON TO LEARN A SKILL."
"THEY SEPARATED THIS TEENAGER FROM ALL HE KNEW, AND RENTED HIM OUT TO STRANGERS, ALL BECAUSE HE BALKED AT BEING CAPTIVE. WHAT A SHAME."
"IT WOULD GET WORSE, BUT IN THE END ROBERT WOULD MAKE THEM PAY, AND PAY HANDSOMELY."

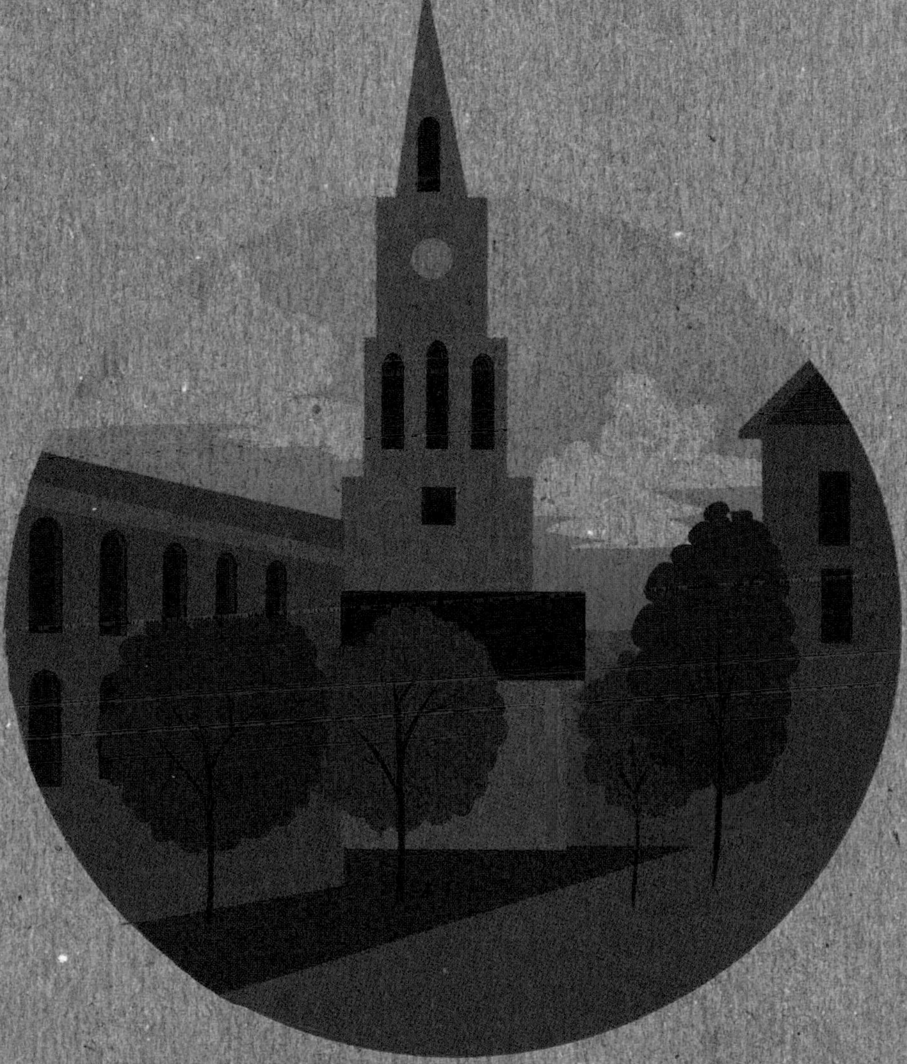

CHAPTER TWO

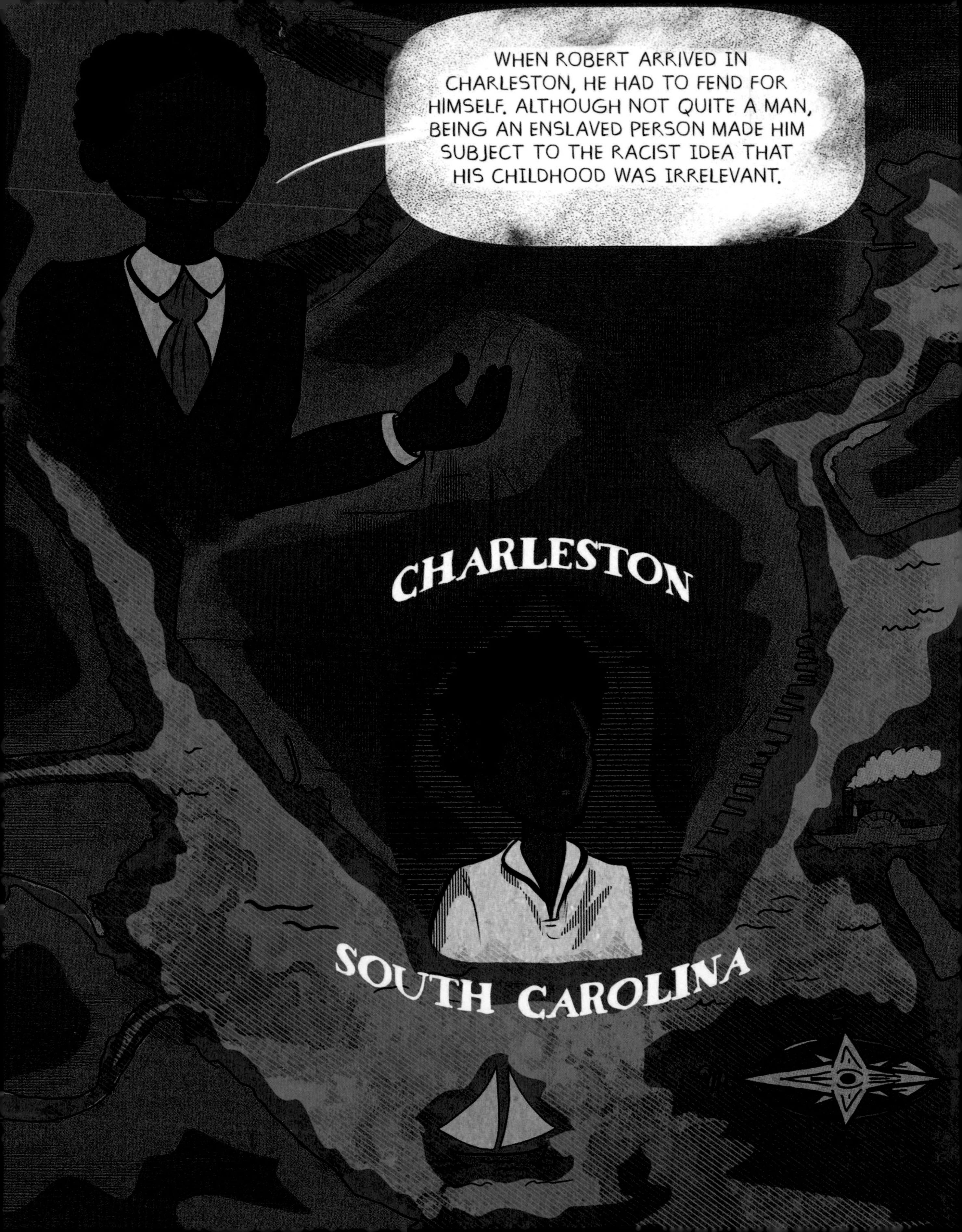
WHEN ROBERT ARRIVED IN CHARLESTON, HE HAD TO FEND FOR HIMSELF. ALTHOUGH NOT QUITE A MAN, BEING AN ENSLAVED PERSON MADE HIM SUBJECT TO THE RACIST IDEA THAT HIS CHILDHOOD WAS IRRELEVANT.
CHARLESTON
SOUTH CAROLINA

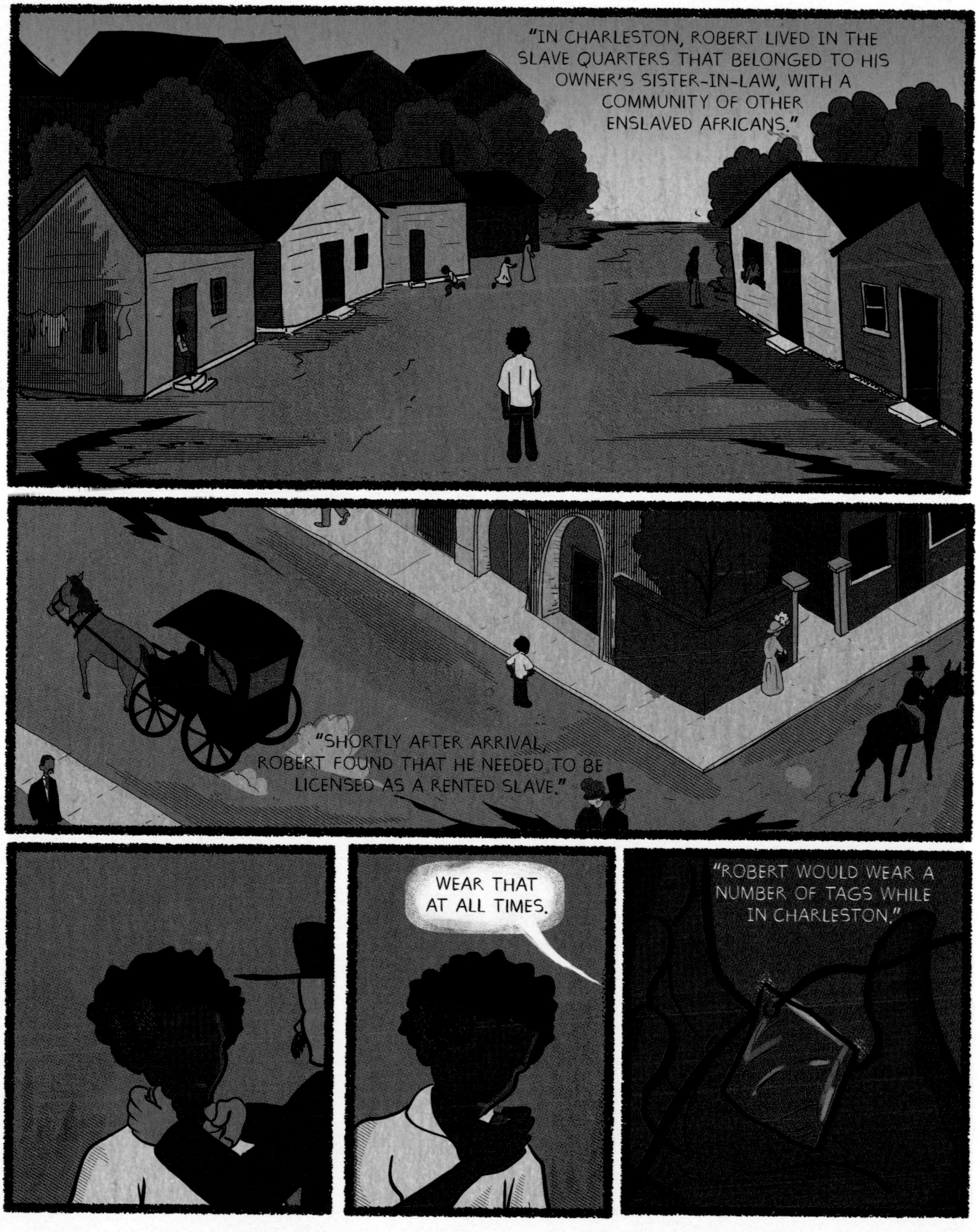
"IN CHARLESTON, ROBERT LIVED IN THE SLAVE QUARTERS THAT BELONGED TO HIS OWNER'S SISTER-IN-LAW, WITH A COMMUNITY OF OTHER ENSLAVED AFRICANS."
"SHORTLY AFTER ARRIVAL, ROBERT FOUND THAT HE NEEDED TO BE LICENSED AS A RENTED SLAVE."
WEAR THAT AT ALL TIMES.
"ROBERT WOULD WEAR A NUMBER OF TAGS WHILE IN CHARLESTON."

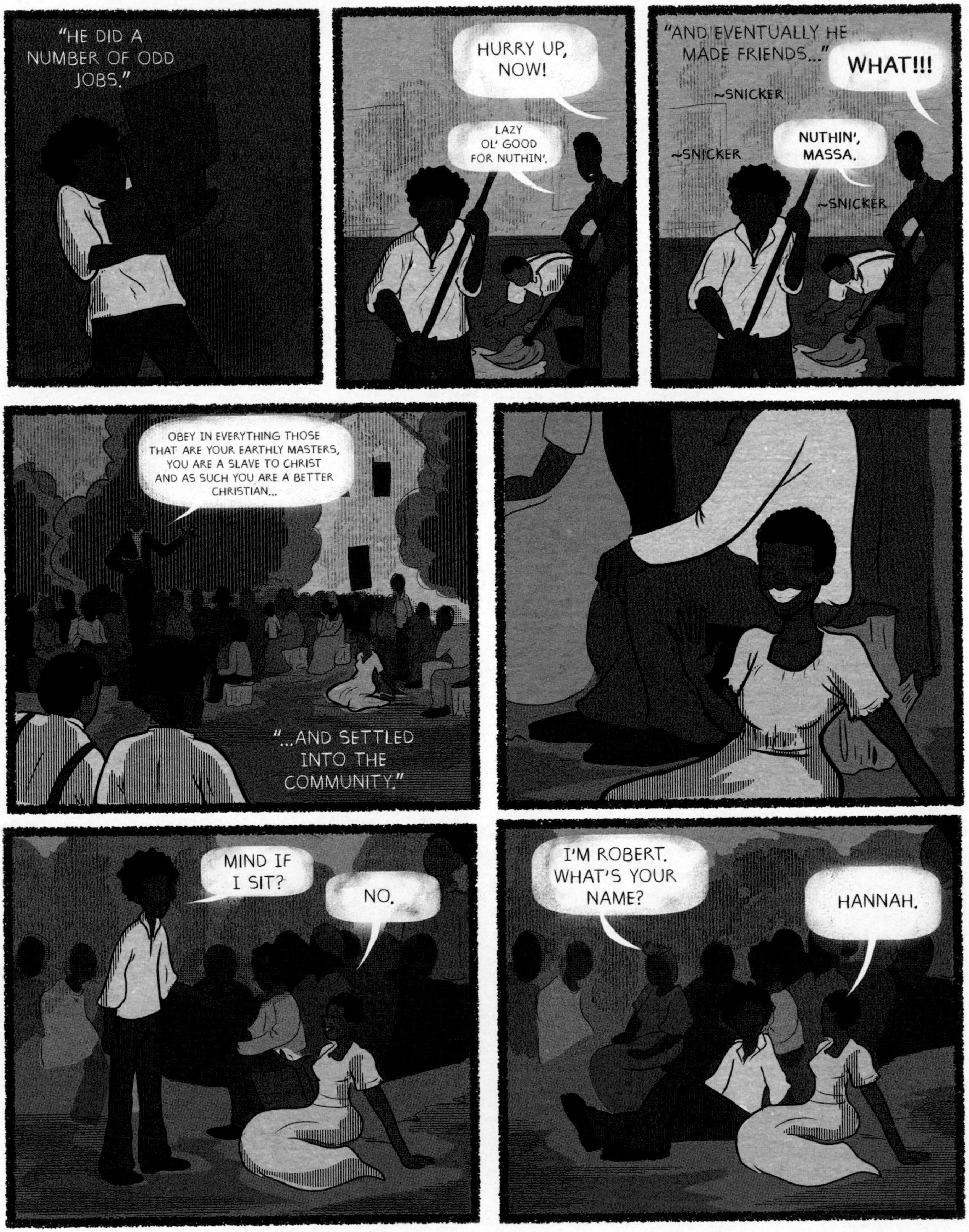
"HE DID A NUMBER OF ODD JOBS."
HURRY UP, NOW!
LAZY OL' GOOD FOR NUTHIN'.
"AND EVENTUALLY HE MADE FRIENDS..."
WHAT!!!
~SNICKER
~SNICKER
NUTHIN', MASSA.
~SNICKER
OBEY IN EVERYTHING THOSE THAT ARE YOUR EARTHLY MASTERS, YOU ARE A SLAVE TO CHRIST AND AS SUCH YOU ARE A BETTER CHRISTIAN...
"...AND SETTLED INTO THE COMMUNITY."
MIND IF I SIT?
NO.
I'M ROBERT. WHAT'S YOUR NAME?
HANNAH.

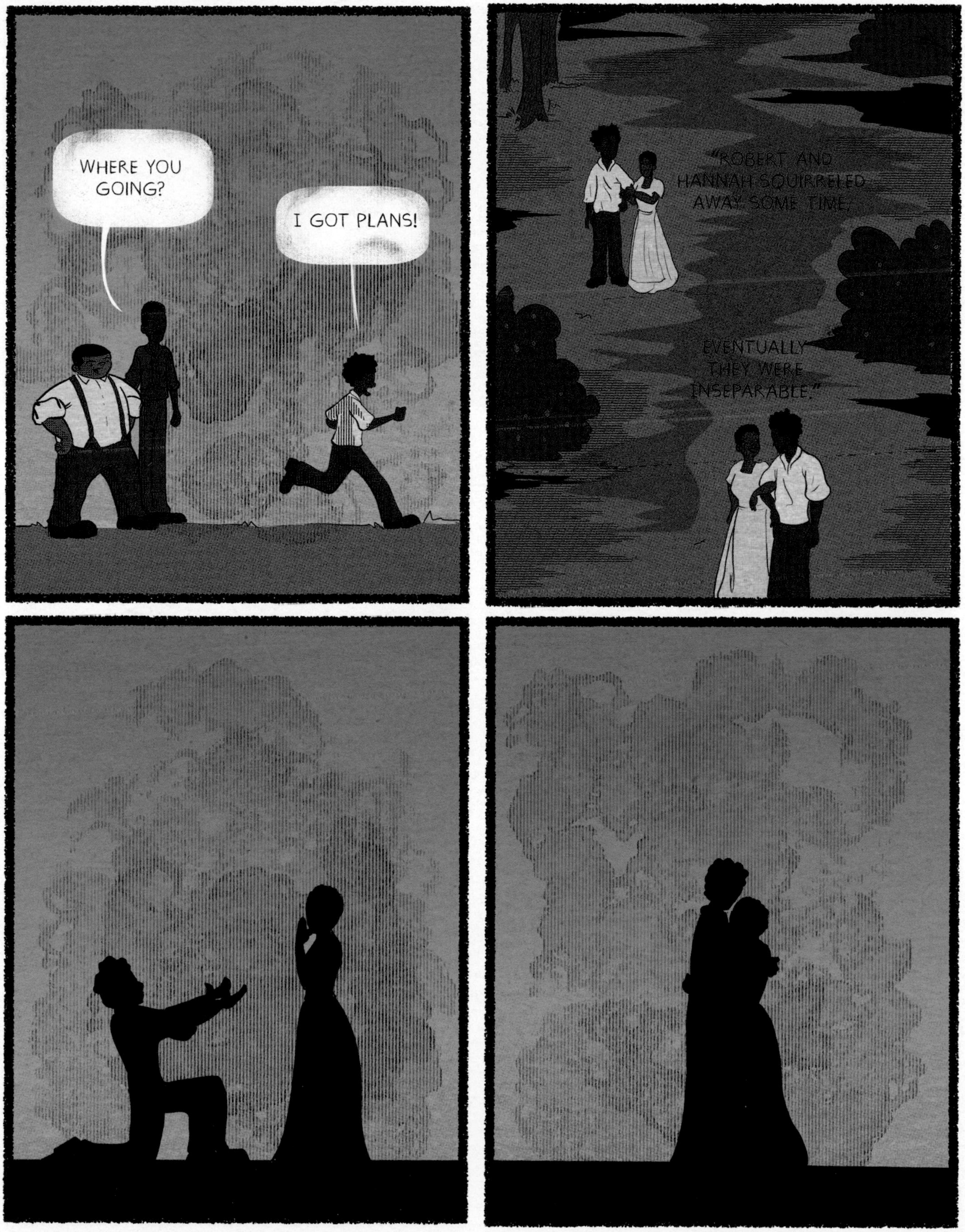
WHERE YOU GOING?
I GOT PLANS!
“ROBERT AND HANNAH SQUIRRELED AWAY SOME TIME.
EVENTUALLY THEY WERE INSEPARABLE.”

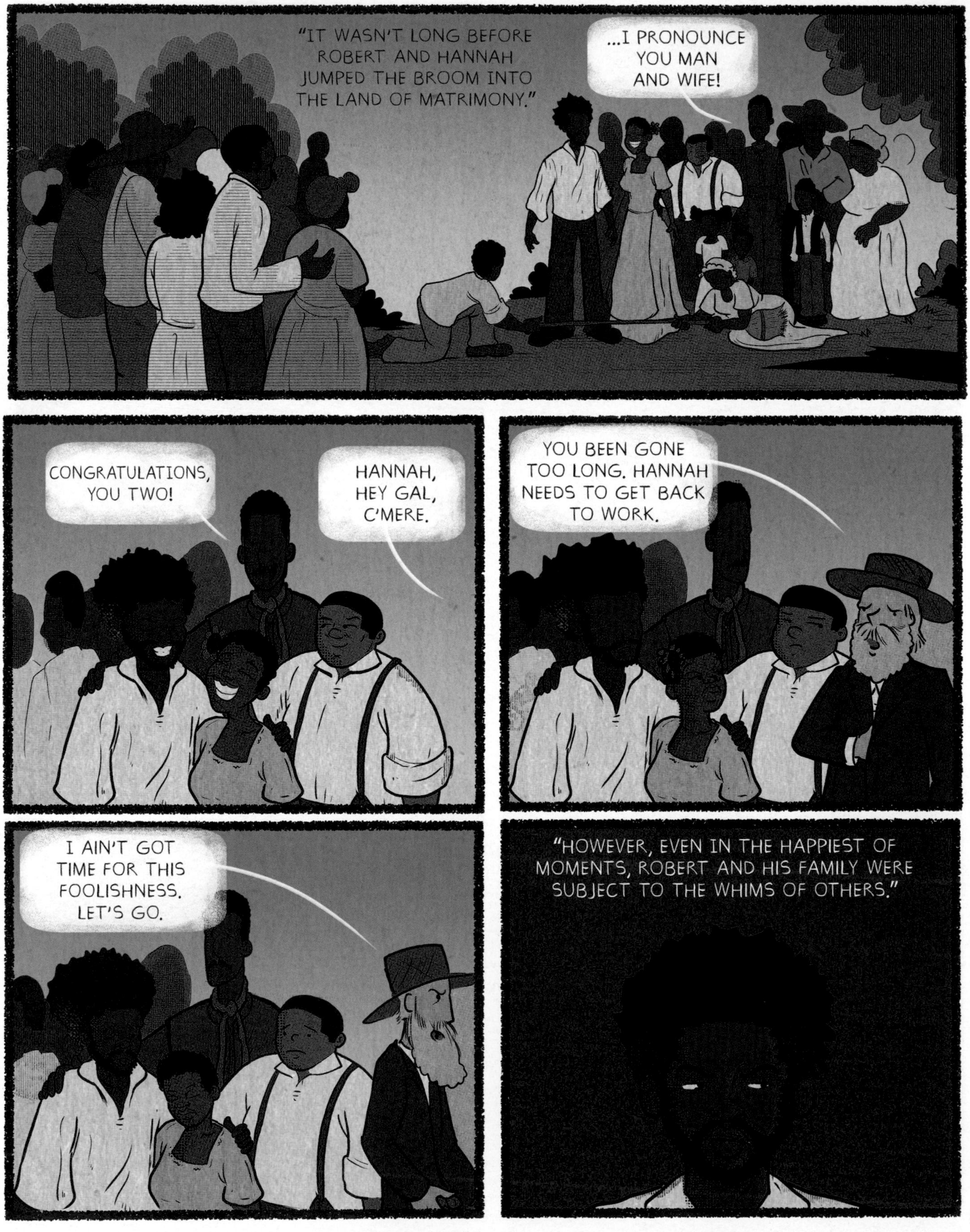
"IT WASN'T LONG BEFORE ROBERT AND HANNAH JUMPED THE BROOM INTO THE LAND OF MATRIMONY."
...I PRONOUNCE YOU MAN AND WIFE!
CONGRATULATIONS, YOU TWO!
HANNAH, HEY GAL, C'MERE.
YOU BEEN GONE TOO LONG. HANNAH NEEDS TO GET BACK TO WORK.
I AIN'T GOT TIME FOR THIS FOOLISHNESS. LET'S GO.
"HOWEVER, EVEN IN THE HAPPIEST OF MOMENTS, ROBERT AND HIS FAMILY WERE SUBJECT TO THE WHIMS OF OTHERS."

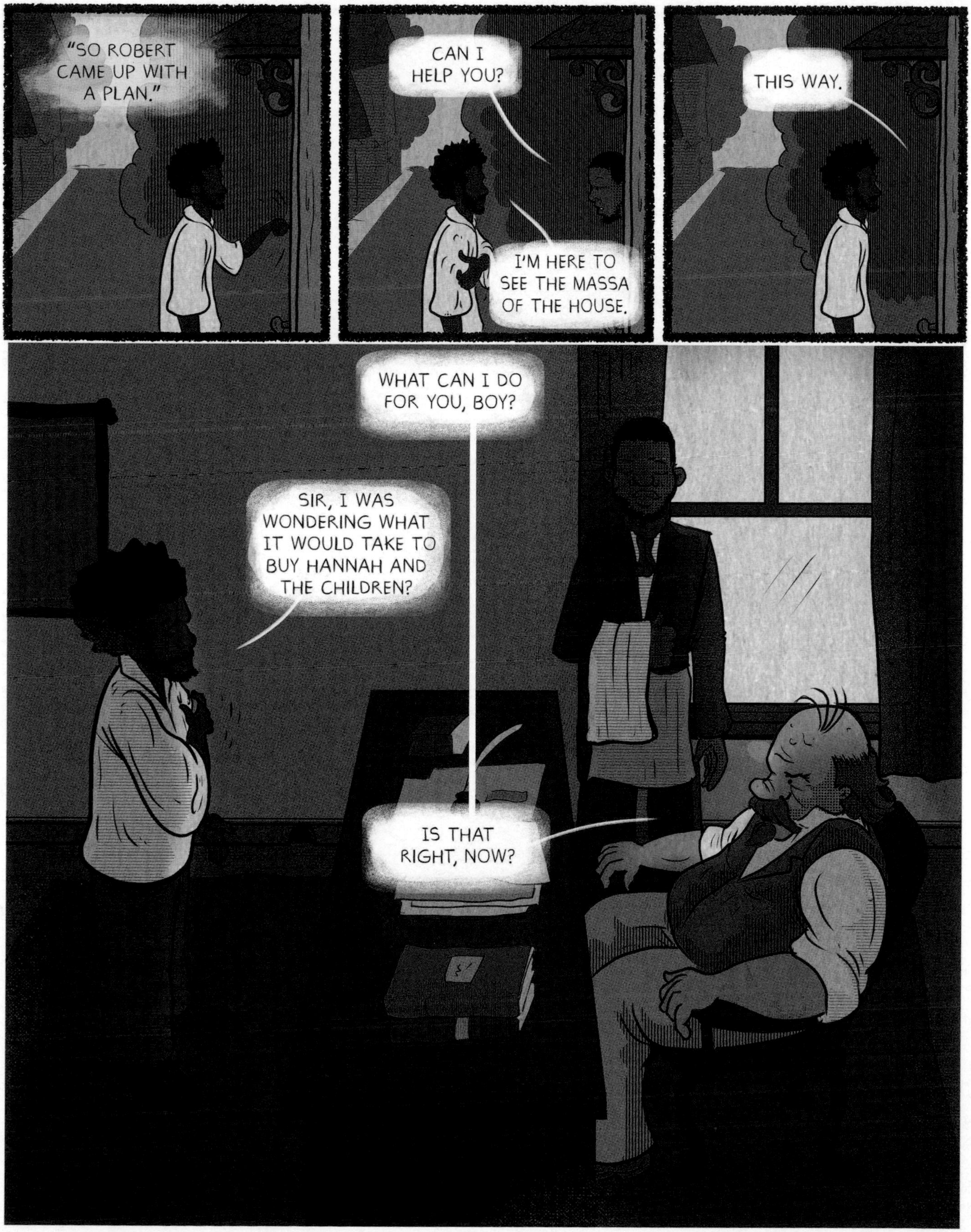
"SO ROBERT CAME UP WITH A PLAN."
CAN I HELP YOU?
I'M HERE TO SEE THE MASSA OF THE HOUSE.
THIS WAY.
WHAT CAN I DO FOR YOU, BOY?
SIR, I WAS WONDERING WHAT IT WOULD TAKE TO BUY HANNAH AND THE CHILDREN?
IS THAT RIGHT, NOW?

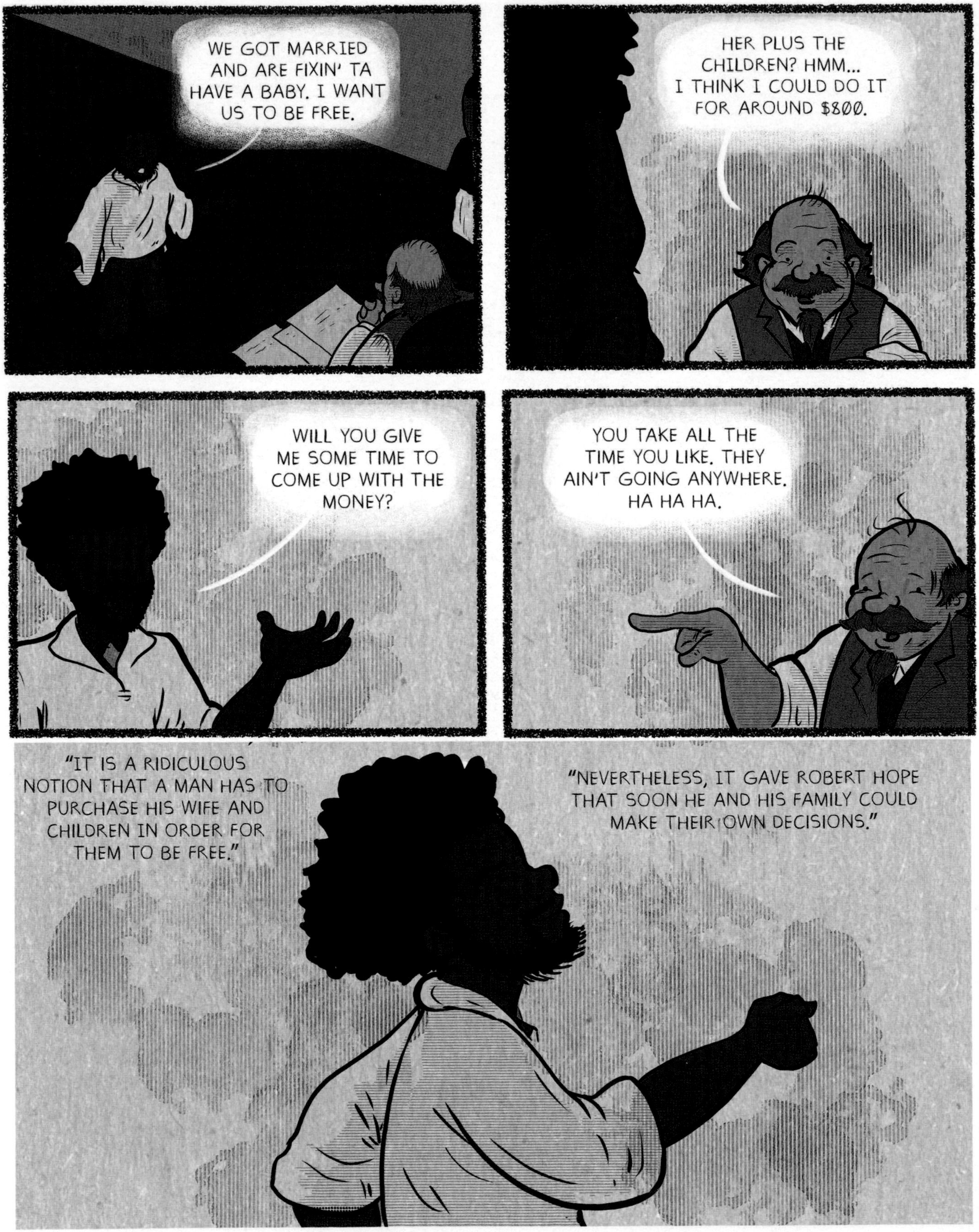
WE GOT MARRIED AND ARE FIXIN' TA HAVE A BABY. I WANT US TO BE FREE.
HER PLUS THE CHILDREN? HMM... I THINK I COULD DO IT FOR AROUND $800.
WILL YOU GIVE ME SOME TIME TO COME UP WITH THE MONEY?
YOU TAKE ALL THE TIME YOU LIKE. THEY AIN'T GOING ANYWHERE. HA HA HA.
"IT IS A RIDICULOUS NOTION THAT A MAN HAS TO PURCHASE HIS WIFE AND CHILDREN IN ORDER FOR THEM TO BE FREE."
"NEVERTHELESS, IT GAVE ROBERT HOPE THAT SOON HE AND HIS FAMILY COULD MAKE THEIR OWN DECISIONS."

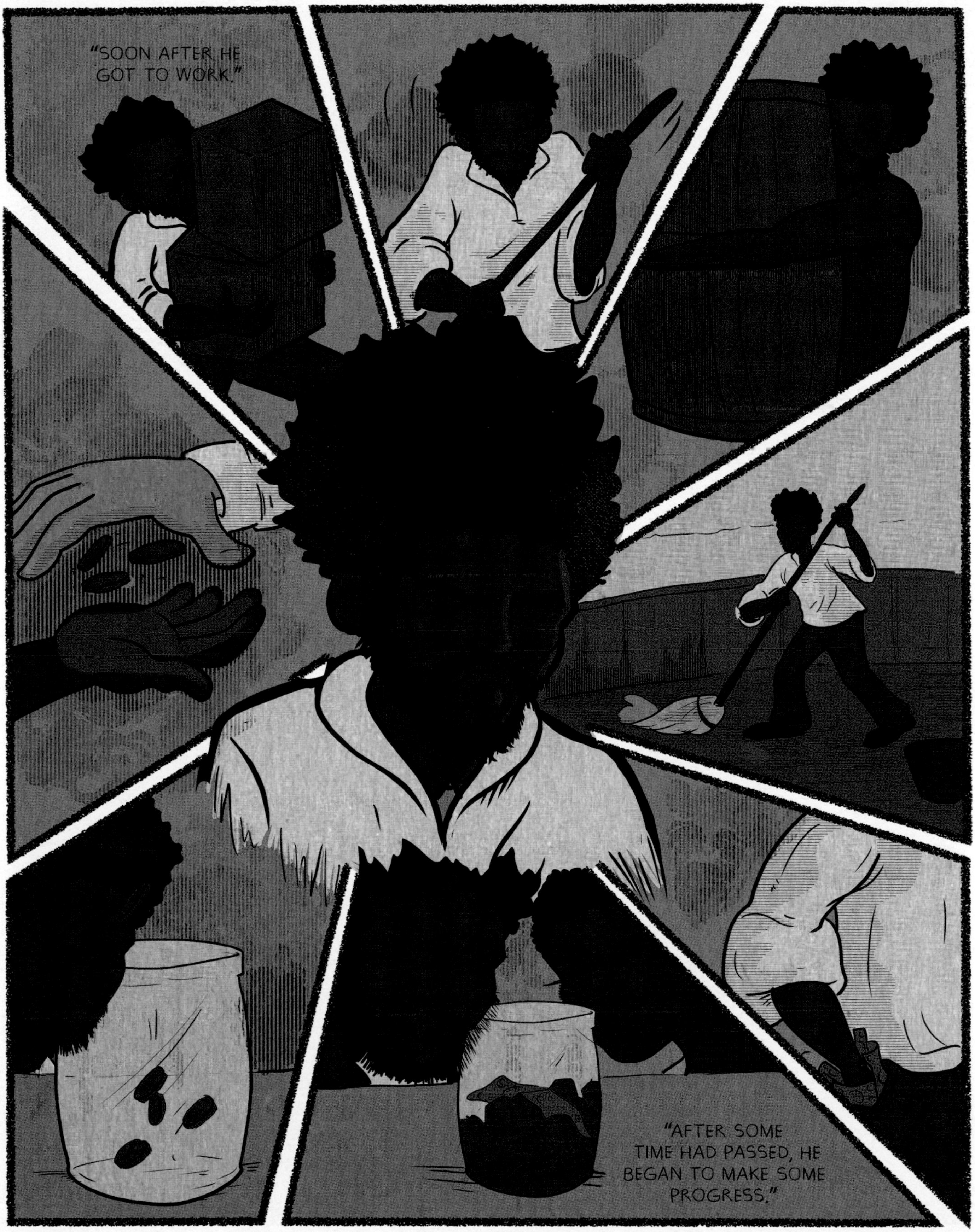
"SOON AFTER HE GOT TO WORK."
"AFTER SOME TIME HAD PASSED, HE BEGAN TO MAKE SOME PROGRESS."

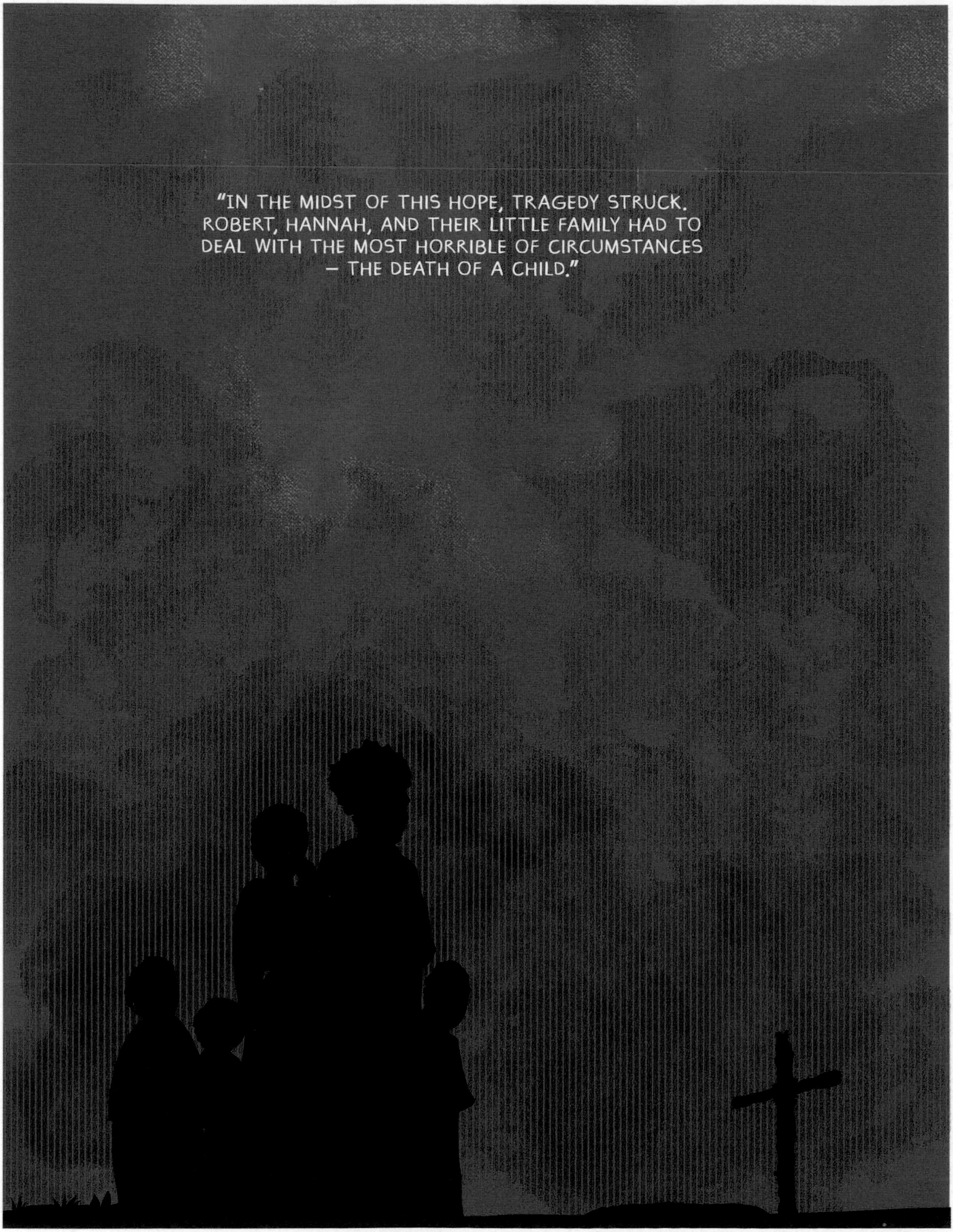
"IN THE MIDST OF THIS HOPE, TRAGEDY STRUCK. ROBERT, HANNAH, AND THEIR LITTLE FAMILY HAD TO DEAL WITH THE MOST HORRIBLE OF CIRCUMSTANCES – THE DEATH OF A CHILD."

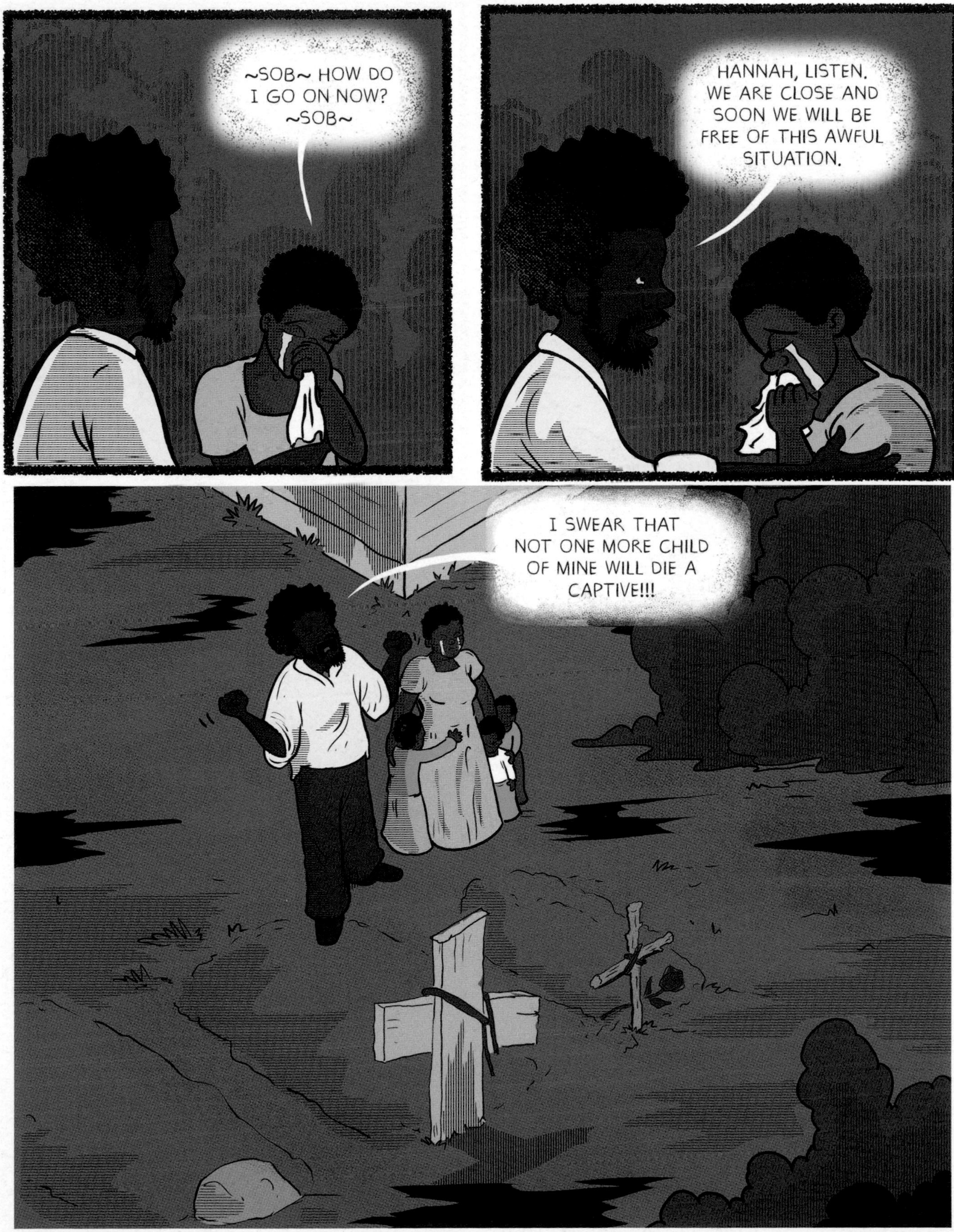
~SOB~ HOW DO I GO ON NOW? ~SOB~
HANNAH, LISTEN. WE ARE CLOSE AND SOON WE WILL BE FREE OF THIS AWFUL SITUATION.
I SWEAR THAT NOT ONE MORE CHILD OF MINE WILL DIE A CAPTIVE!!!

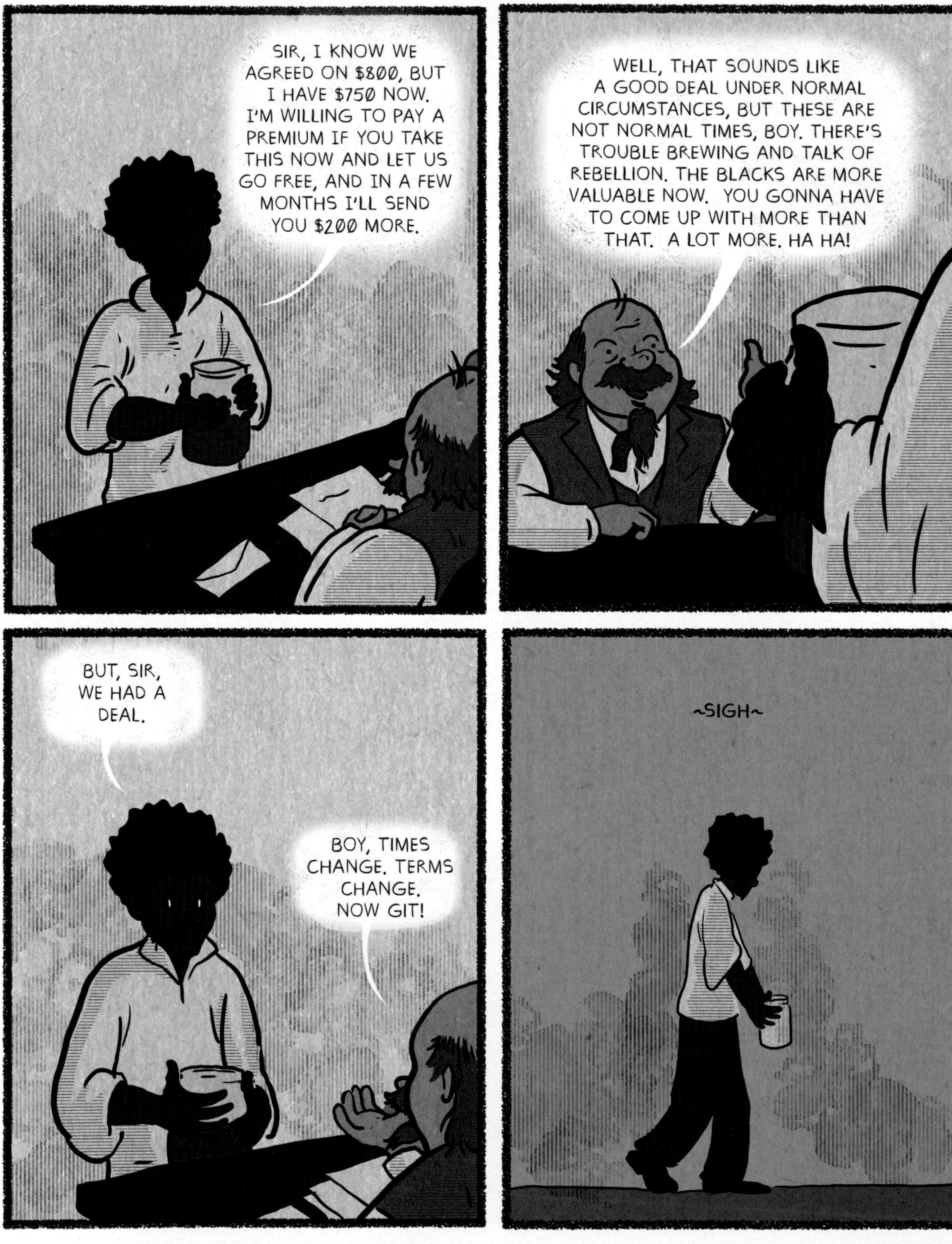
SIR, I KNOW WE AGREED ON $800, BUT I HAVE $750 NOW. I'M WILLING TO PAY A PREMIUM IF YOU TAKE THIS NOW AND LET US GO FREE, AND IN A FEW MONTHS I'LL SEND YOU $200 MORE.
WELL, THAT SOUNDS LIKE A GOOD DEAL UNDER NORMAL CIRCUMSTANCES, BUT THESE ARE NOT NORMAL TIMES, BOY. THERE'S TROUBLE BREWING AND TALK OF REBELLION. THE BLACKS ARE MORE VALUABLE NOW. YOU GONNA HAVE TO COME UP WITH MORE THAN THAT. A LOT MORE. HA HA!
BUT, SIR, WE HAD A DEAL.
BOY, TIMES CHANGE. TERMS CHANGE. NOW GIT!
~SIGH~

CHAPTER THREE

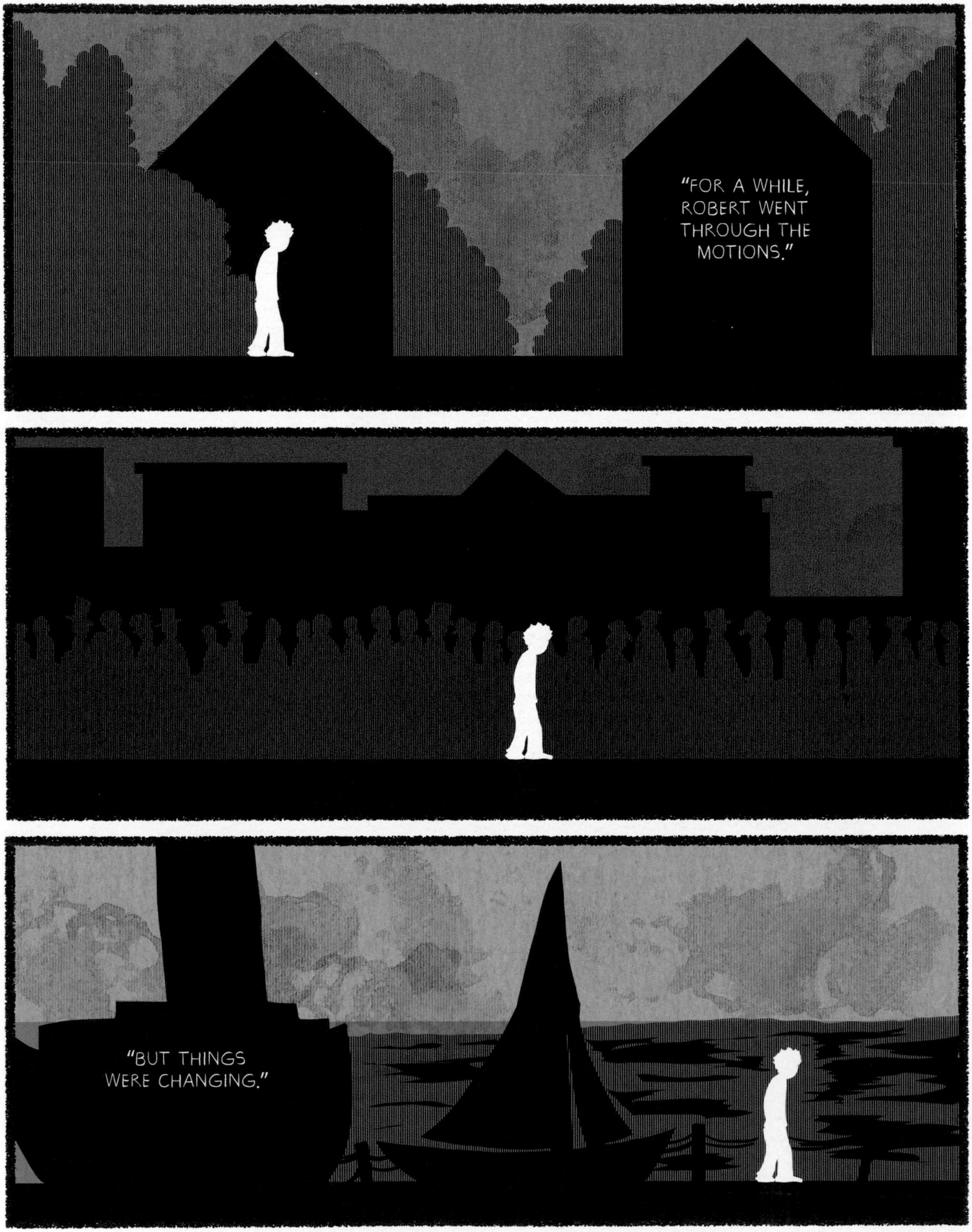
"FOR A WHILE, ROBERT WENT THROUGH THE MOTIONS."
"BUT THINGS WERE CHANGING."

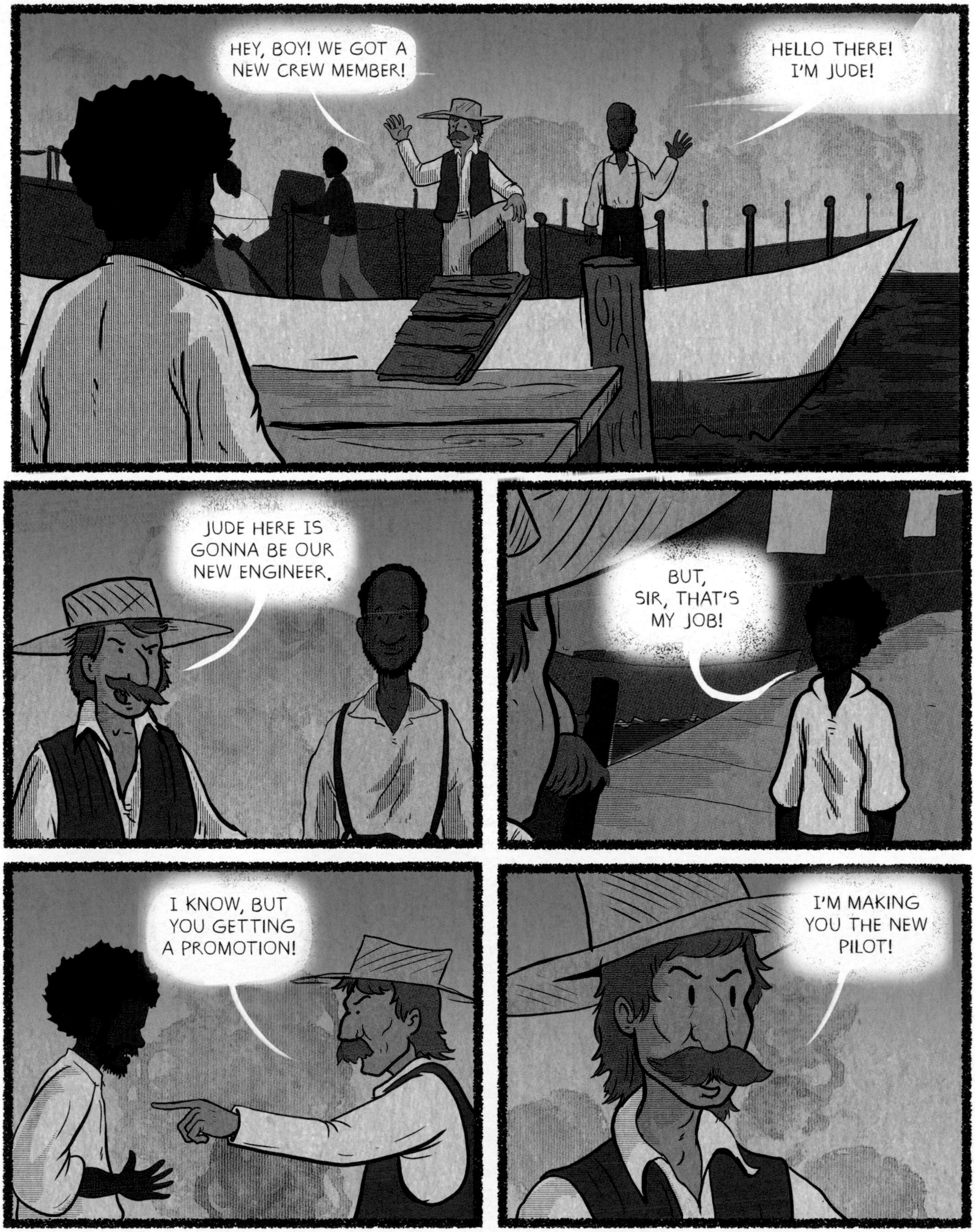
HEY, BOY! WE GOT A NEW CREW MEMBER!
HELLO THERE! I'M JUDE!
JUDE HERE IS GONNA BE OUR NEW ENGINEER.
BUT, SIR, THAT'S MY JOB!
I KNOW, BUT YOU GETTING A PROMOTION!
I'M MAKING YOU THE NEW PILOT!

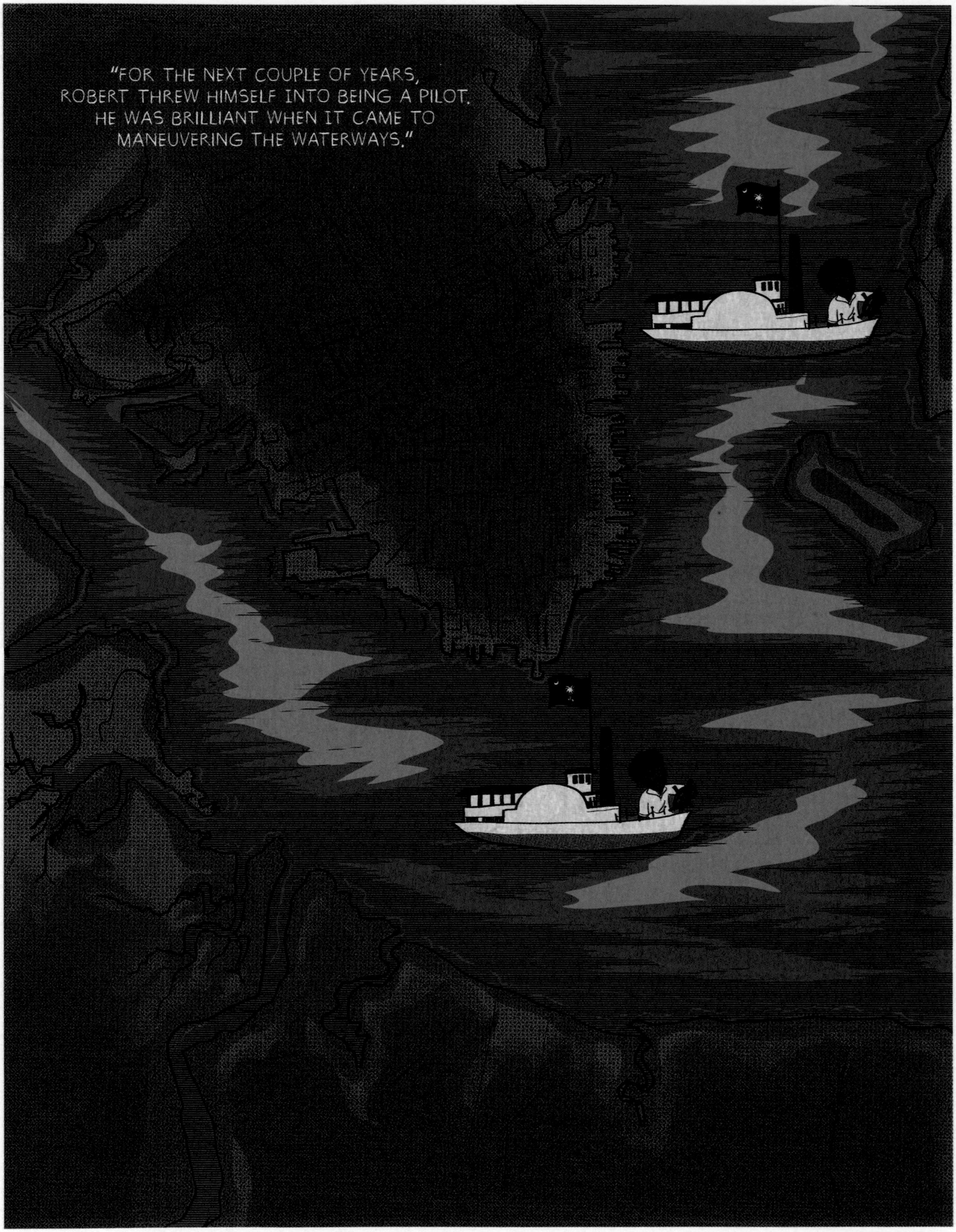
"FOR THE NEXT COUPLE OF YEARS, ROBERT THREW HIMSELF INTO BEING A PILOT. HE WAS BRILLIANT WHEN IT CAME TO MANEUVERING THE WATERWAYS."

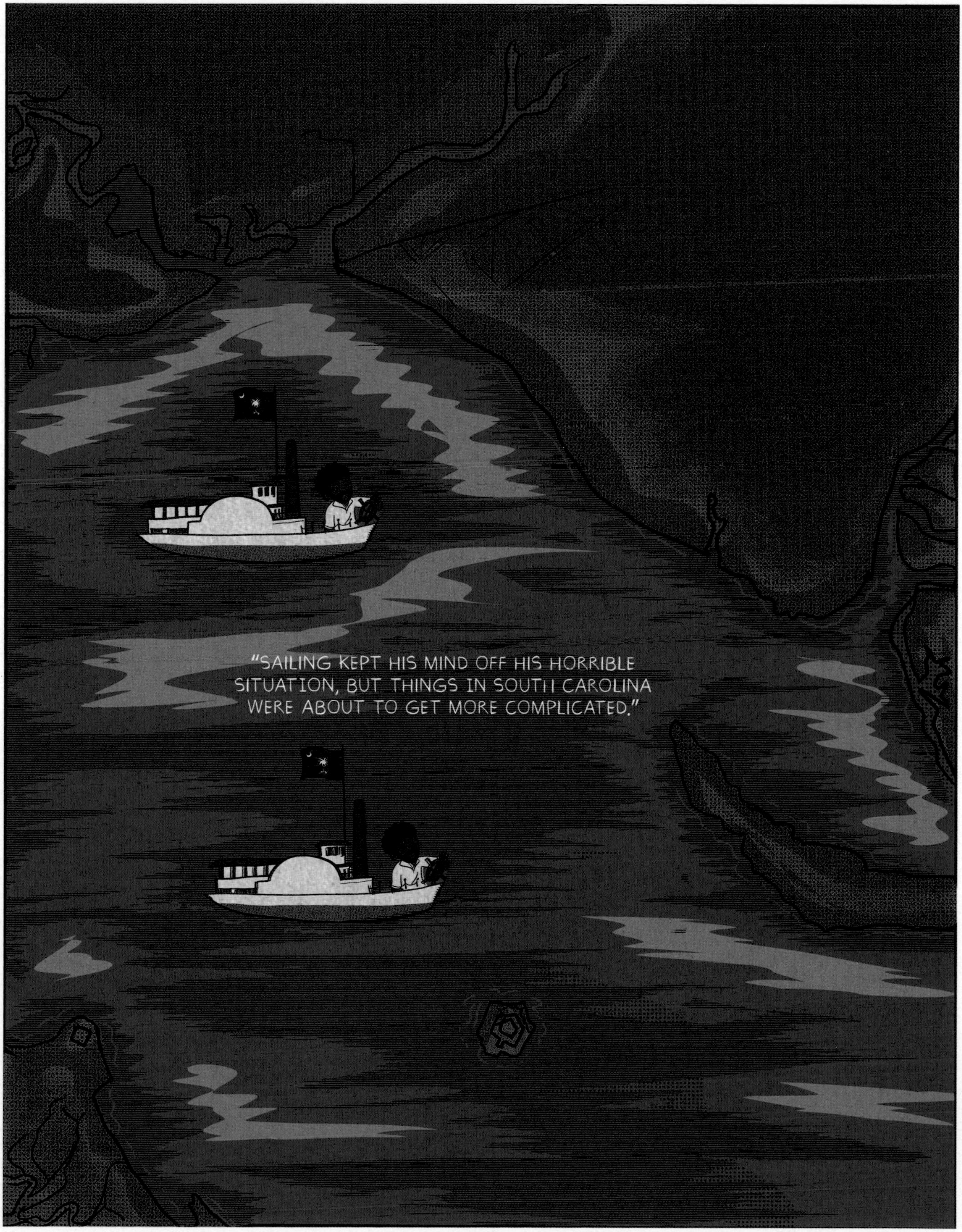
"SAILING KEPT HIS MIND OFF HIS HORRIBLE SITUATION, BUT THINGS IN SOUTH CAROLINA WERE ABOUT TO GET MORE COMPLICATED."

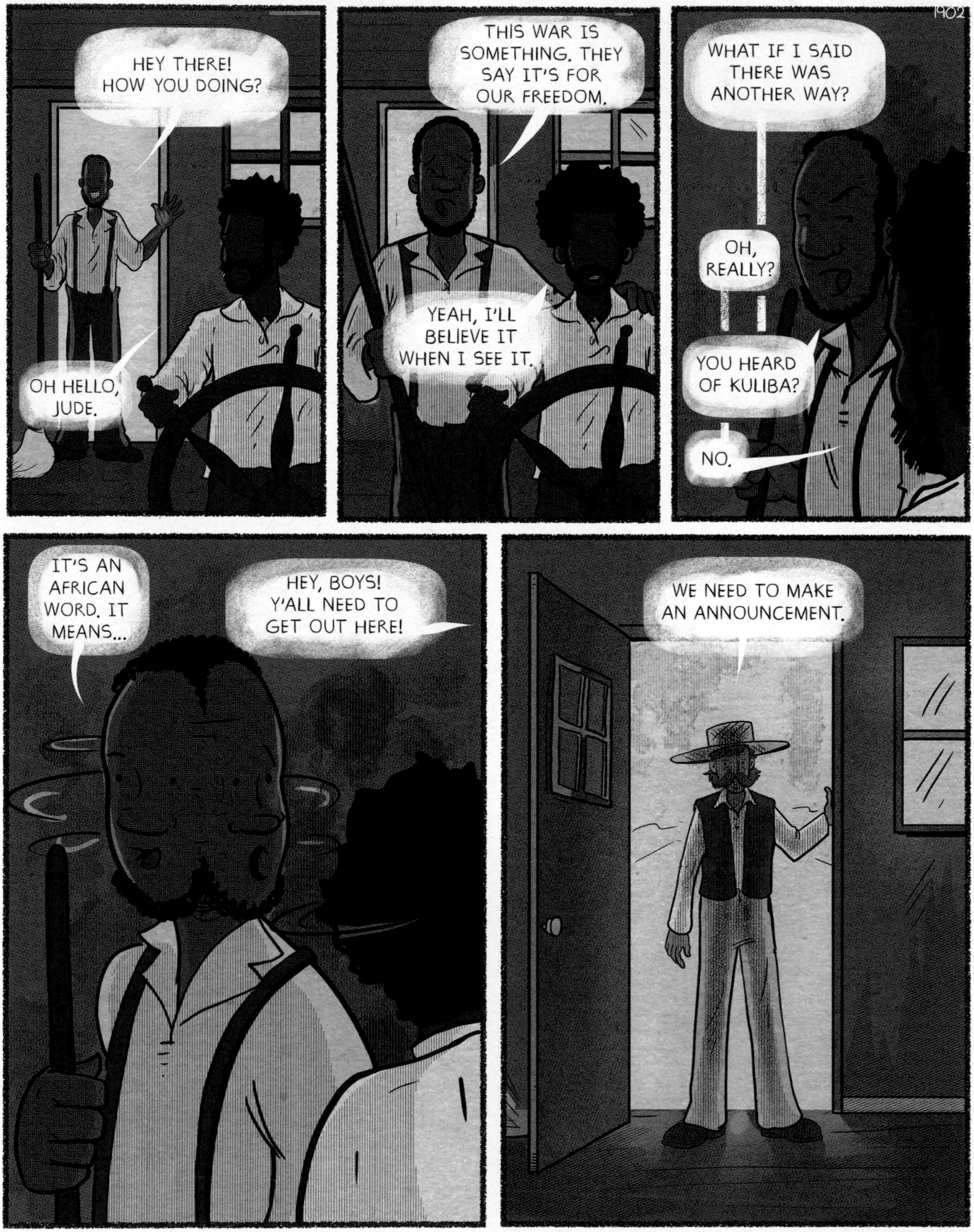
HEY THERE! HOW YOU DOING?
OH HELLO, JUDE.
THIS WAR IS SOMETHING. THEY SAY IT'S FOR OUR FREEDOM.
YEAH, I'LL BELIEVE IT WHEN I SEE IT.
1902
WHAT IF I SAID THERE WAS ANOTHER WAY?
OH, REALLY?
YOU HEARD OF KULIBA?
NO.
IT'S AN AFRICAN WORD. IT MEANS...
HEY, BOYS! Y'ALL NEED TO GET OUT HERE!
WE NEED TO MAKE AN ANNOUNCEMENT.

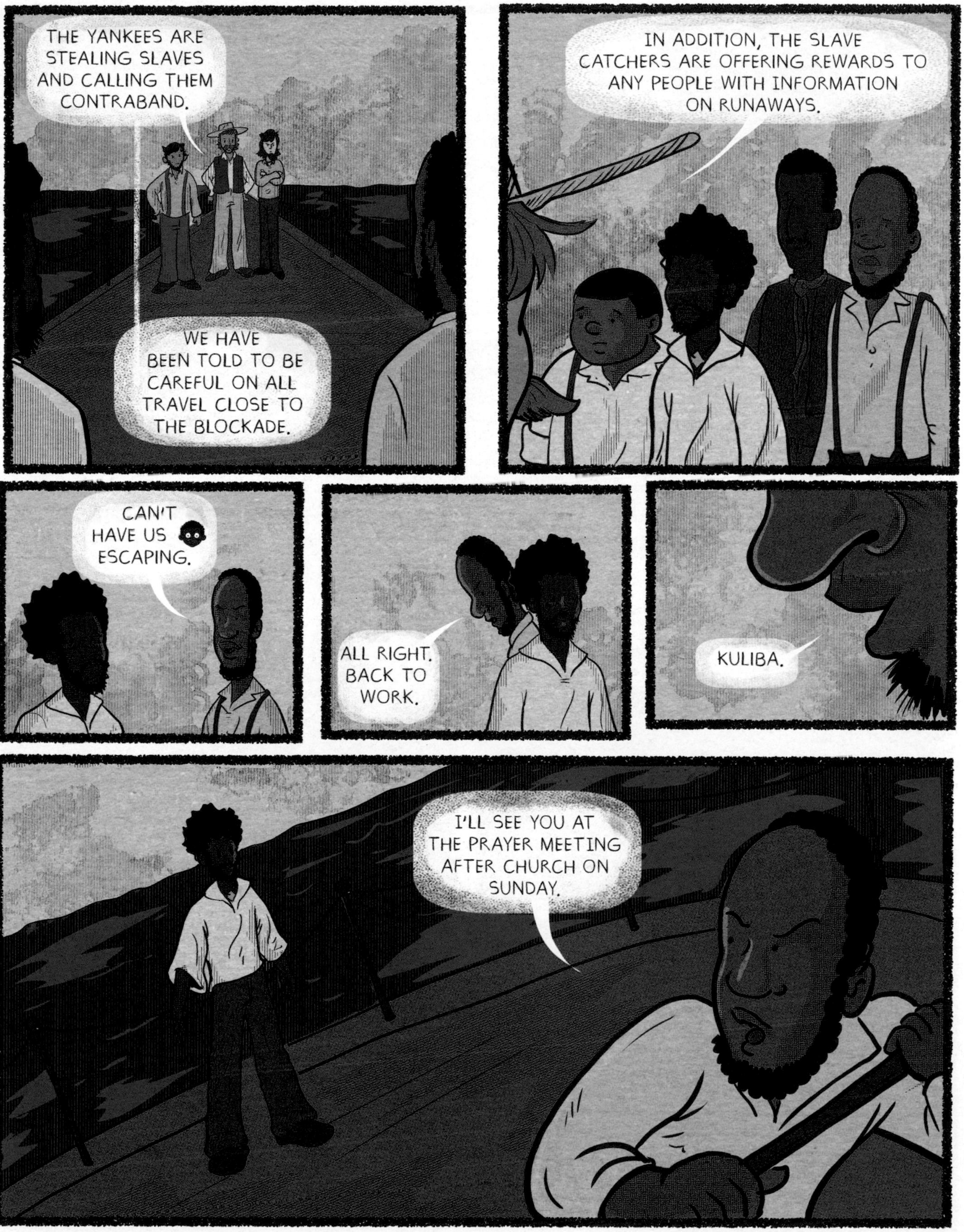
THE YANKEES ARE STEALING SLAVES AND CALLING THEM CONTRABAND.
WE HAVE BEEN TOLD TO BE CAREFUL ON ALL TRAVEL CLOSE TO THE BLOCKADE.
IN ADDITION, THE SLAVE CATCHERS ARE OFFERING REWARDS TO ANY PEOPLE WITH INFORMATION ON RUNAWAYS.
CAN'T HAVE US ESCAPING.
ALL RIGHT. BACK TO WORK.
KULIBA.
I'LL SEE YOU AT THE PRAYER MEETING AFTER CHURCH ON SUNDAY.

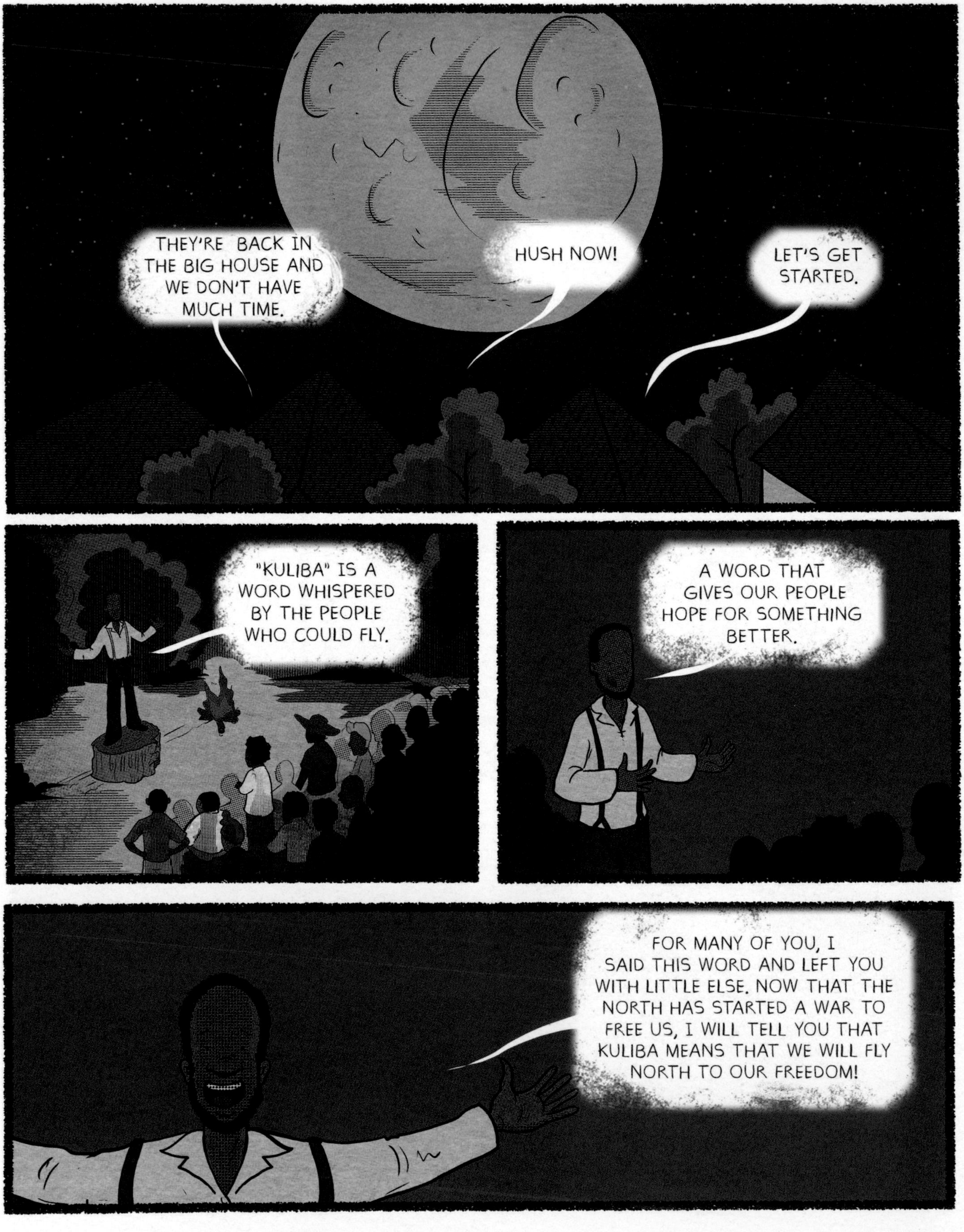
THEY'RE BACK IN THE BIG HOUSE AND WE DON'T HAVE MUCH TIME.
HUSH NOW!
LET'S GET STARTED.
"KULIBA" IS A WORD WHISPERED BY THE PEOPLE WHO COULD FLY.
A WORD THAT GIVES OUR PEOPLE HOPE FOR SOMETHING BETTER.
FOR MANY OF YOU, I SAID THIS WORD AND LEFT YOU WITH LITTLE ELSE. NOW THAT THE NORTH HAS STARTED A WAR TO FREE US, I WILL TELL YOU THAT KULIBA MEANS THAT WE WILL FLY NORTH TO OUR FREEDOM!

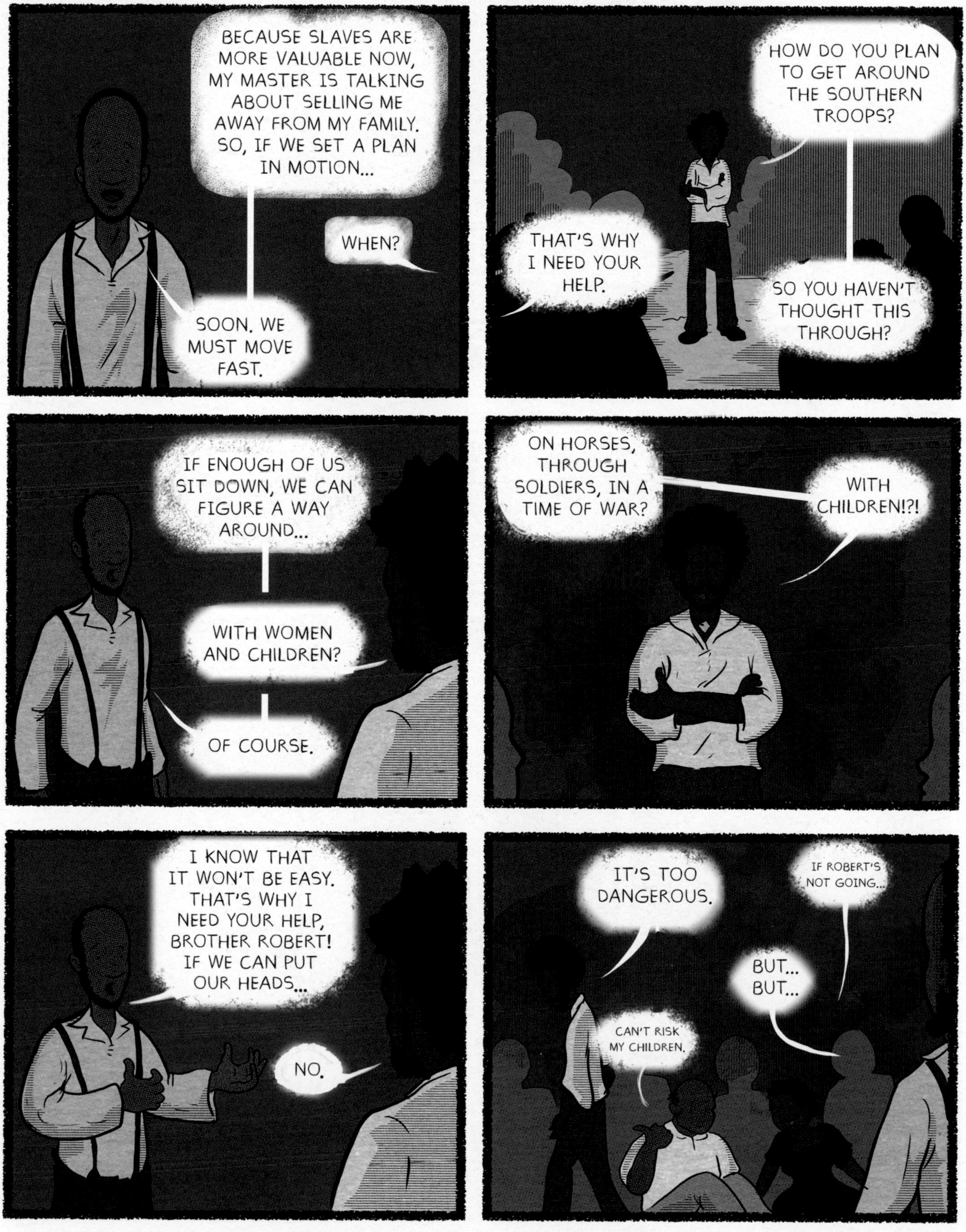
BECAUSE SLAVES ARE MORE VALUABLE NOW, MY MASTER IS TALKING ABOUT SELLING ME AWAY FROM MY FAMILY. SO, IF WE SET A PLAN IN MOTION...
WHEN?
SOON. WE MUST MOVE FAST.
HOW DO YOU PLAN TO GET AROUND THE SOUTHERN TROOPS?
THAT'S WHY I NEED YOUR HELP.
SO YOU HAVEN'T THOUGHT THIS THROUGH?
IF ENOUGH OF US SIT DOWN, WE CAN FIGURE A WAY AROUND...
WITH WOMEN AND CHILDREN?
OF COURSE.
ON HORSES, THROUGH SOLDIERS, IN A TIME OF WAR?
WITH CHILDREN!?!
I KNOW THAT IT WON'T BE EASY. THAT'S WHY I NEED YOUR HELP, BROTHER ROBERT! IF WE CAN PUT OUR HEADS...
NO.
IT'S TOO DANGEROUS.
IF ROBERT'S NOT GOING...
BUT... BUT...
CAN'T RISK MY CHILDREN.

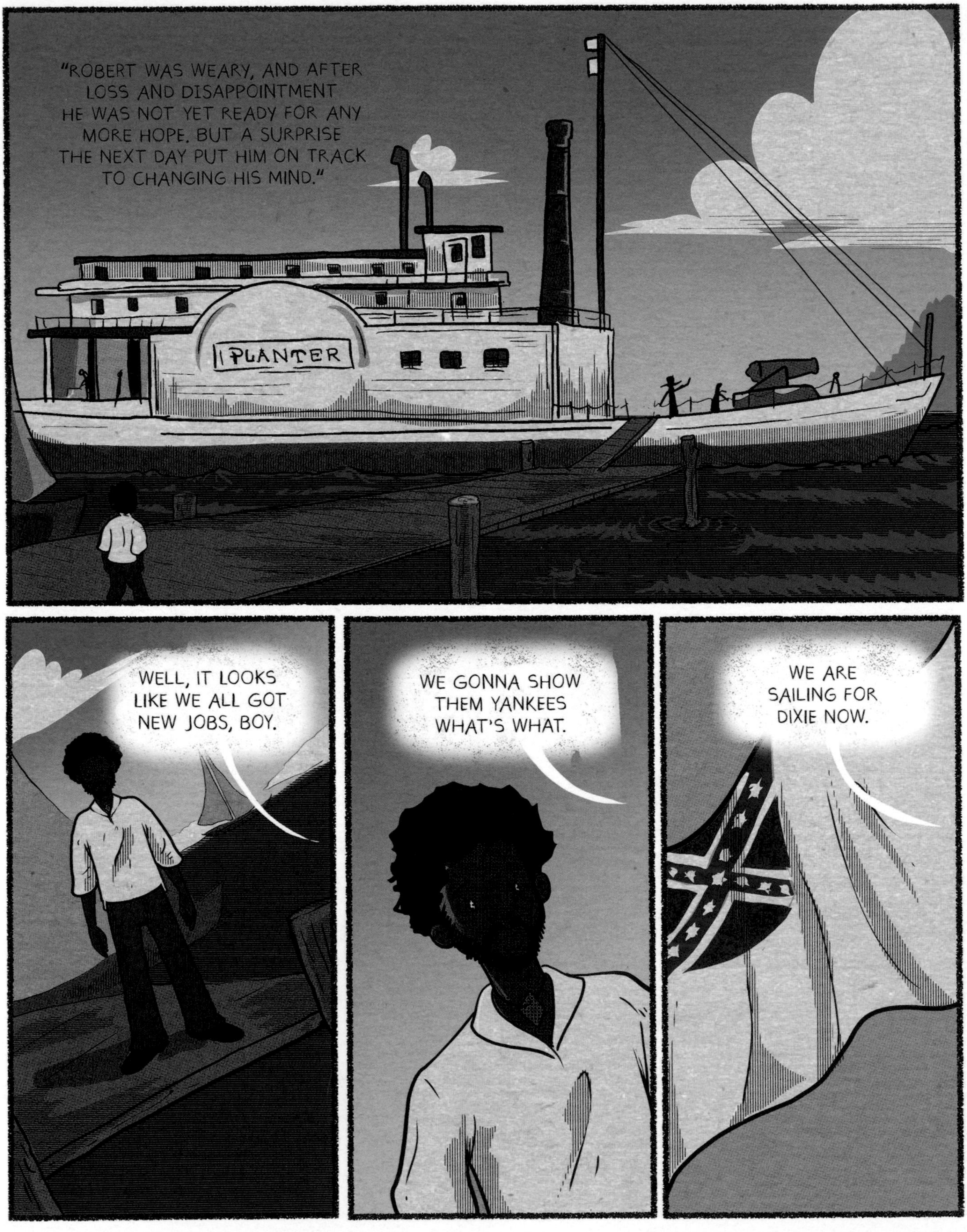
"ROBERT WAS WEARY, AND AFTER LOSS AND DISAPPOINTMENT HE WAS NOT YET READY FOR ANY MORE HOPE. BUT A SURPRISE THE NEXT DAY PUT HIM ON TRACK TO CHANGING HIS MIND."
PLANTER
WELL, IT LOOKS LIKE WE ALL GOT NEW JOBS, BOY.
WE GONNA SHOW THEM YANKEES WHAT'S WHAT.
WE ARE SAILING FOR DIXIE NOW.

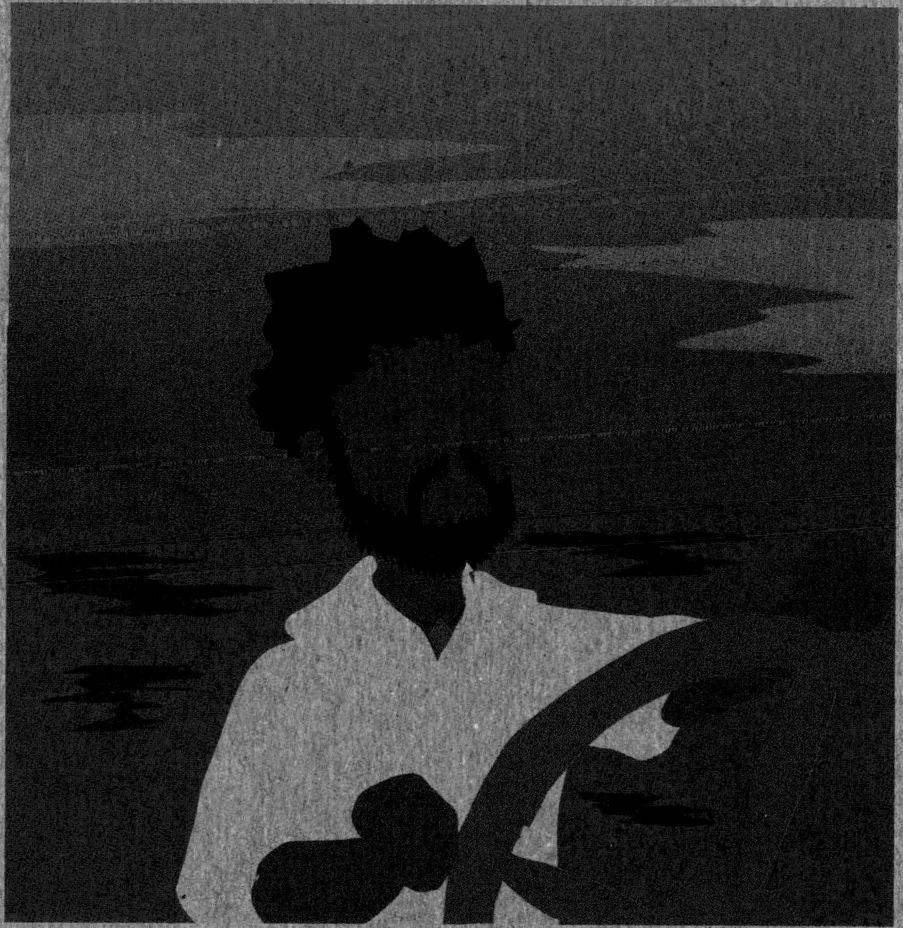

CHAPTER FOUR

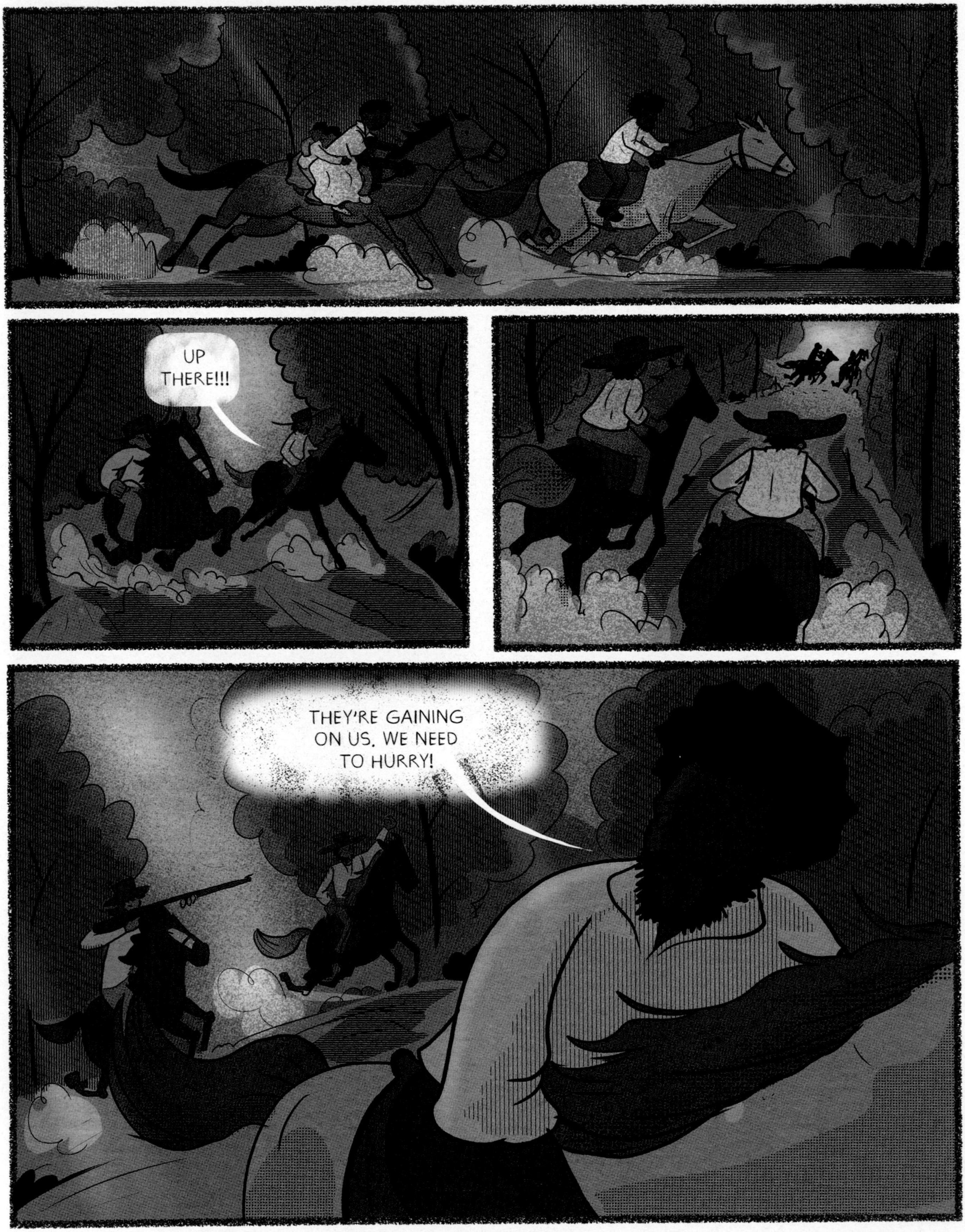
UP THERE!!!
THEY'RE GAINING ON US. WE NEED TO HURRY!

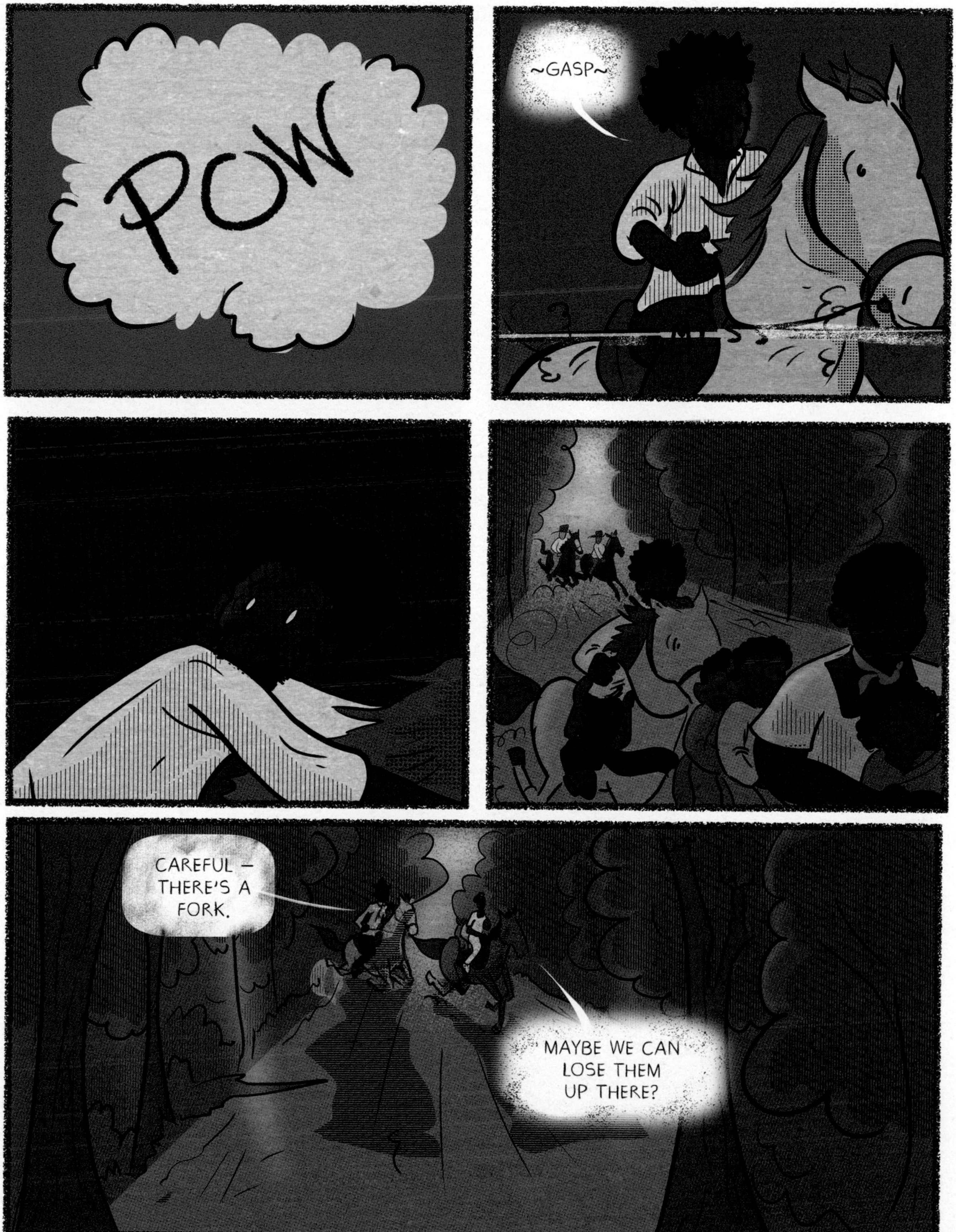
POW
~GASP~
CAREFUL — THERE'S A FORK.
MAYBE WE CAN LOSE THEM UP THERE?

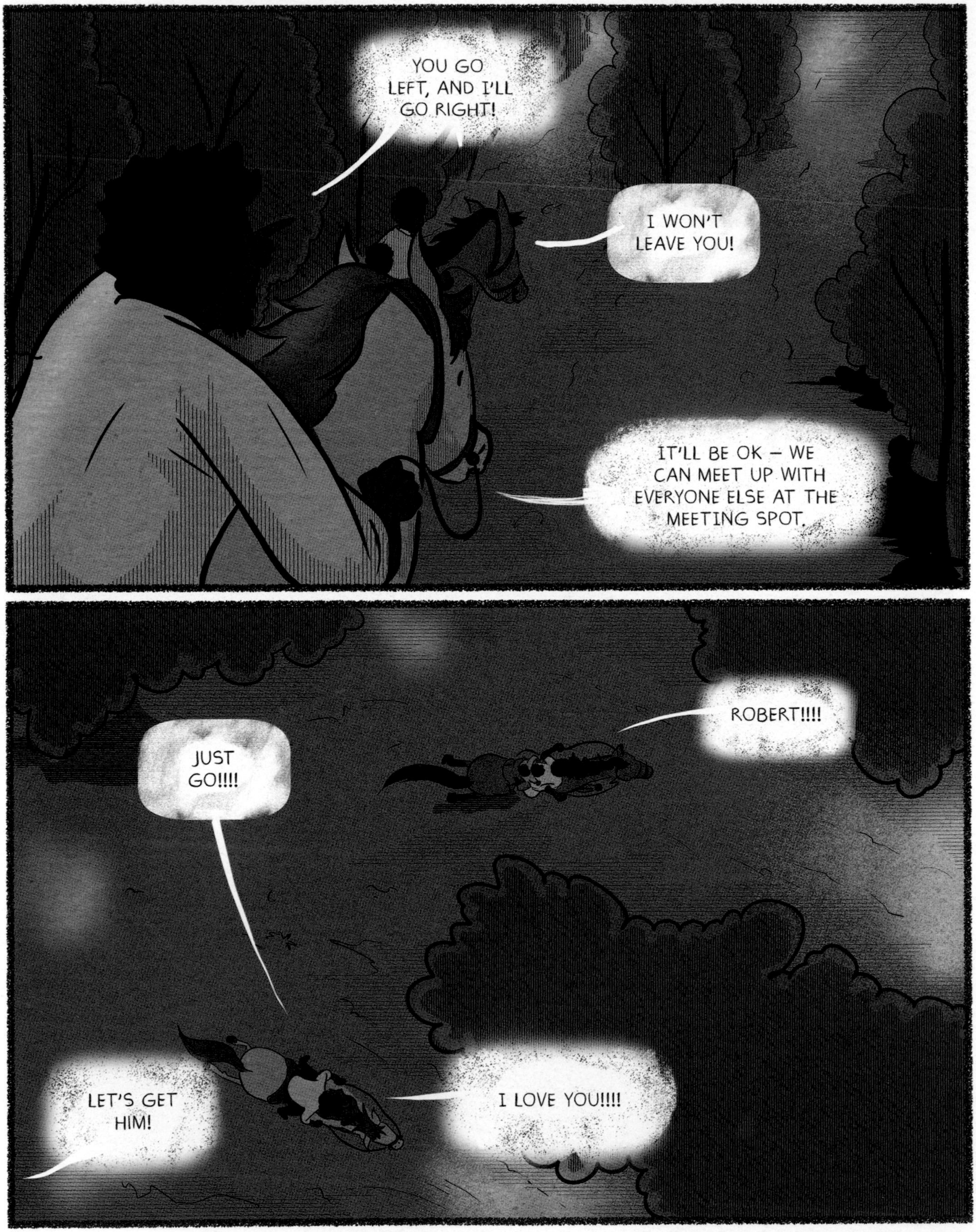
YOU GO LEFT, AND I'LL GO RIGHT!
I WON'T LEAVE YOU!
IT'LL BE OK – WE CAN MEET UP WITH EVERYONE ELSE AT THE MEETING SPOT.
ROBERT!!!!
JUST GO!!!!
LET'S GET HIM!
I LOVE YOU!!!!

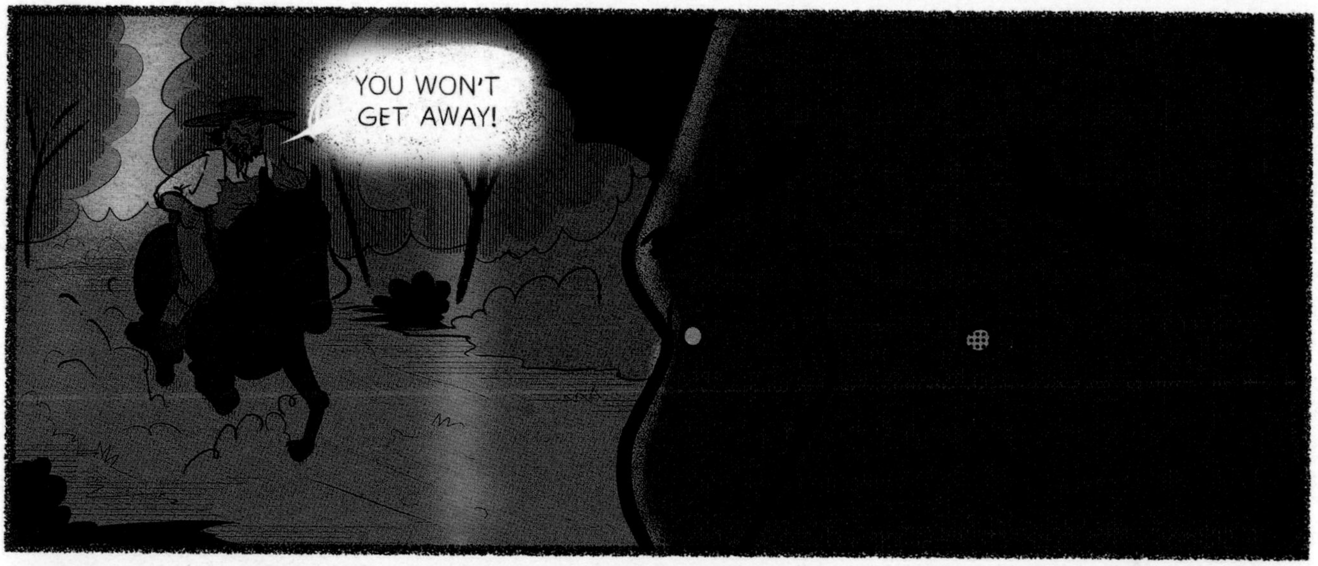
YOU WON'T GET AWAY!

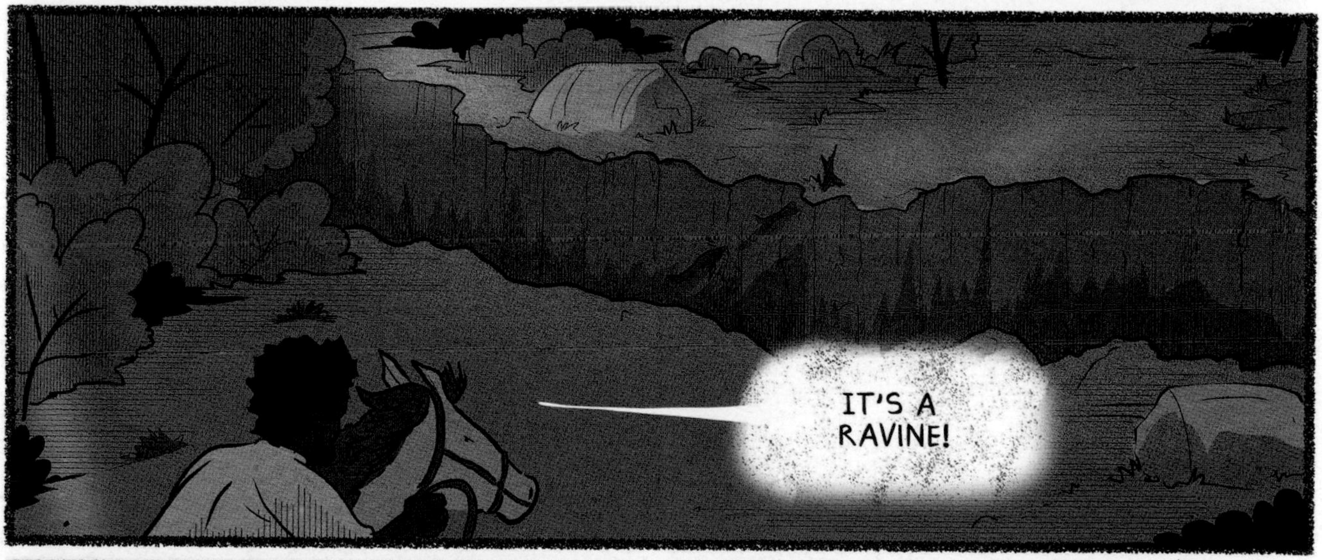
IT'S A RAVINE!

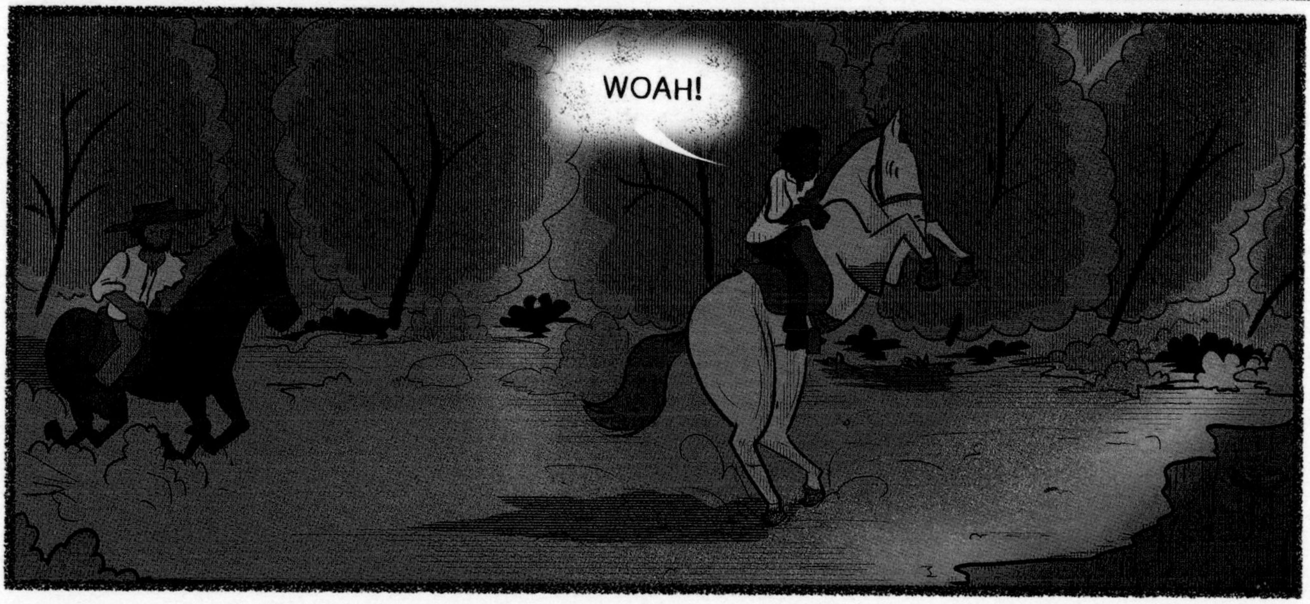
WOAH!

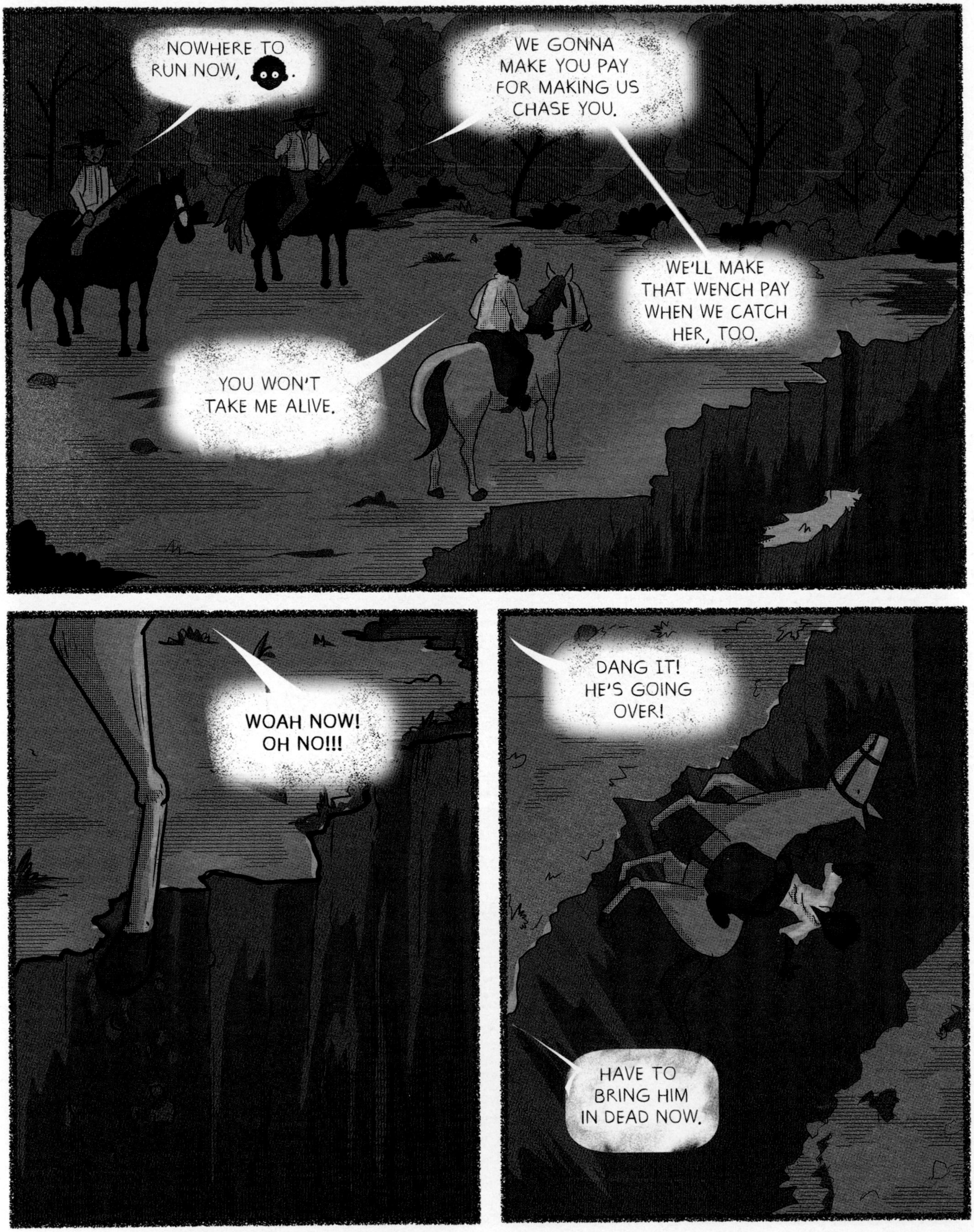
NOWHERE TO RUN NOW, .
WE GONNA MAKE YOU PAY FOR MAKING US CHASE YOU.
WE'LL MAKE THAT WENCH PAY WHEN WE CATCH HER, TOO.
YOU WON'T TAKE ME ALIVE.
WOAH NOW! OH NO!!!
DANG IT! HE'S GOING OVER!
HAVE TO BRING HIM IN DEAD NOW.

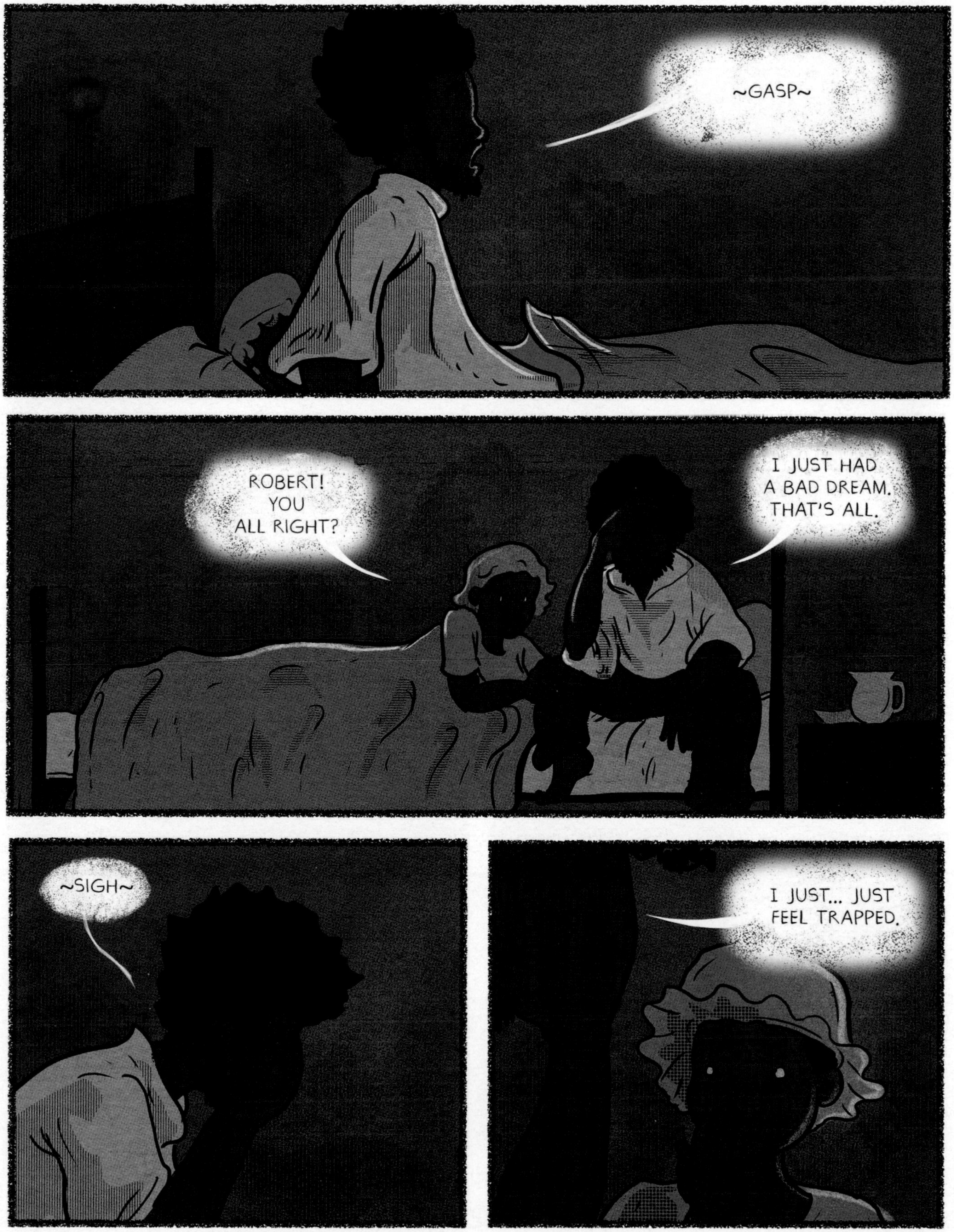
~GASP~
ROBERT! YOU ALL RIGHT?
I JUST HAD A BAD DREAM. THAT'S ALL.
~SIGH~
I JUST... JUST FEEL TRAPPED.

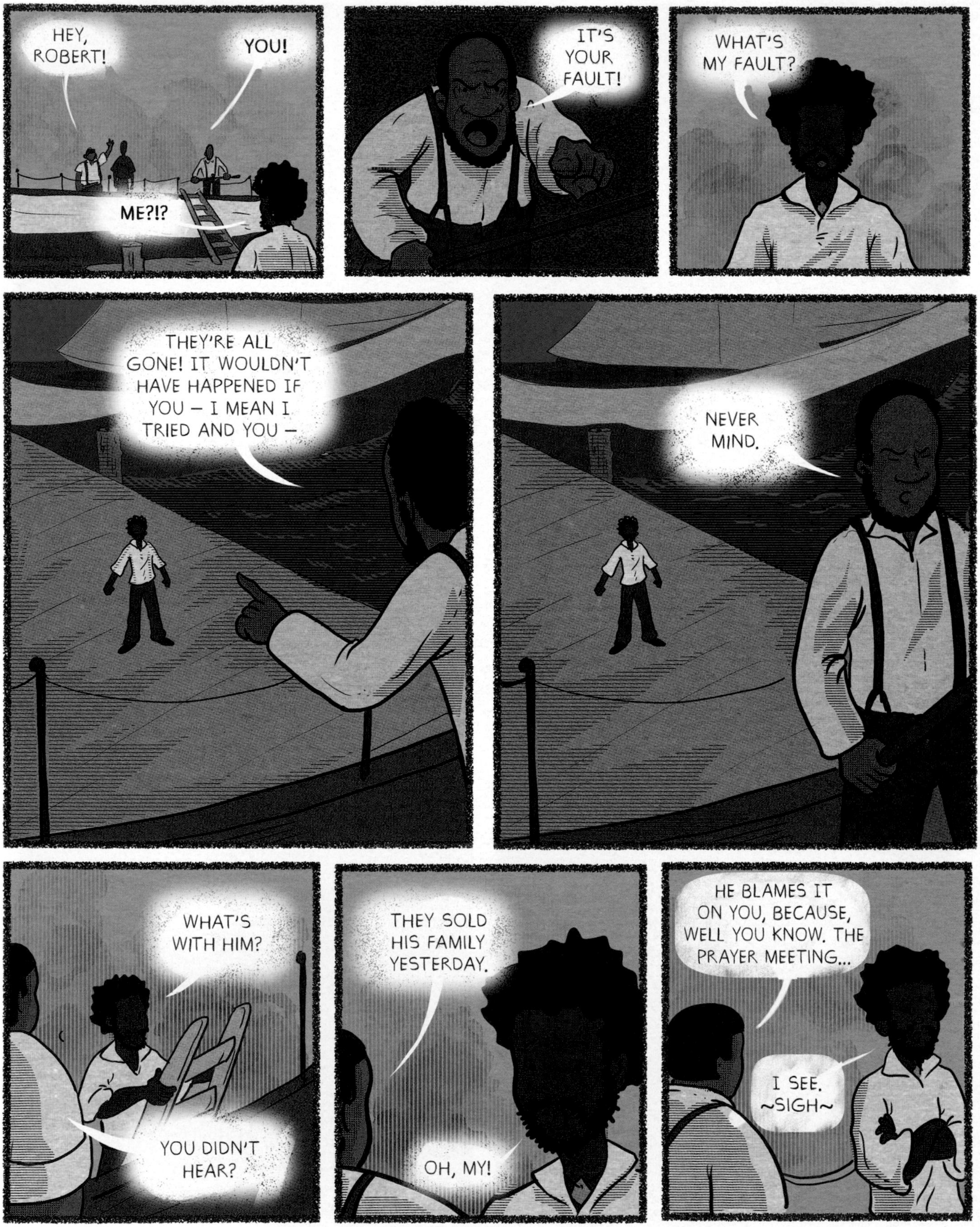
HEY, ROBERT!
YOU!
ME?!?
IT'S YOUR FAULT!
WHAT'S MY FAULT?
THEY'RE ALL GONE! IT WOULDN'T HAVE HAPPENED IF YOU – I MEAN I TRIED AND YOU –
NEVER MIND.
WHAT'S WITH HIM?
YOU DIDN'T HEAR?
THEY SOLD HIS FAMILY YESTERDAY.
OH, MY!
HE BLAMES IT ON YOU, BECAUSE, WELL YOU KNOW. THE PRAYER MEETING...
I SEE. ~SIGH~

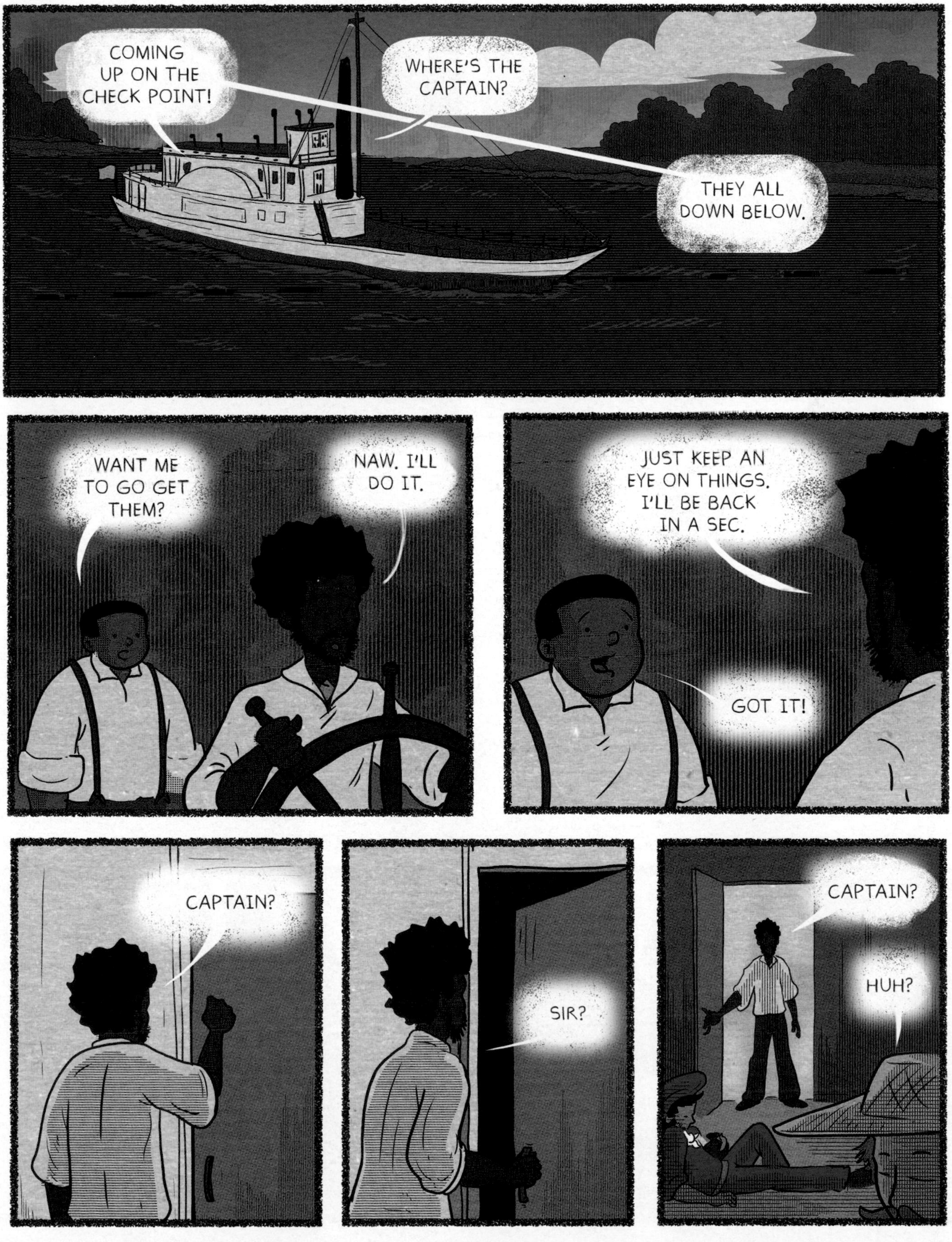
COMING UP ON THE CHECK POINT!
WHERE'S THE CAPTAIN?
THEY ALL DOWN BELOW.
WANT ME TO GO GET THEM?
NAW. I'LL DO IT.
JUST KEEP AN EYE ON THINGS. I'LL BE BACK IN A SEC.
GOT IT!
CAPTAIN?
SIR?
CAPTAIN?
HUH?

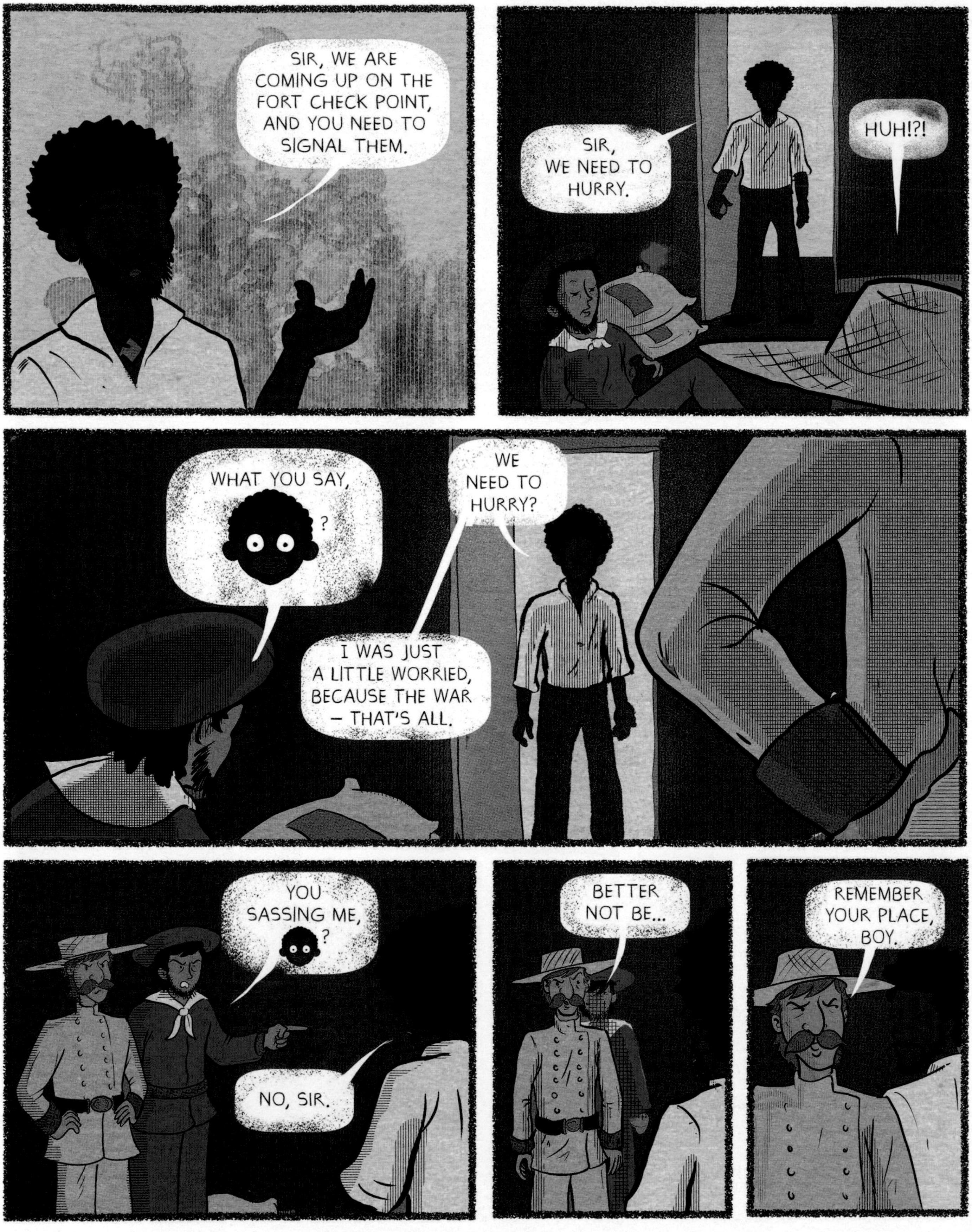
SIR, WE ARE COMING UP ON THE FORT CHECK POINT, AND YOU NEED TO SIGNAL THEM.
SIR, WE NEED TO HURRY.
HUH!?!
WHAT YOU SAY, ?
WE NEED TO HURRY?
I WAS JUST A LITTLE WORRIED, BECAUSE THE WAR – THAT'S ALL.
YOU SASSING ME, ?
NO, SIR.
BETTER NOT BE...
REMEMBER YOUR PLACE, BOY.

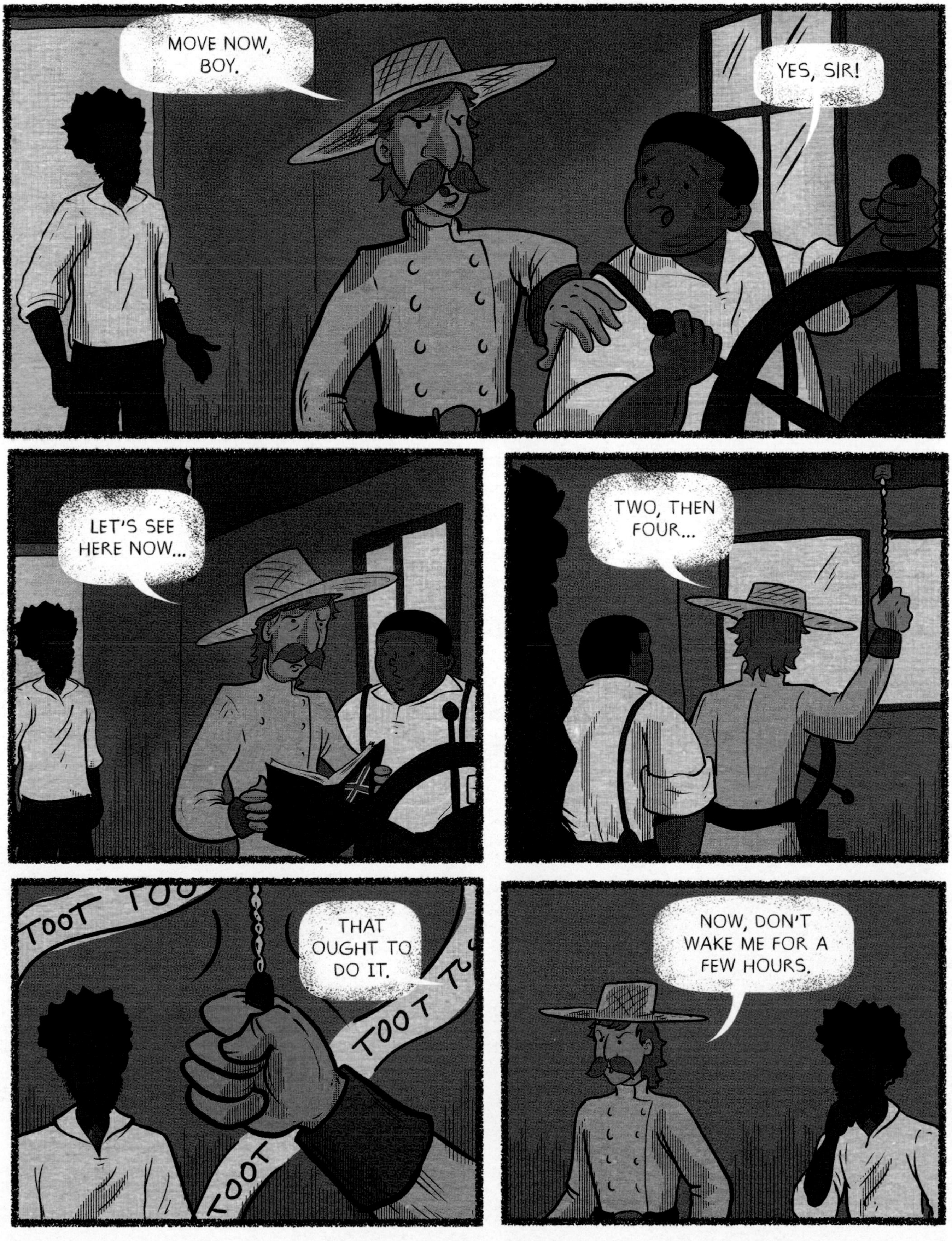
MOVE NOW, BOY.
YES, SIR!
LET'S SEE HERE NOW...
TWO, THEN FOUR...
TOOT TOO
THAT OUGHT TO DO IT.
TOOT
TOOT
NOW, DON'T WAKE ME FOR A FEW HOURS.

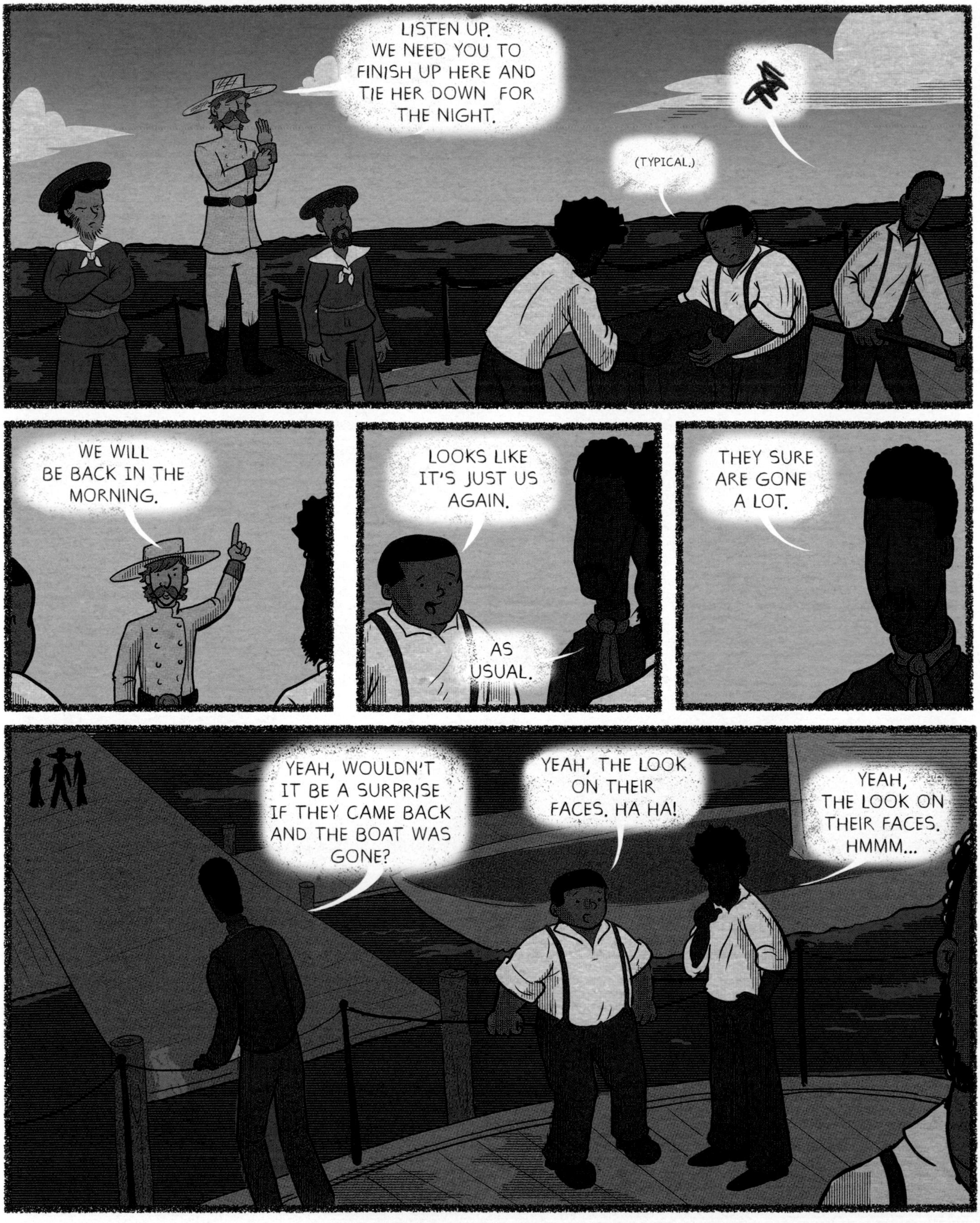
LISTEN UP. WE NEED YOU TO FINISH UP HERE AND TIE HER DOWN FOR THE NIGHT.
(TYPICAL.)
WE WILL BE BACK IN THE MORNING.
LOOKS LIKE IT'S JUST US AGAIN.
AS USUAL.
THEY SURE ARE GONE A LOT.
YEAH, WOULDN'T IT BE A SURPRISE IF THEY CAME BACK AND THE BOAT WAS GONE?
YEAH, THE LOOK ON THEIR FACES. HA HA!
YEAH, THE LOOK ON THEIR FACES. HMMM...

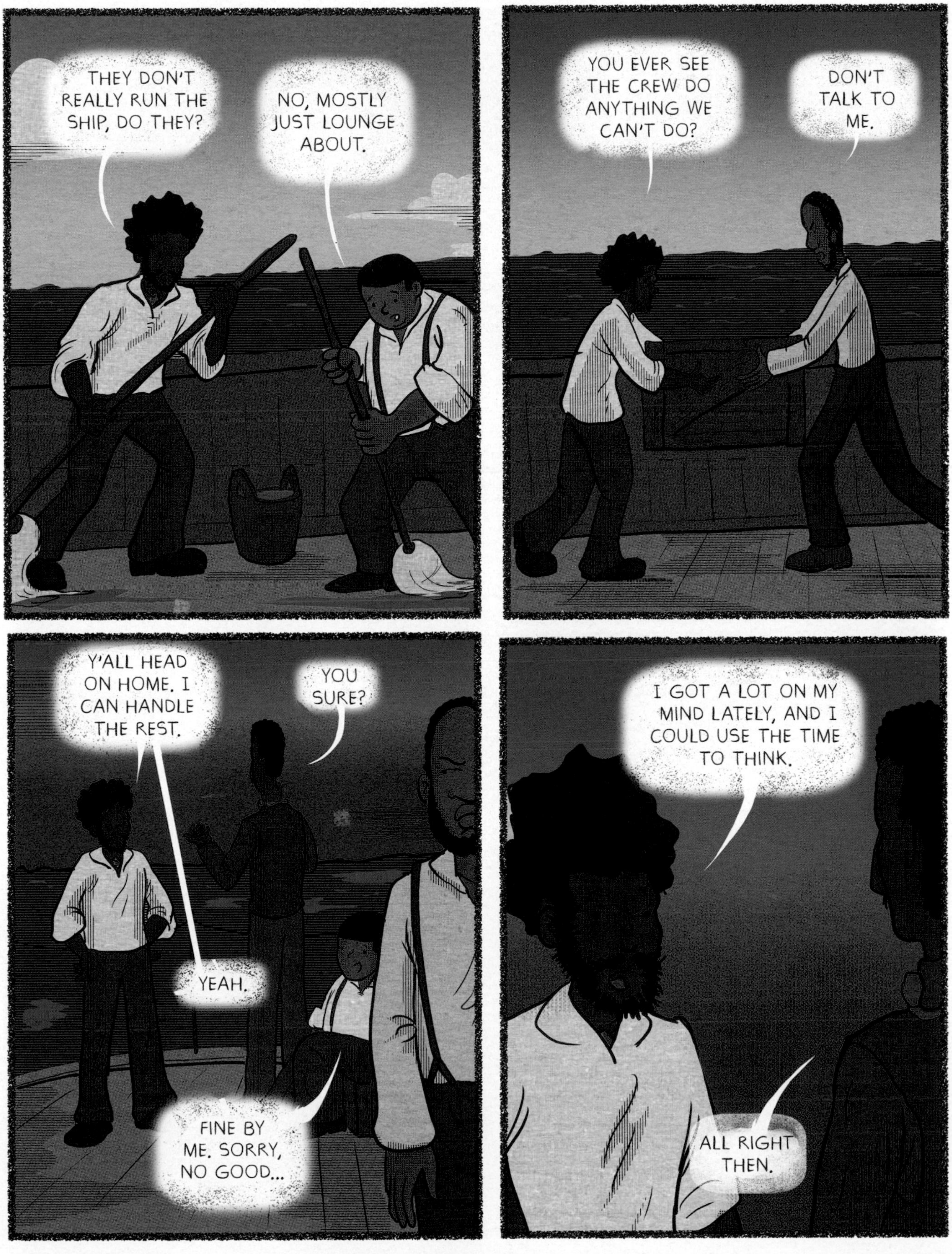
THEY DON'T REALLY RUN THE SHIP, DO THEY?
NO, MOSTLY JUST LOUNGE ABOUT.
YOU EVER SEE THE CREW DO ANYTHING WE CAN'T DO?
DON'T TALK TO ME.
Y'ALL HEAD ON HOME. I CAN HANDLE THE REST.
YOU SURE?
YEAH.
FINE BY ME. SORRY, NO GOOD...
I GOT A LOT ON MY MIND LATELY, AND I COULD USE THE TIME TO THINK.
ALL RIGHT THEN.

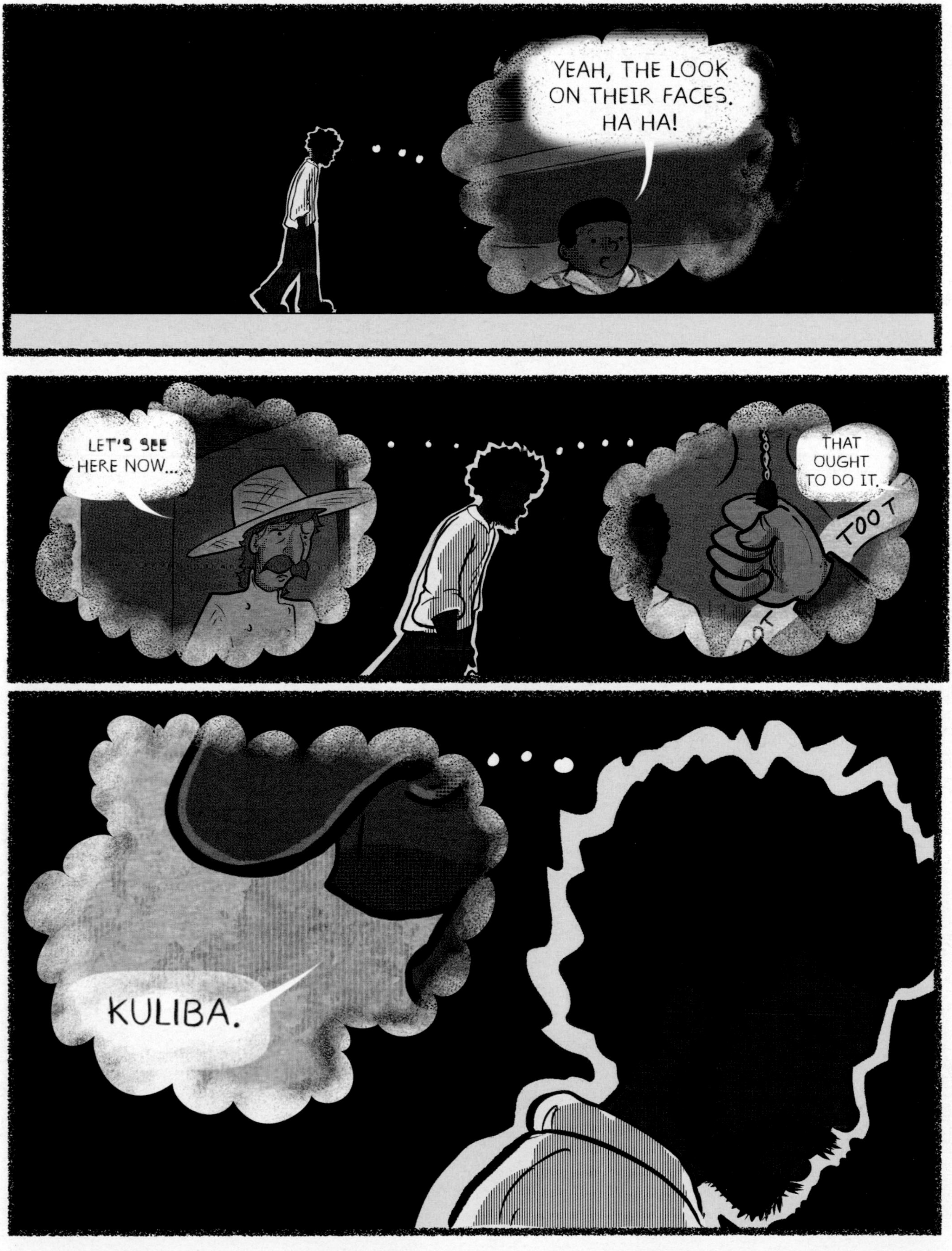
YEAH, THE LOOK ON THEIR FACES. HA HA!
LET'S SEE HERE NOW...
THAT OUGHT TO DO IT.
TOOT
KULIBA.

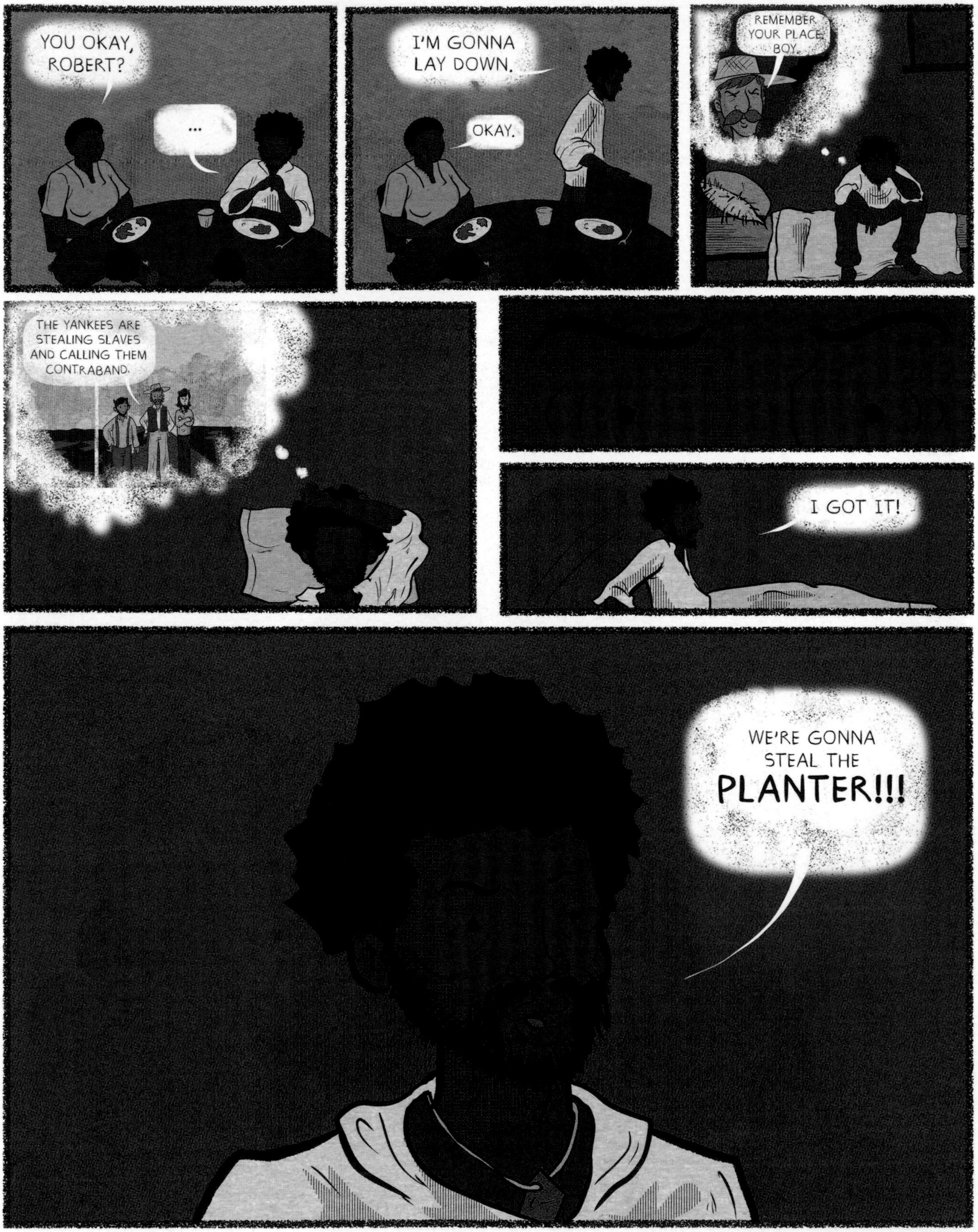
YOU OKAY, ROBERT?
...
I'M GONNA LAY DOWN.
OKAY.
REMEMBER YOUR PLACE, BOY.
THE YANKEES ARE STEALING SLAVES AND CALLING THEM CONTRABAND.
I GOT IT!
WE'RE GONNA STEAL THE PLANTER!!!

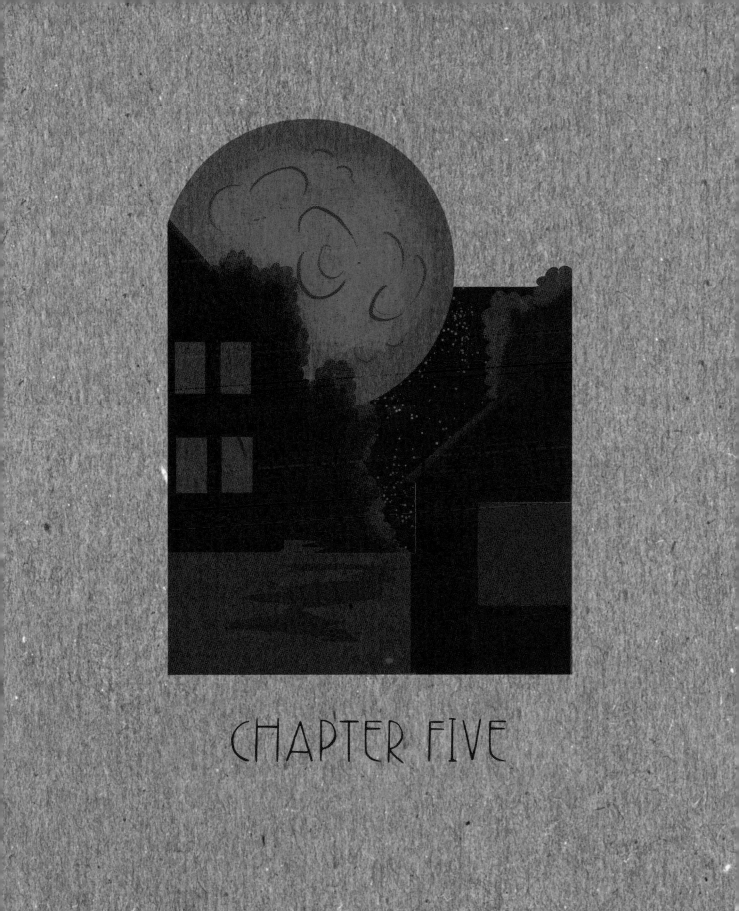

CHAPTER FIVE

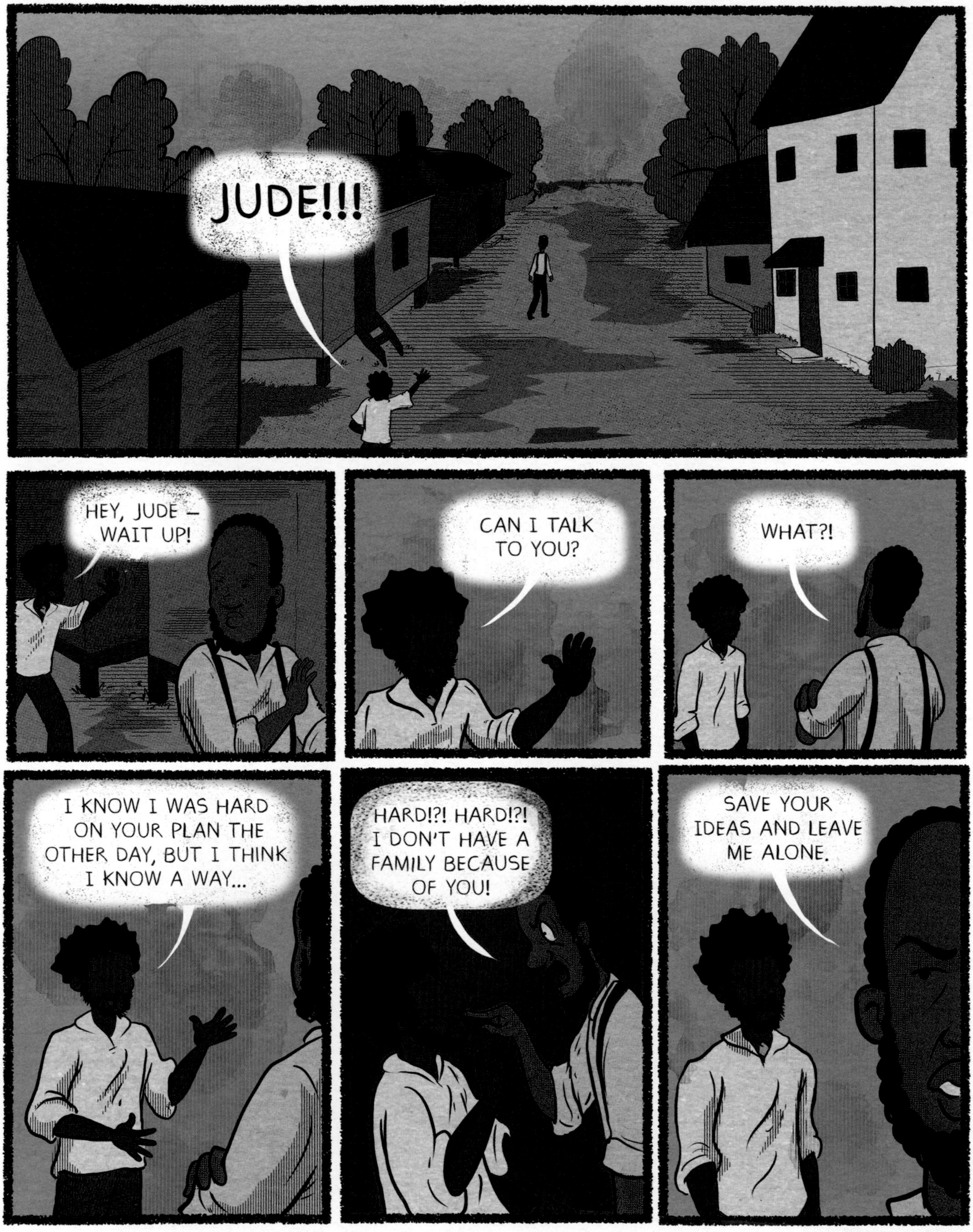
JUDE!!!
HEY, JUDE — WAIT UP!
CAN I TALK TO YOU?
WHAT?!
I KNOW I WAS HARD ON YOUR PLAN THE OTHER DAY, BUT I THINK I KNOW A WAY...
HARD!?! HARD!?! I DON'T HAVE A FAMILY BECAUSE OF YOU!
SAVE YOUR IDEAS AND LEAVE ME ALONE.

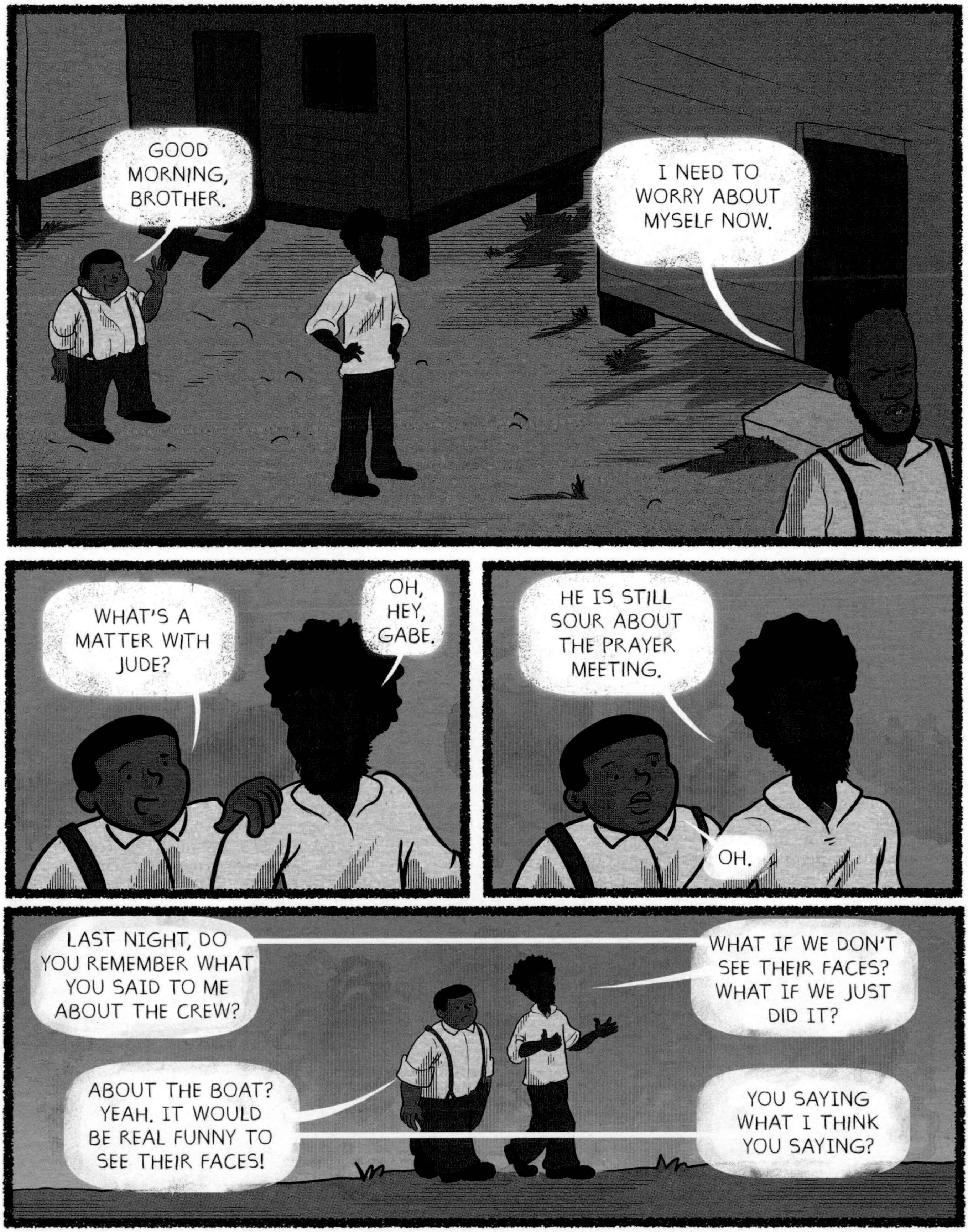
GOOD MORNING, BROTHER.
I NEED TO WORRY ABOUT MYSELF NOW.
WHAT'S A MATTER WITH JUDE?
OH, HEY, GABE.
HE IS STILL SOUR ABOUT THE PRAYER MEETING.
OH.
LAST NIGHT, DO YOU REMEMBER WHAT YOU SAID TO ME ABOUT THE CREW?
ABOUT THE BOAT? YEAH. IT WOULD BE REAL FUNNY TO SEE THEIR FACES!
WHAT IF WE DON'T SEE THEIR FACES? WHAT IF WE JUST DID IT?
YOU SAYING WHAT I THINK YOU SAYING?

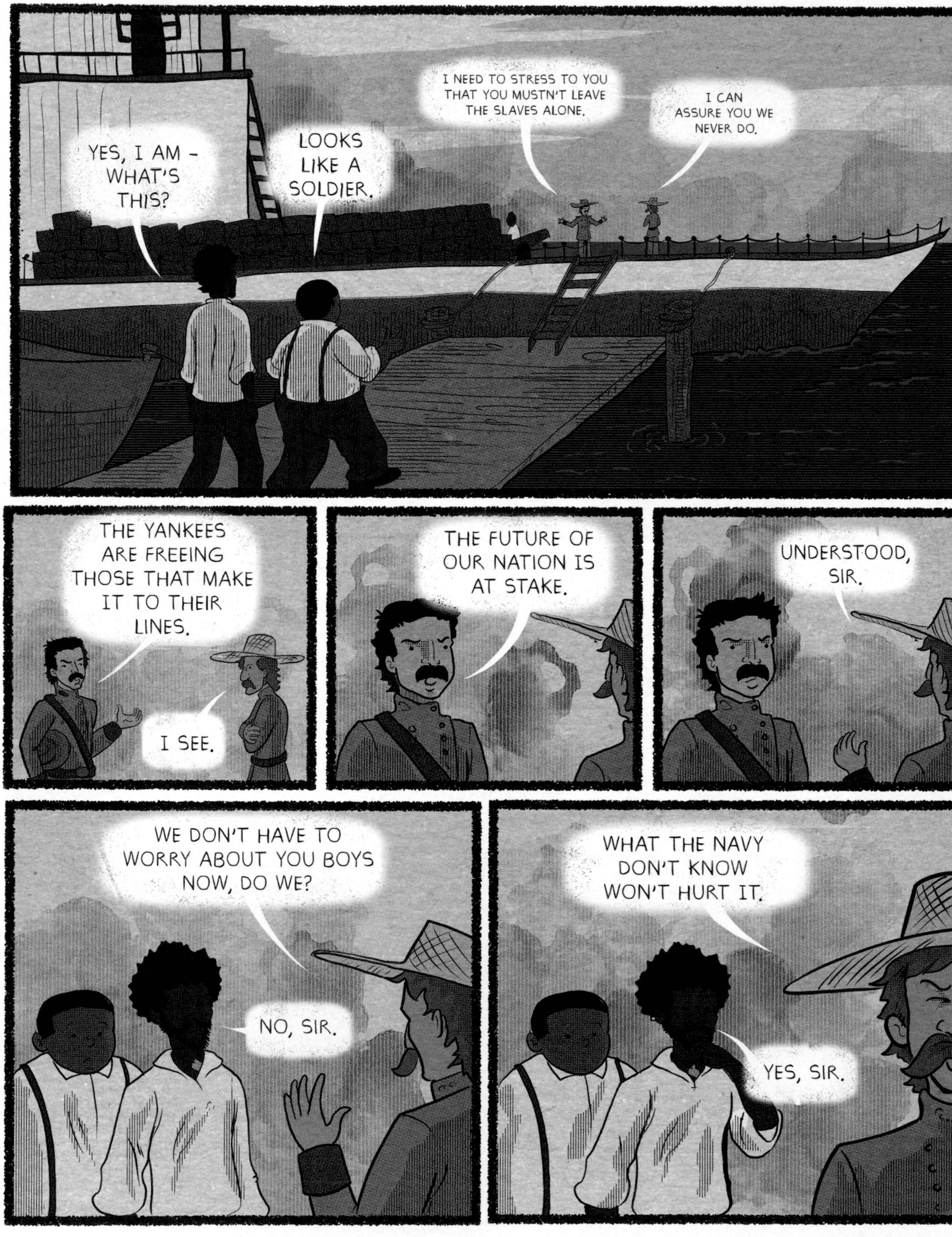
YES, I AM - WHAT'S THIS?
LOOKS LIKE A SOLDIER.
I NEED TO STRESS TO YOU THAT YOU MUSTN'T LEAVE THE SLAVES ALONE.
I CAN ASSURE YOU WE NEVER DO.
THE YANKEES ARE FREEING THOSE THAT MAKE IT TO THEIR LINES.
I SEE.
THE FUTURE OF OUR NATION IS AT STAKE.
UNDERSTOOD, SIR.
WE DON'T HAVE TO WORRY ABOUT YOU BOYS NOW, DO WE?
NO, SIR.
WHAT THE NAVY DON'T KNOW WON'T HURT IT.
YES, SIR.

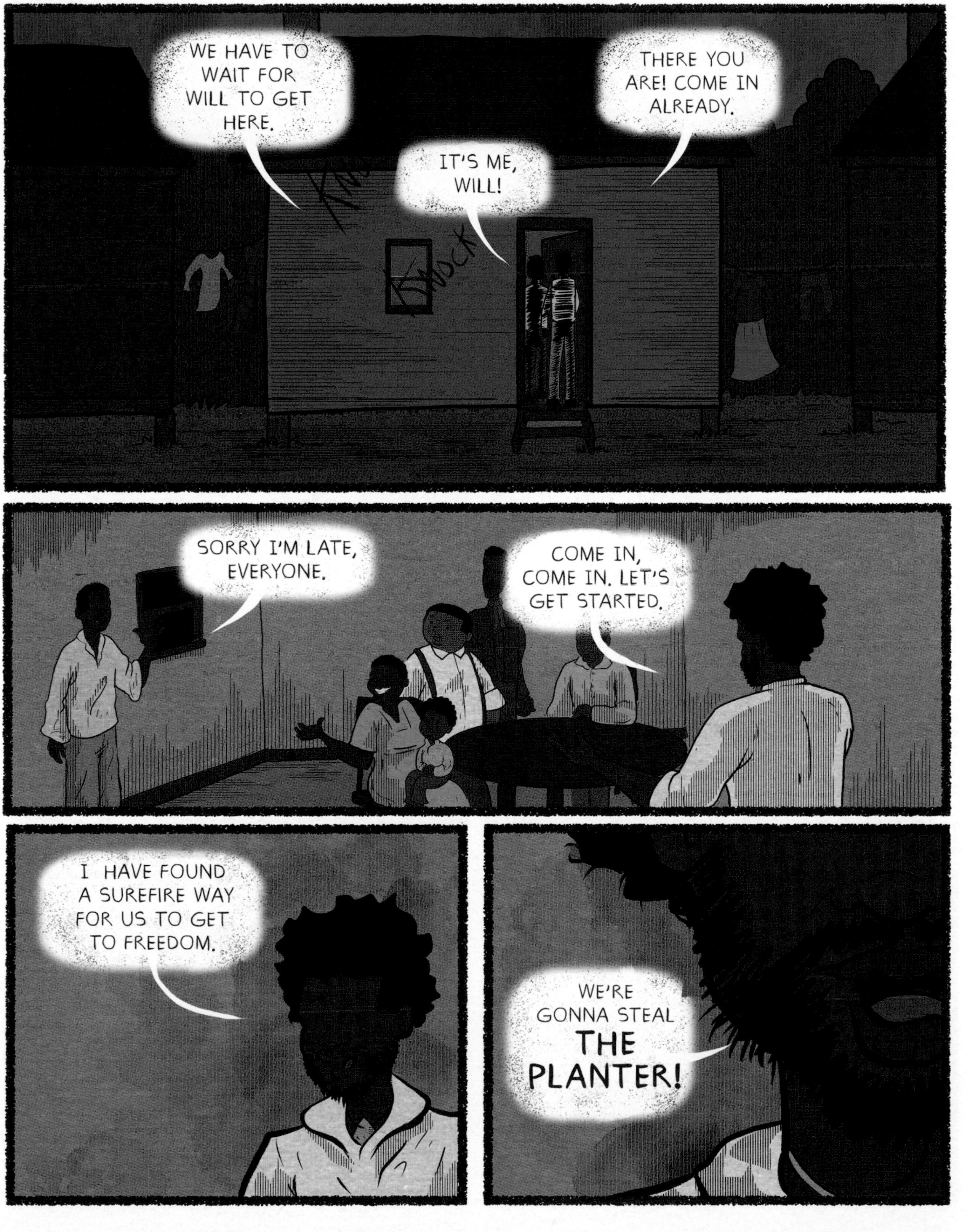
WE HAVE TO WAIT FOR WILL TO GET HERE.
KNOCK
IT'S ME, WILL!
THERE YOU ARE! COME IN ALREADY.
SORRY I'M LATE, EVERYONE.
COME IN, COME IN. LET'S GET STARTED.
I HAVE FOUND A SUREFIRE WAY FOR US TO GET TO FREEDOM.
WE'RE GONNA STEAL THE PLANTER!

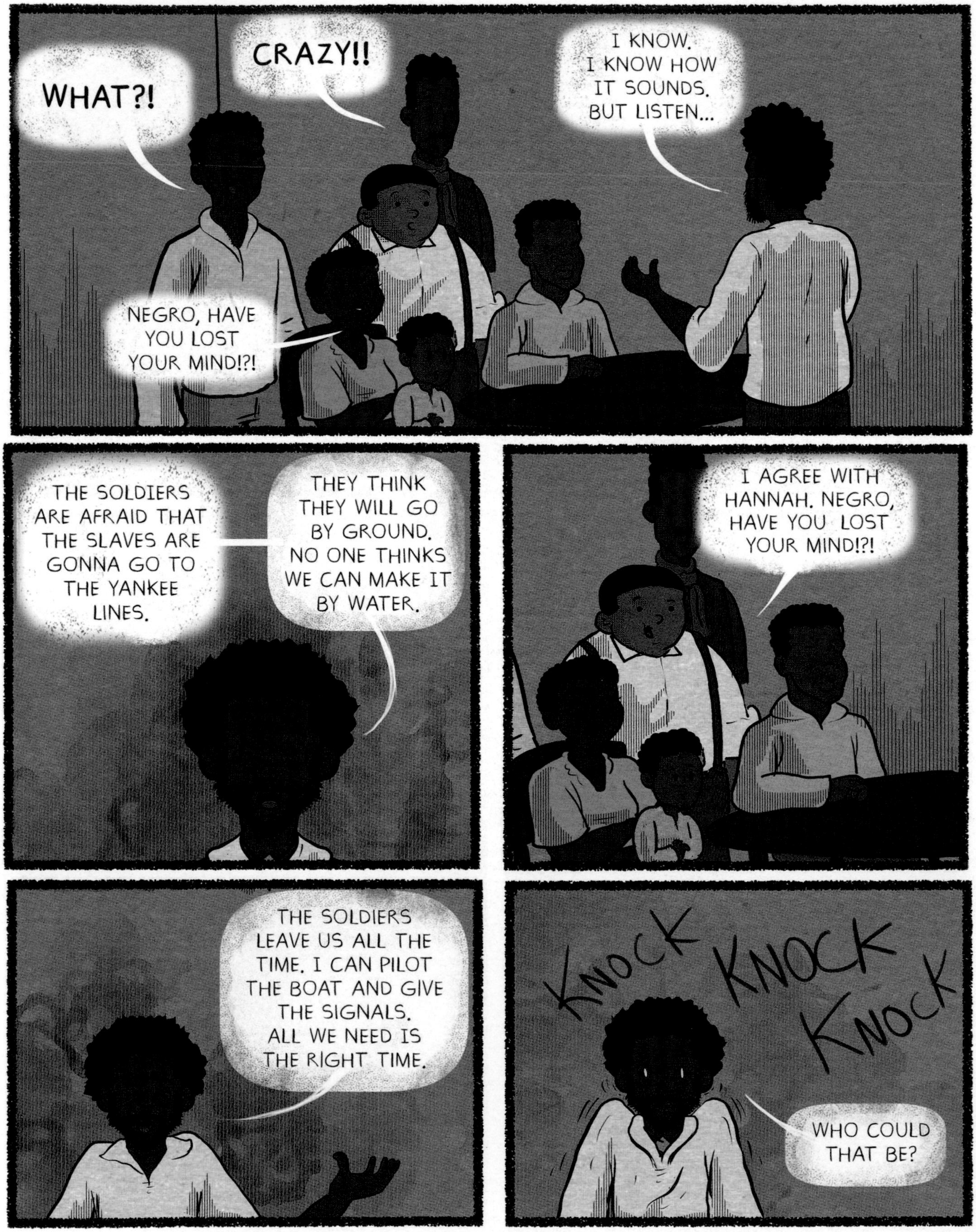
WHAT?!
CRAZY!!
I KNOW. I KNOW HOW IT SOUNDS. BUT LISTEN...
NEGRO, HAVE YOU LOST YOUR MIND!?!
THE SOLDIERS ARE AFRAID THAT THE SLAVES ARE GONNA GO TO THE YANKEE LINES.
THEY THINK THEY WILL GO BY GROUND. NO ONE THINKS WE CAN MAKE IT BY WATER.
I AGREE WITH HANNAH. NEGRO, HAVE YOU LOST YOUR MIND!?!
THE SOLDIERS LEAVE US ALL THE TIME. I CAN PILOT THE BOAT AND GIVE THE SIGNALS. ALL WE NEED IS THE RIGHT TIME.
KNOCK KNOCK KNOCK
WHO COULD THAT BE?

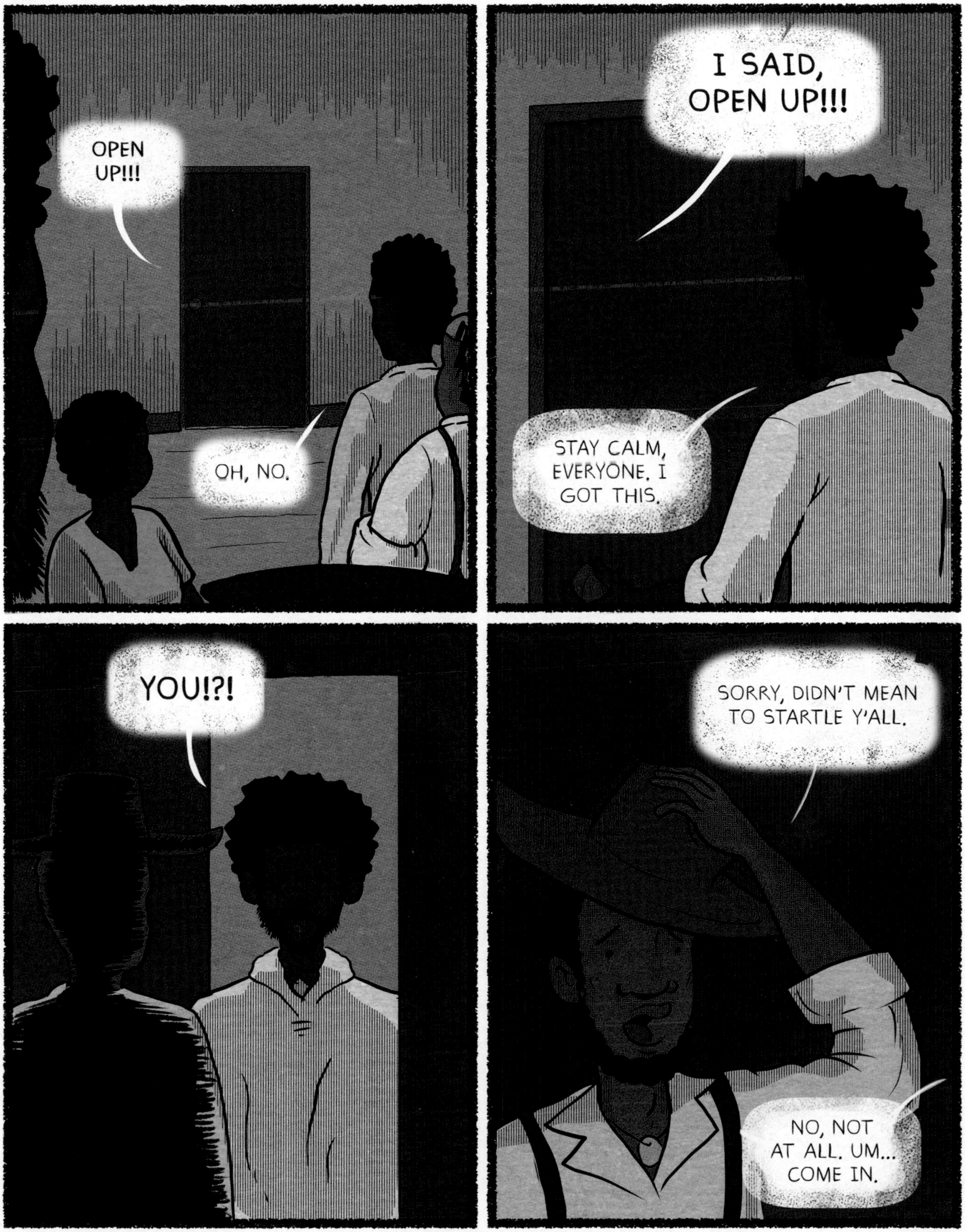
OPEN UP!!!
OH, NO.
I SAID, OPEN UP!!!
STAY CALM, EVERYONE. I GOT THIS.
YOU!?!
SORRY, DIDN'T MEAN TO STARTLE Y'ALL.
NO, NOT AT ALL. UM... COME IN.

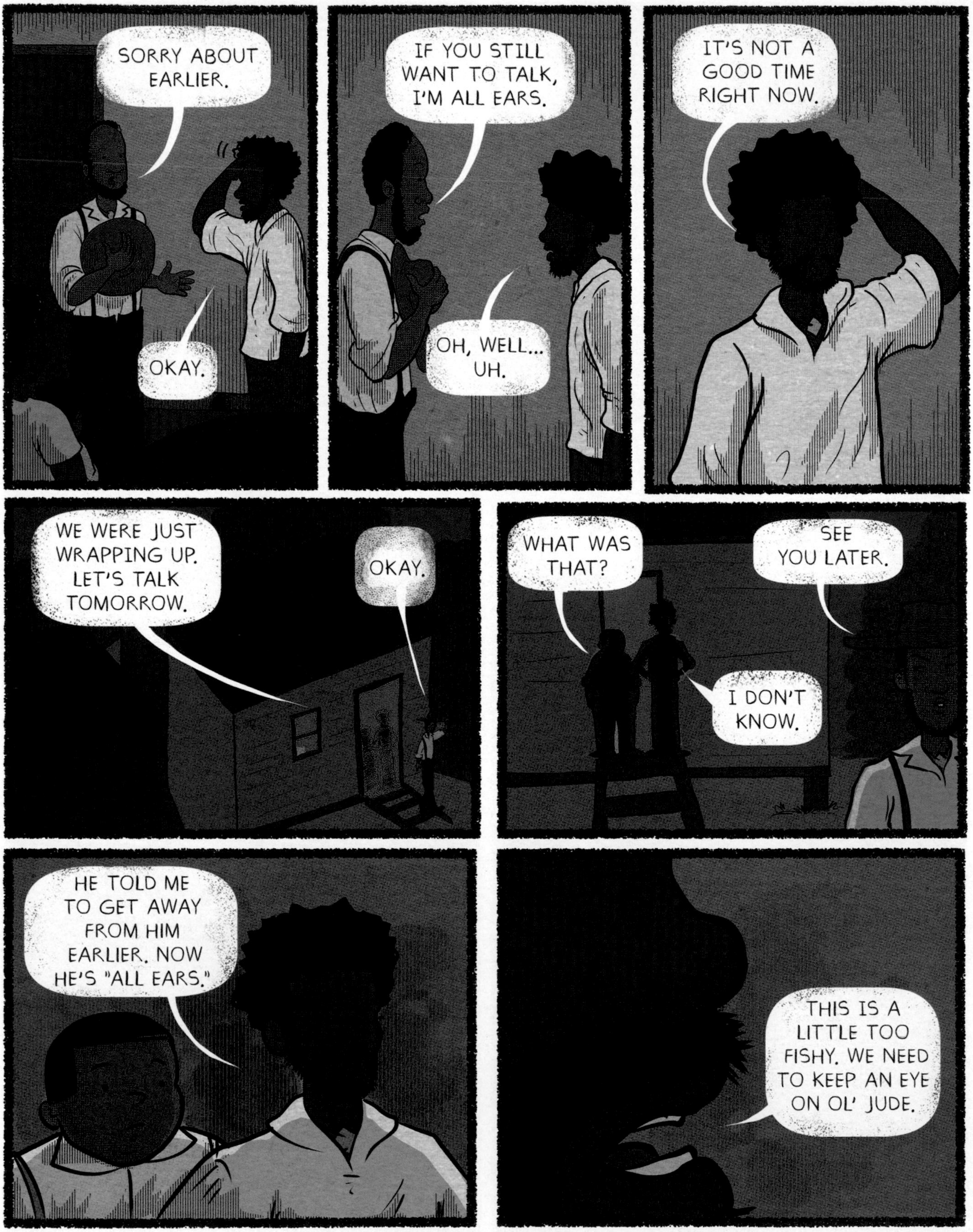
SORRY ABOUT EARLIER.
OKAY.
IF YOU STILL WANT TO TALK, I'M ALL EARS.
OH, WELL... UH.
IT'S NOT A GOOD TIME RIGHT NOW.
WE WERE JUST WRAPPING UP. LET'S TALK TOMORROW.
OKAY.
WHAT WAS THAT?
I DON'T KNOW.
SEE YOU LATER.
HE TOLD ME TO GET AWAY FROM HIM EARLIER. NOW HE'S "ALL EARS."
THIS IS A LITTLE TOO FISHY. WE NEED TO KEEP AN EYE ON OL' JUDE.

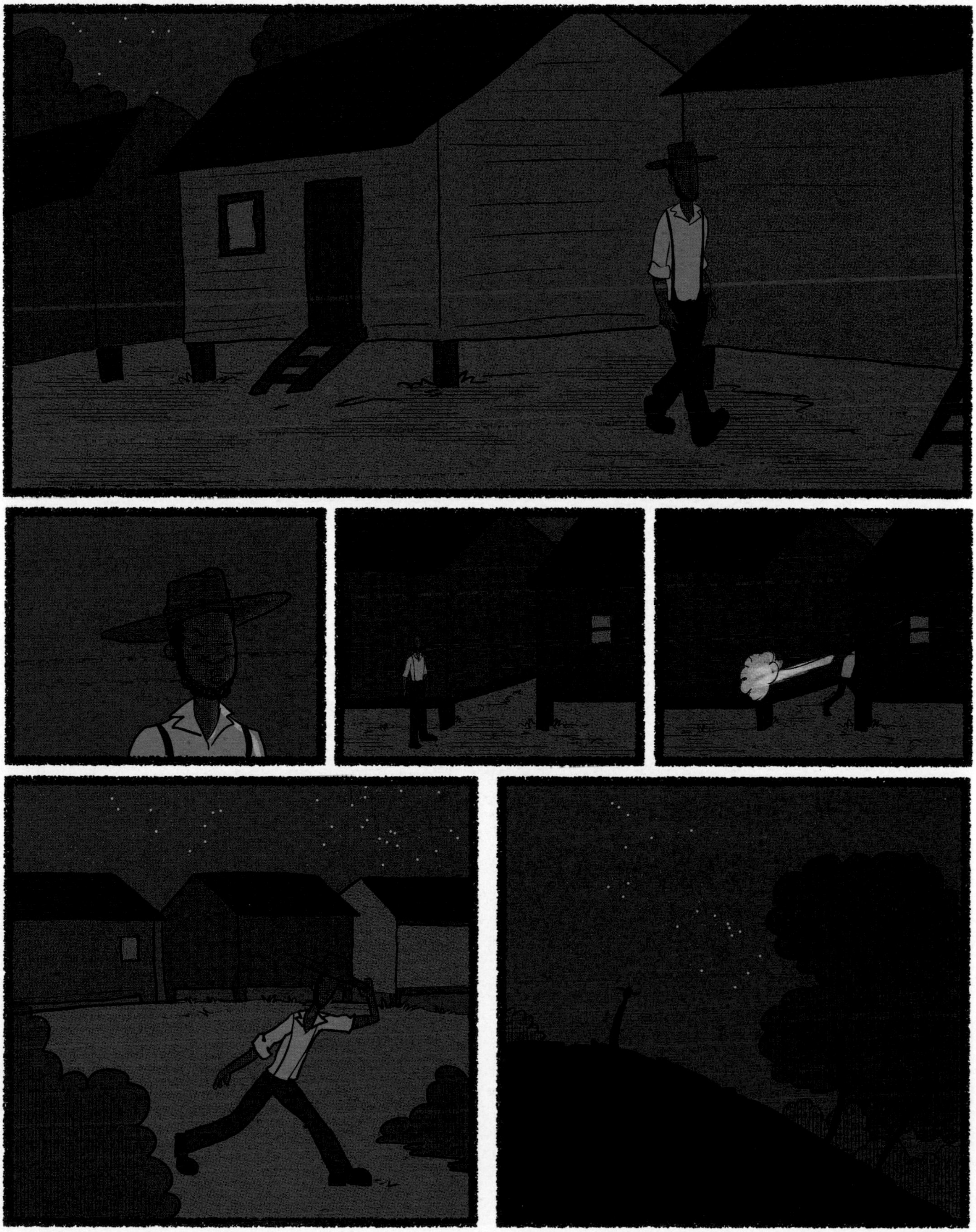

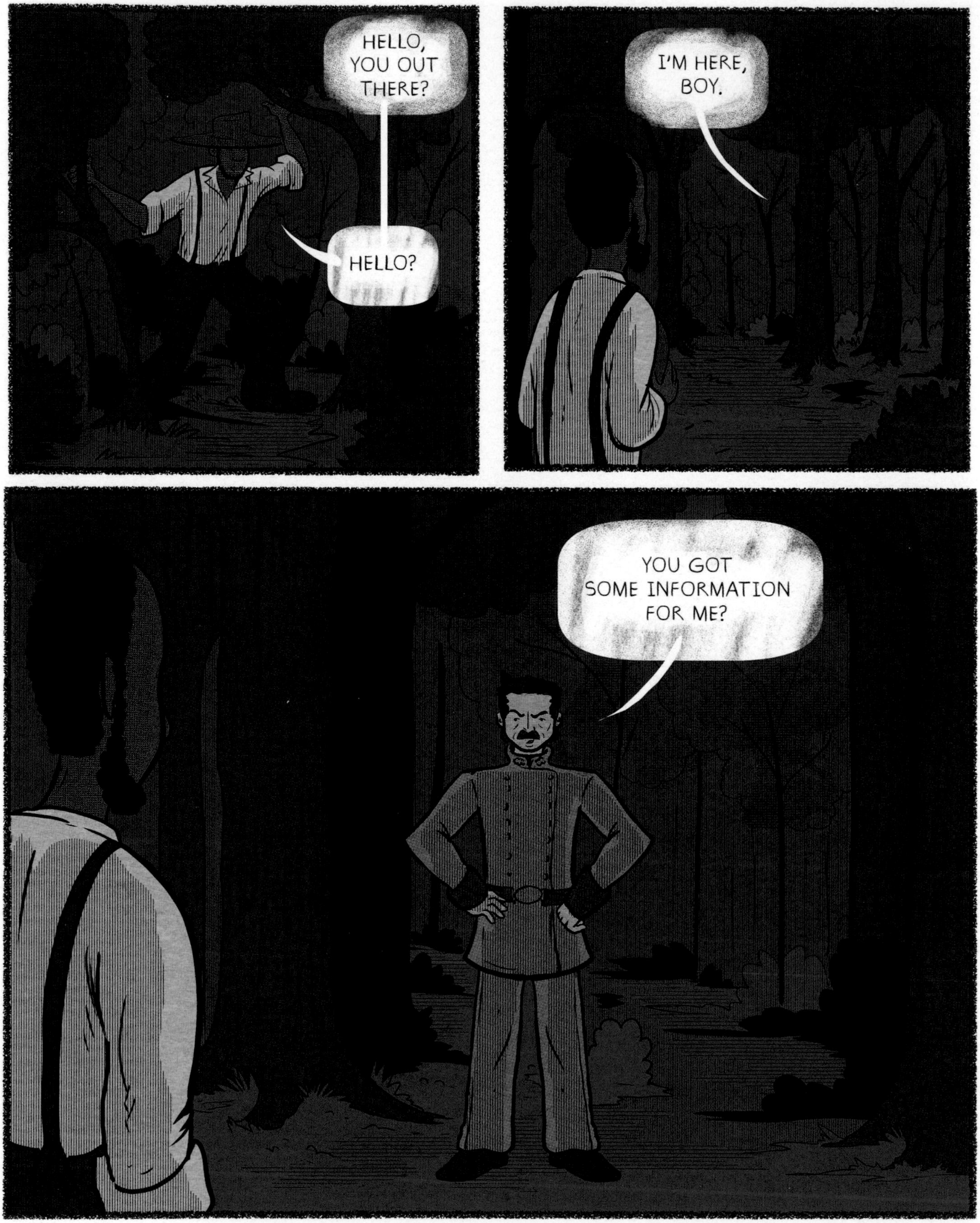
HELLO,
YOU OUT
THERE?
HELLO?
I'M HERE,
BOY.
YOU GOT
SOME INFORMATION
FOR ME?

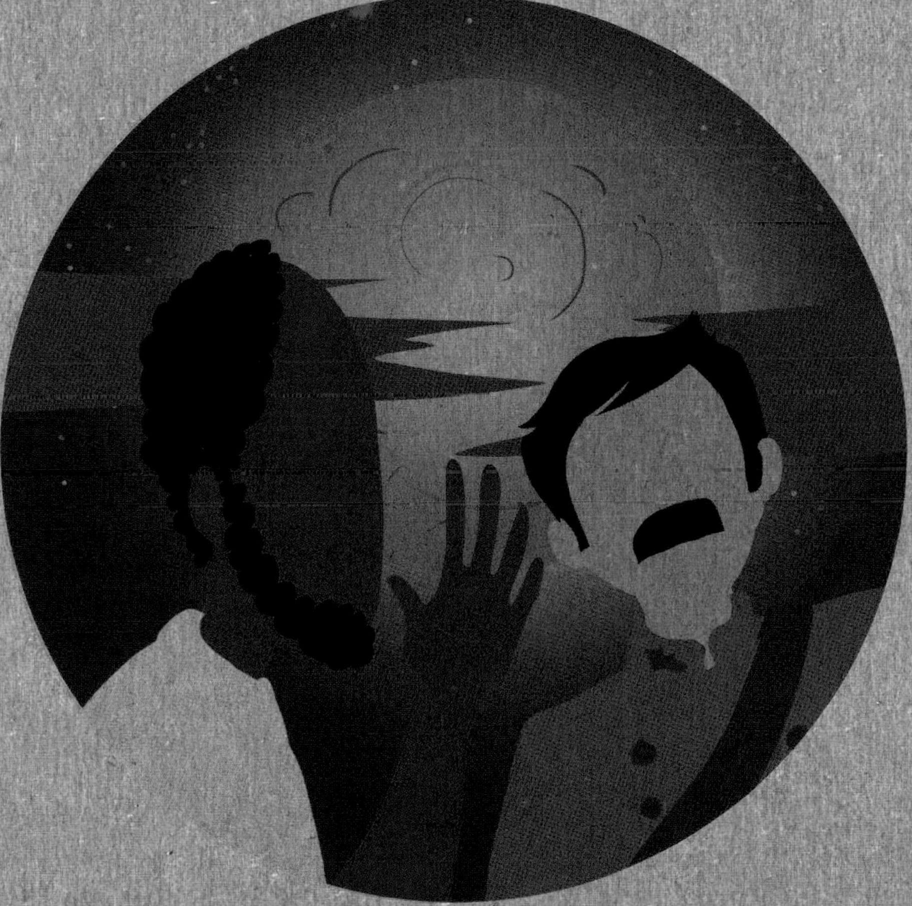

CHAPTER SIX

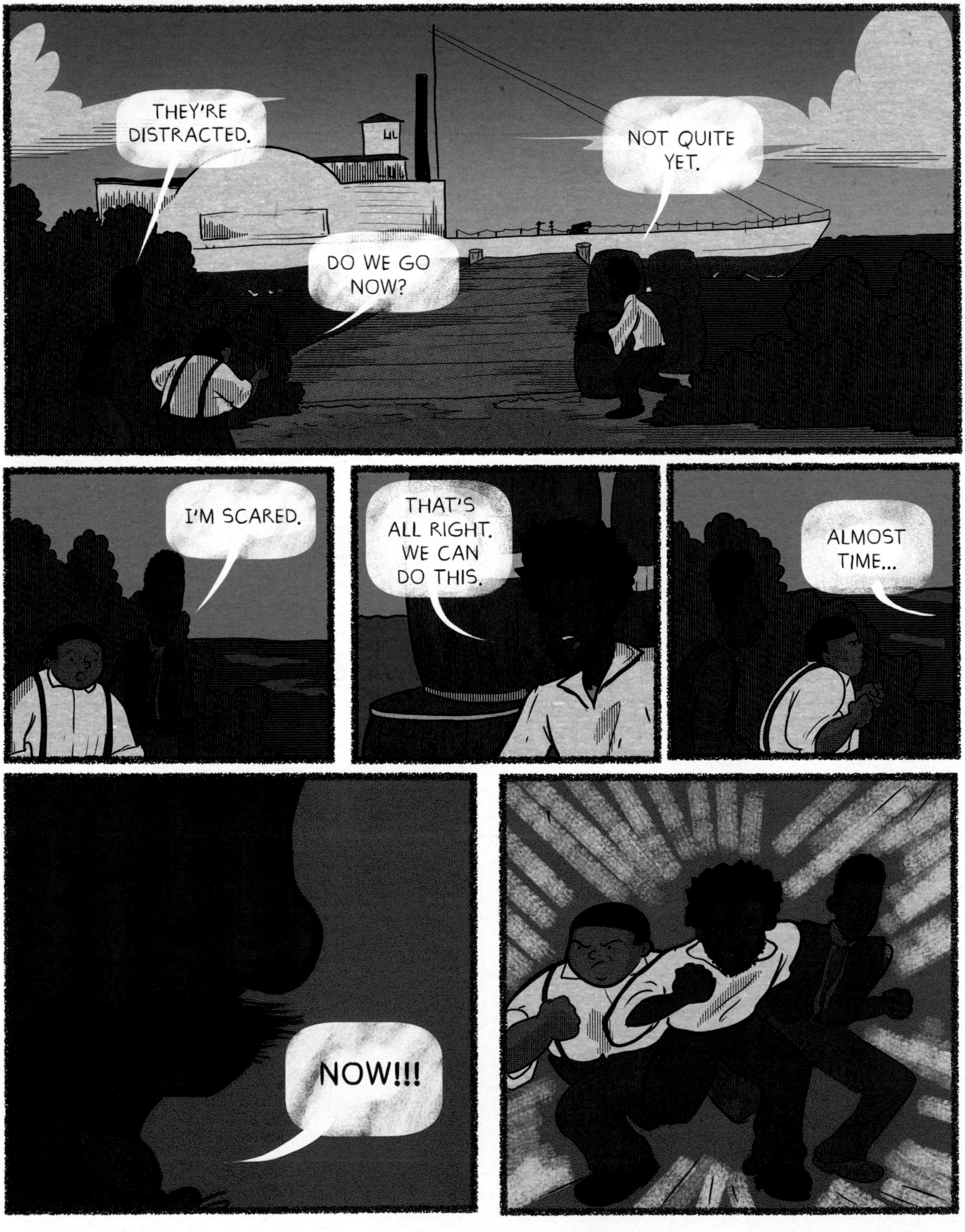
THEY'RE DISTRACTED.
DO WE GO NOW?
NOT QUITE YET.
I'M SCARED.
THAT'S ALL RIGHT. WE CAN DO THIS.
ALMOST TIME...
NOW!!!

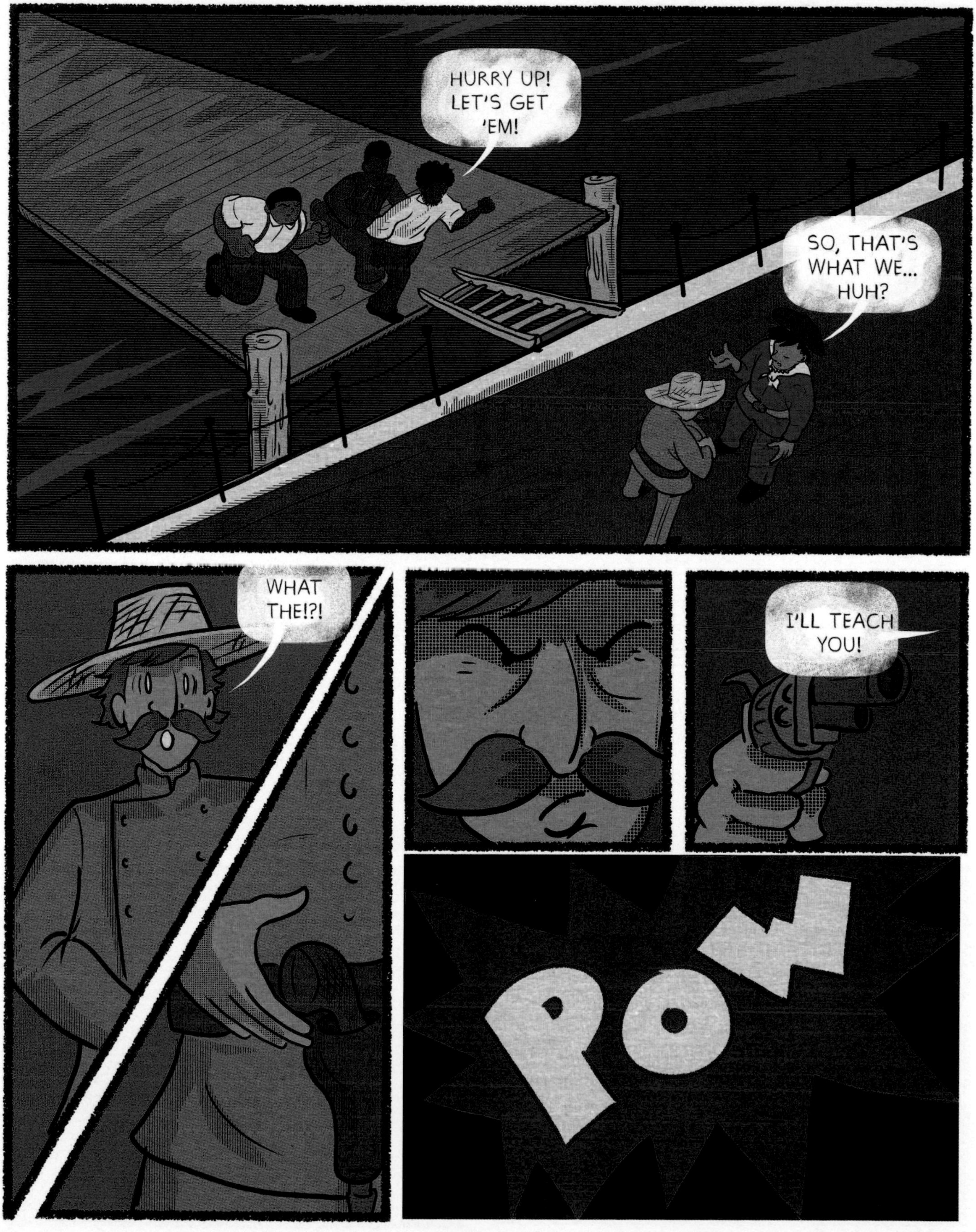
HURRY UP! LET'S GET 'EM!
SO, THAT'S WHAT WE... HUH?
WHAT THE!?!
I'LL TEACH YOU!
POW

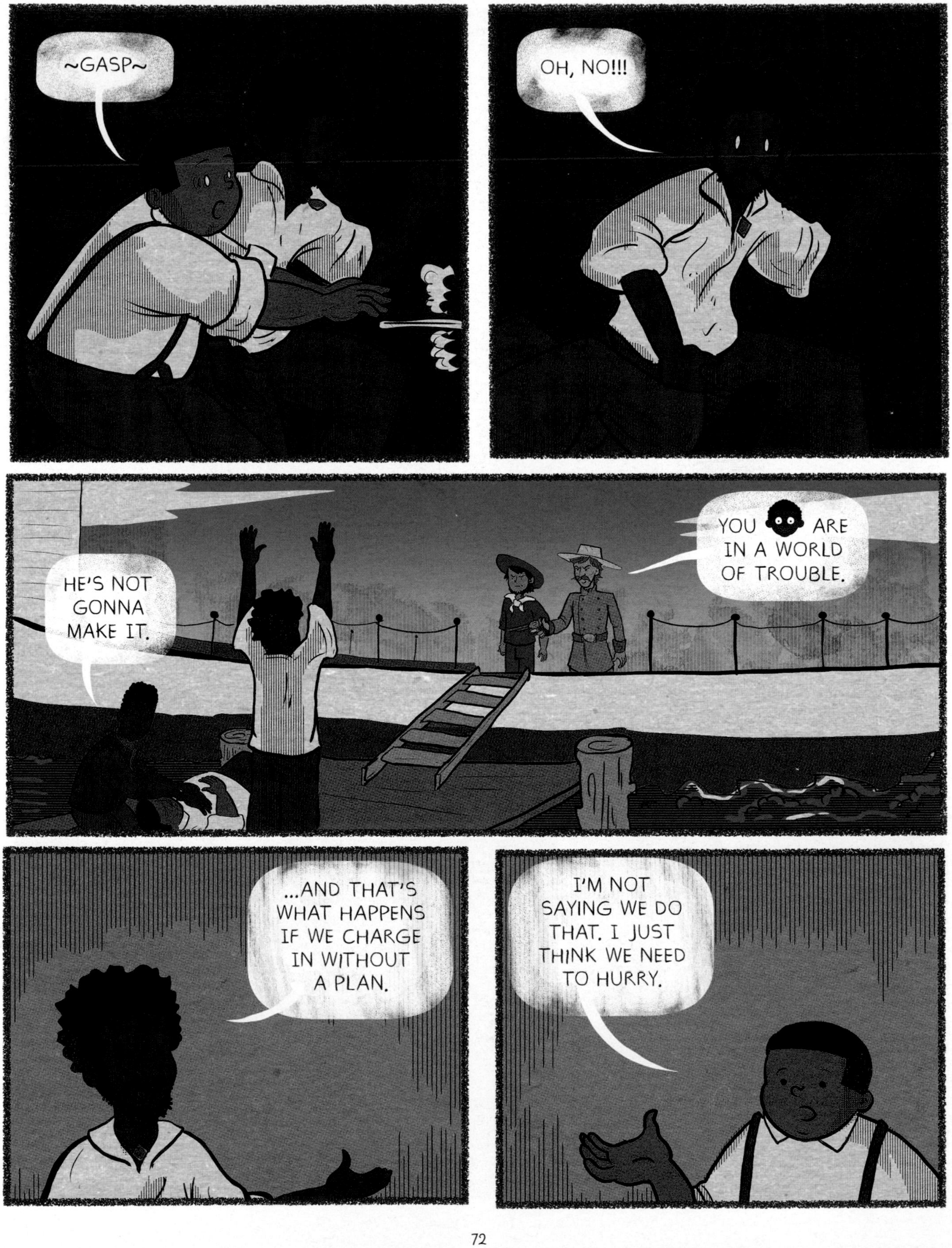
~GASP~
OH, NO!!!
HE'S NOT GONNA MAKE IT.
YOU ARE IN A WORLD OF TROUBLE.
...AND THAT'S WHAT HAPPENS IF WE CHARGE IN WITHOUT A PLAN.
I'M NOT SAYING WE DO THAT. I JUST THINK WE NEED TO HURRY.

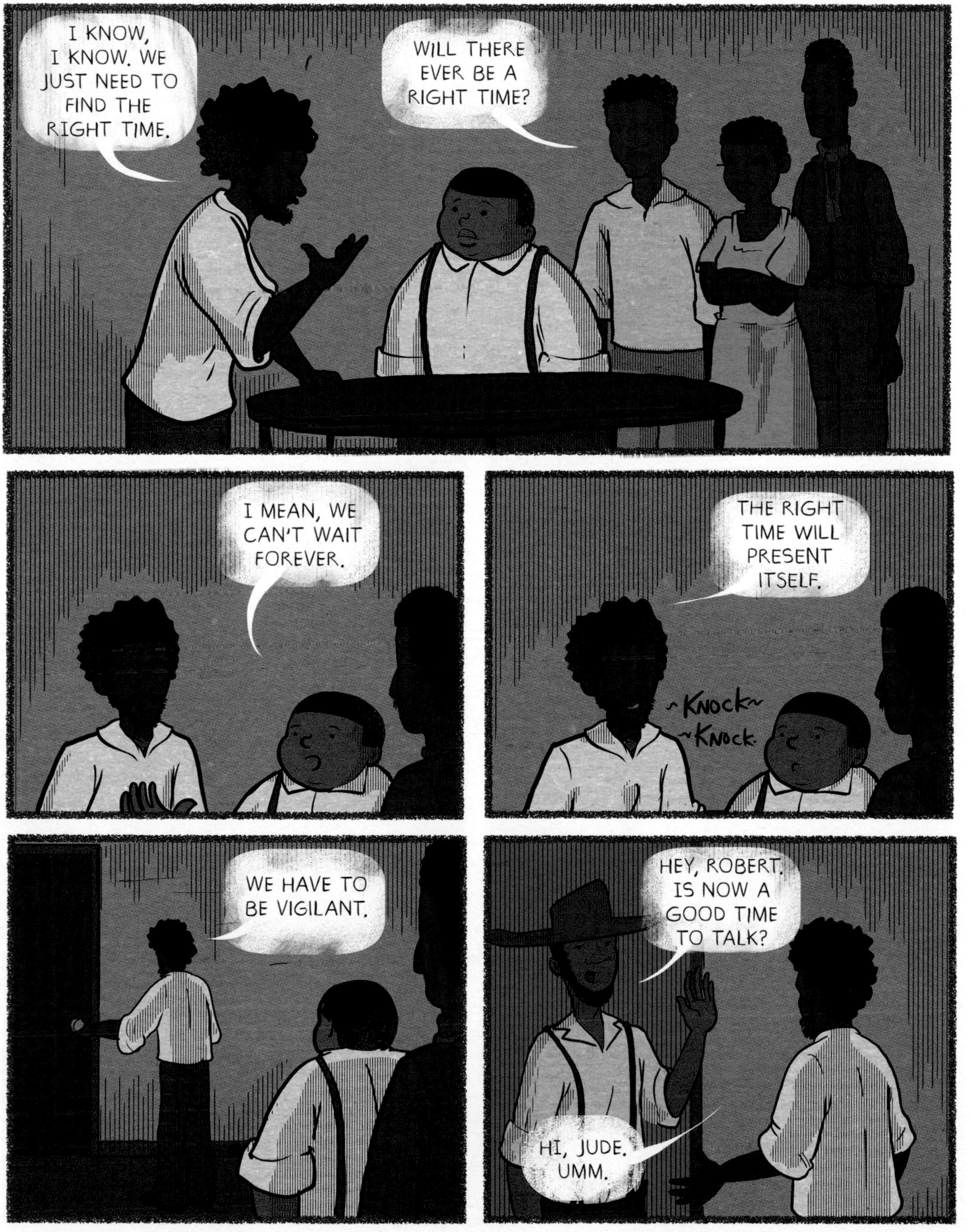
I KNOW, I KNOW. WE JUST NEED TO FIND THE RIGHT TIME.
WILL THERE EVER BE A RIGHT TIME?
I MEAN, WE CAN'T WAIT FOREVER.
THE RIGHT TIME WILL PRESENT ITSELF.
~KNOCK~
~KNOCK
WE HAVE TO BE VIGILANT.
HEY, ROBERT. IS NOW A GOOD TIME TO TALK?
HI, JUDE. UMM.

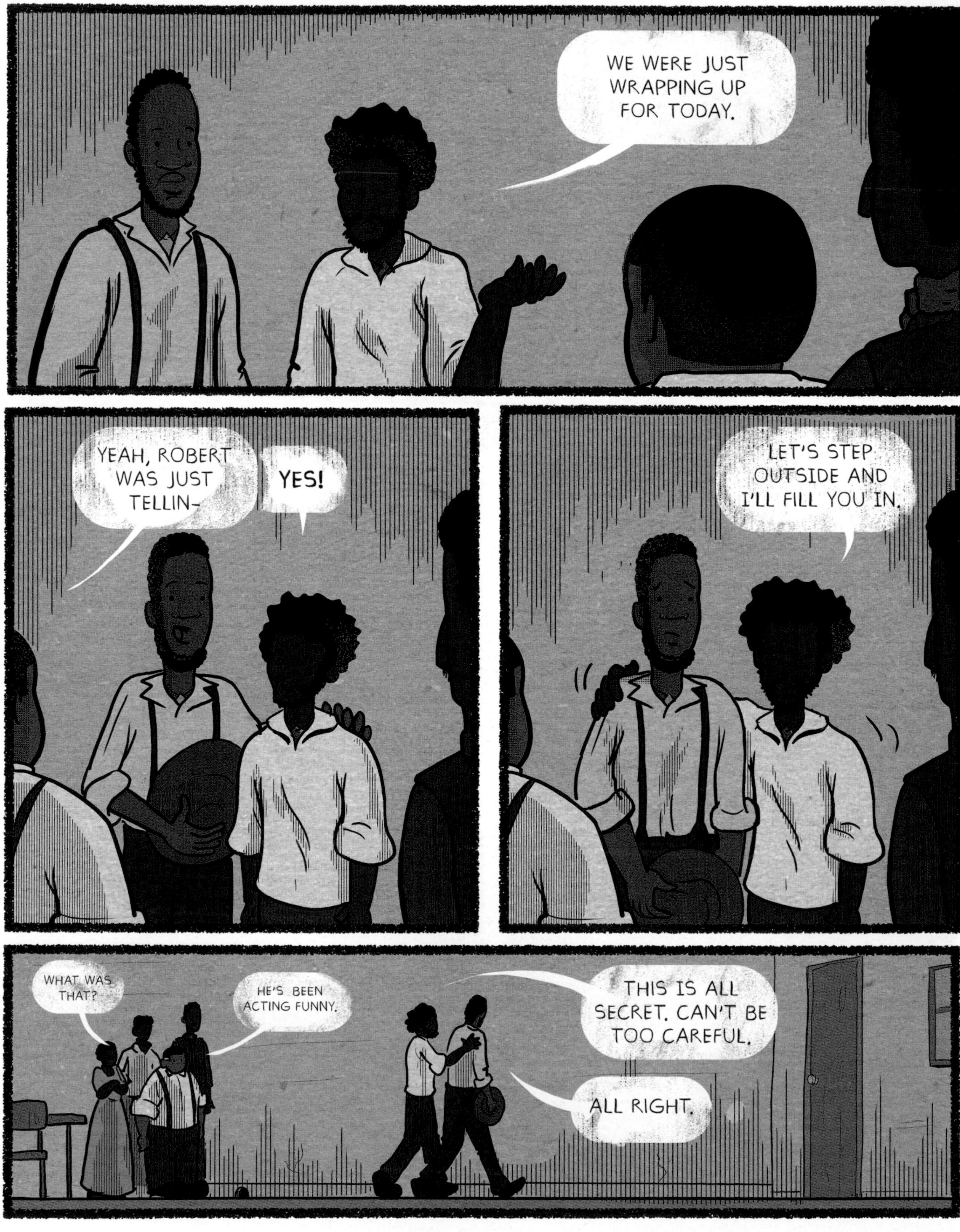
WE WERE JUST WRAPPING UP FOR TODAY.
YEAH, ROBERT WAS JUST TELLIN-
YES!
LET'S STEP OUTSIDE AND I'LL FILL YOU IN.
WHAT WAS THAT?
HE'S BEEN ACTING FUNNY.
THIS IS ALL SECRET. CAN'T BE TOO CAREFUL.
ALL RIGHT.

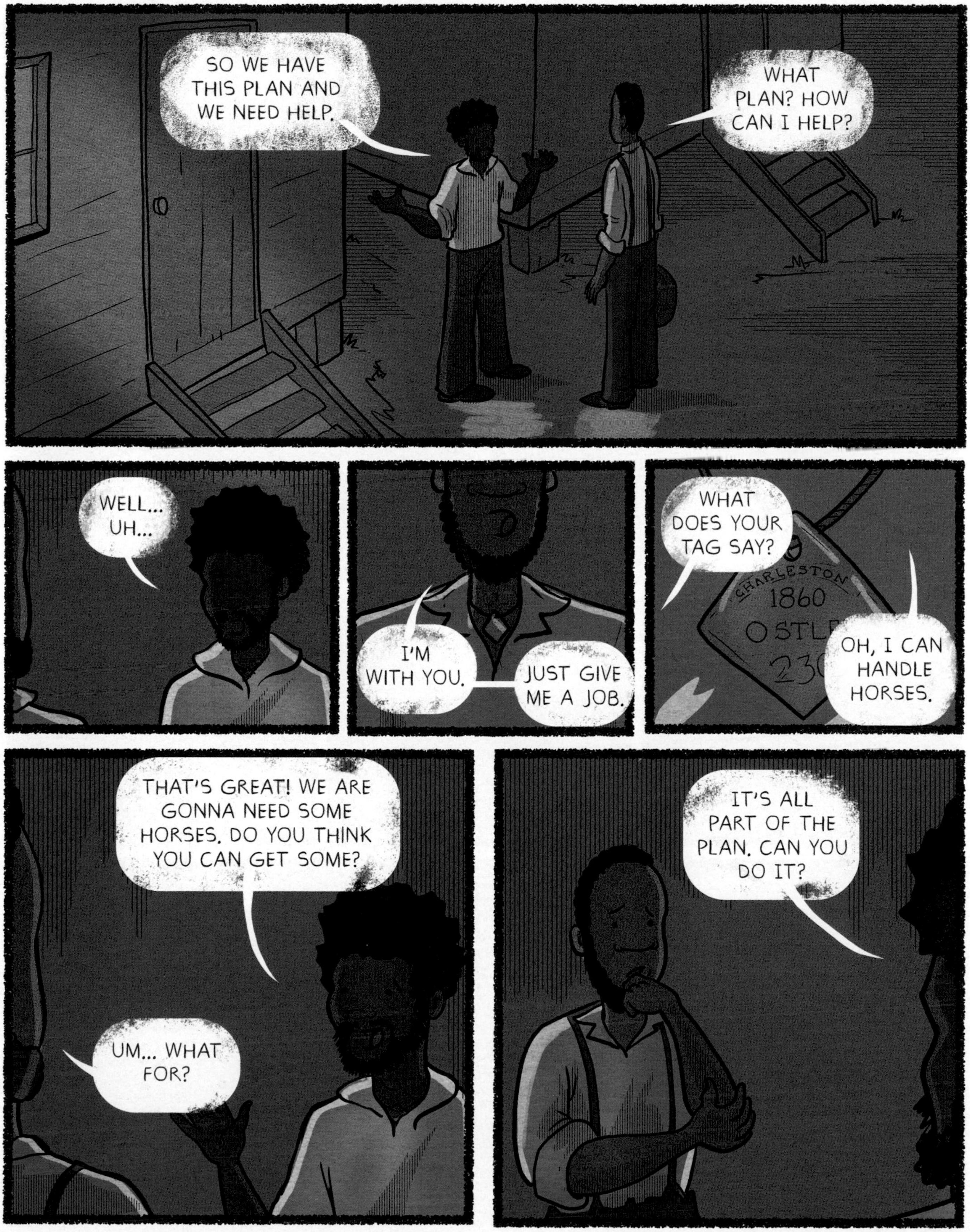
SO WE HAVE THIS PLAN AND WE NEED HELP.
WHAT PLAN? HOW CAN I HELP?
WELL... UH...
I'M WITH YOU.
JUST GIVE ME A JOB.
WHAT DOES YOUR TAG SAY?
CHARLESTON 1860 OSTL 23
OH, I CAN HANDLE HORSES.
THAT'S GREAT! WE ARE GONNA NEED SOME HORSES. DO YOU THINK YOU CAN GET SOME?
UM... WHAT FOR?
IT'S ALL PART OF THE PLAN. CAN YOU DO IT?

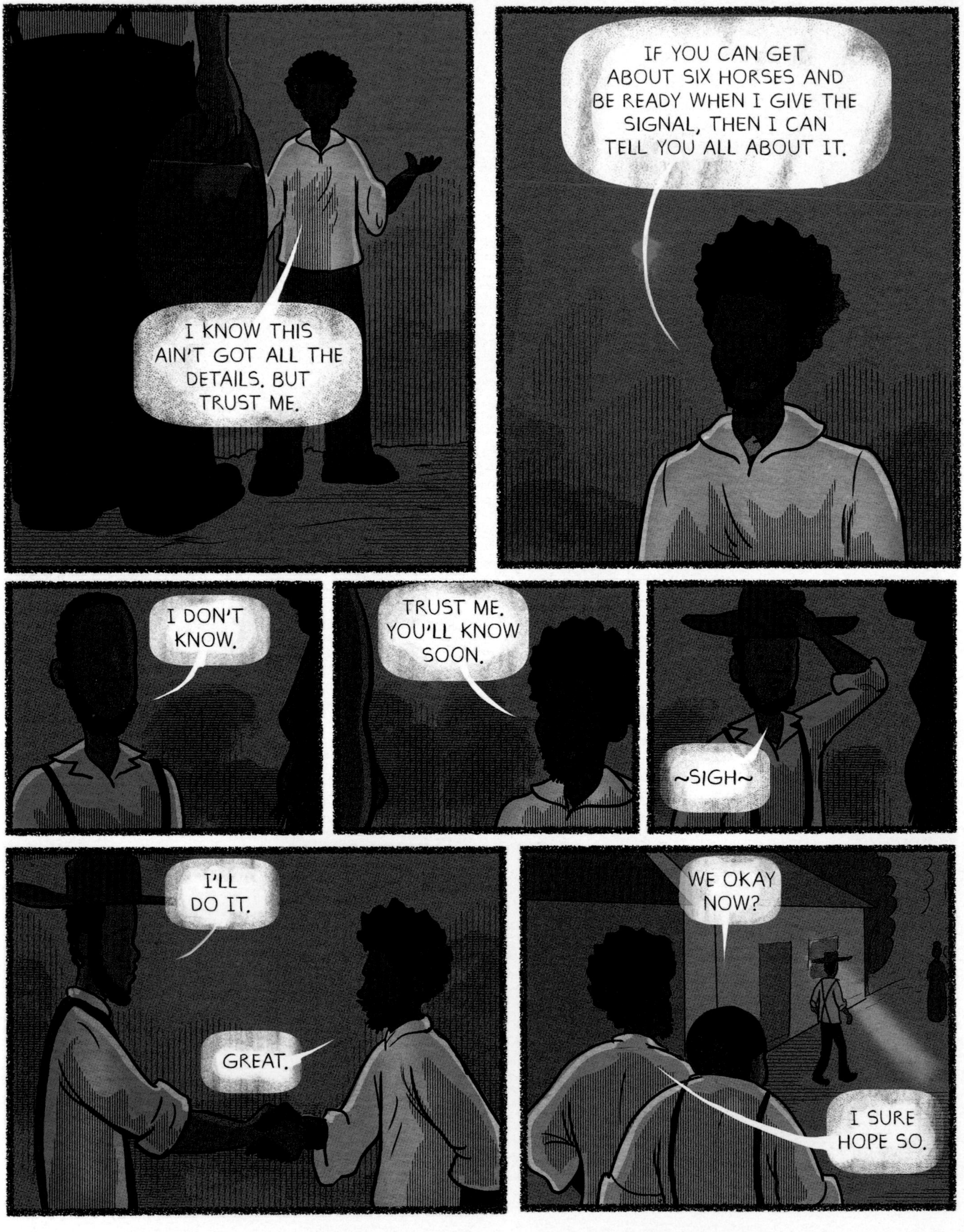
I KNOW THIS AIN'T GOT ALL THE DETAILS. BUT TRUST ME.
IF YOU CAN GET ABOUT SIX HORSES AND BE READY WHEN I GIVE THE SIGNAL, THEN I CAN TELL YOU ALL ABOUT IT.
I DON'T KNOW.
TRUST ME. YOU'LL KNOW SOON.
~SIGH~
I'LL DO IT.
GREAT.
WE OKAY NOW?
I SURE HOPE SO.

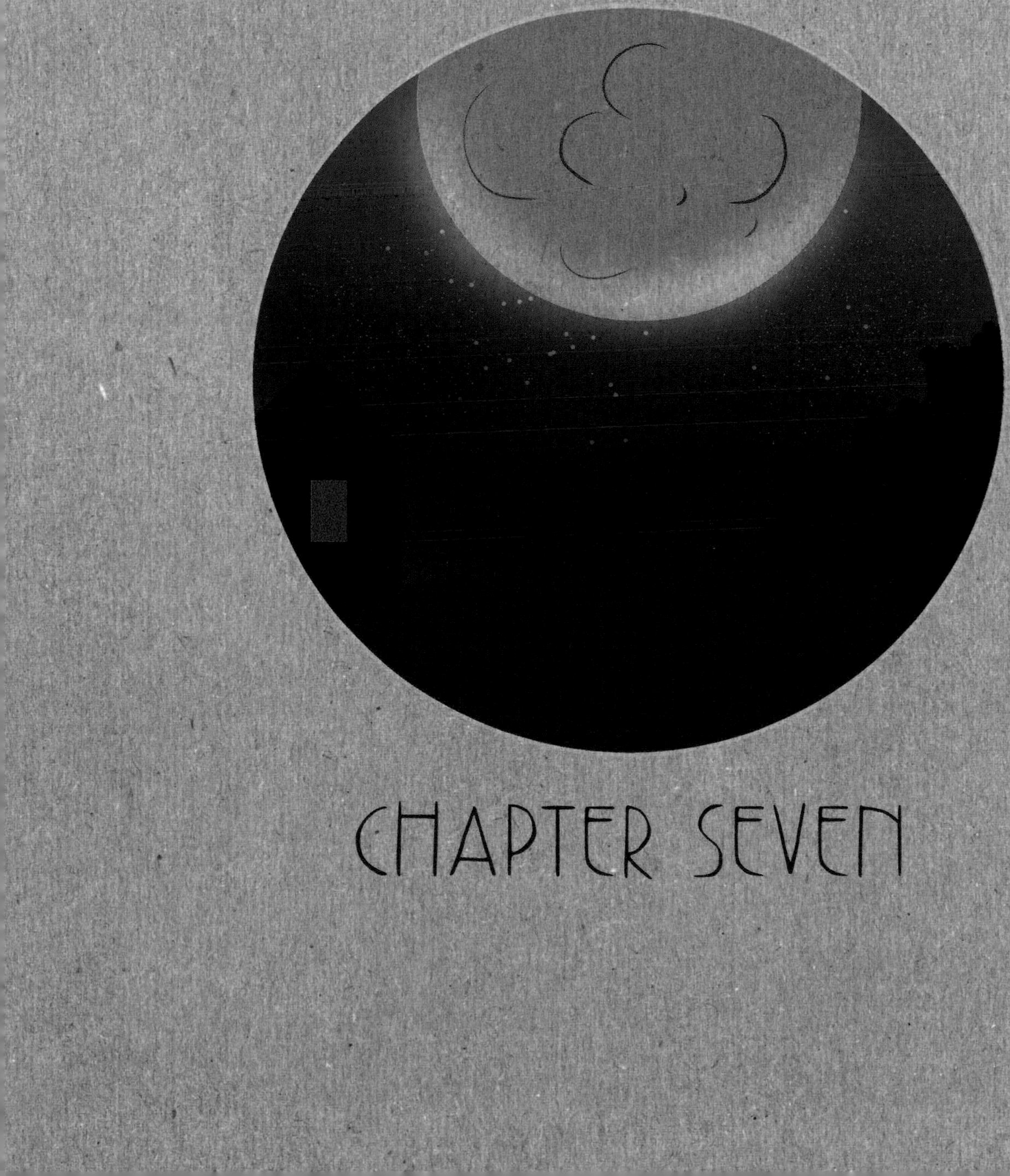

CHAPTER SEVEN

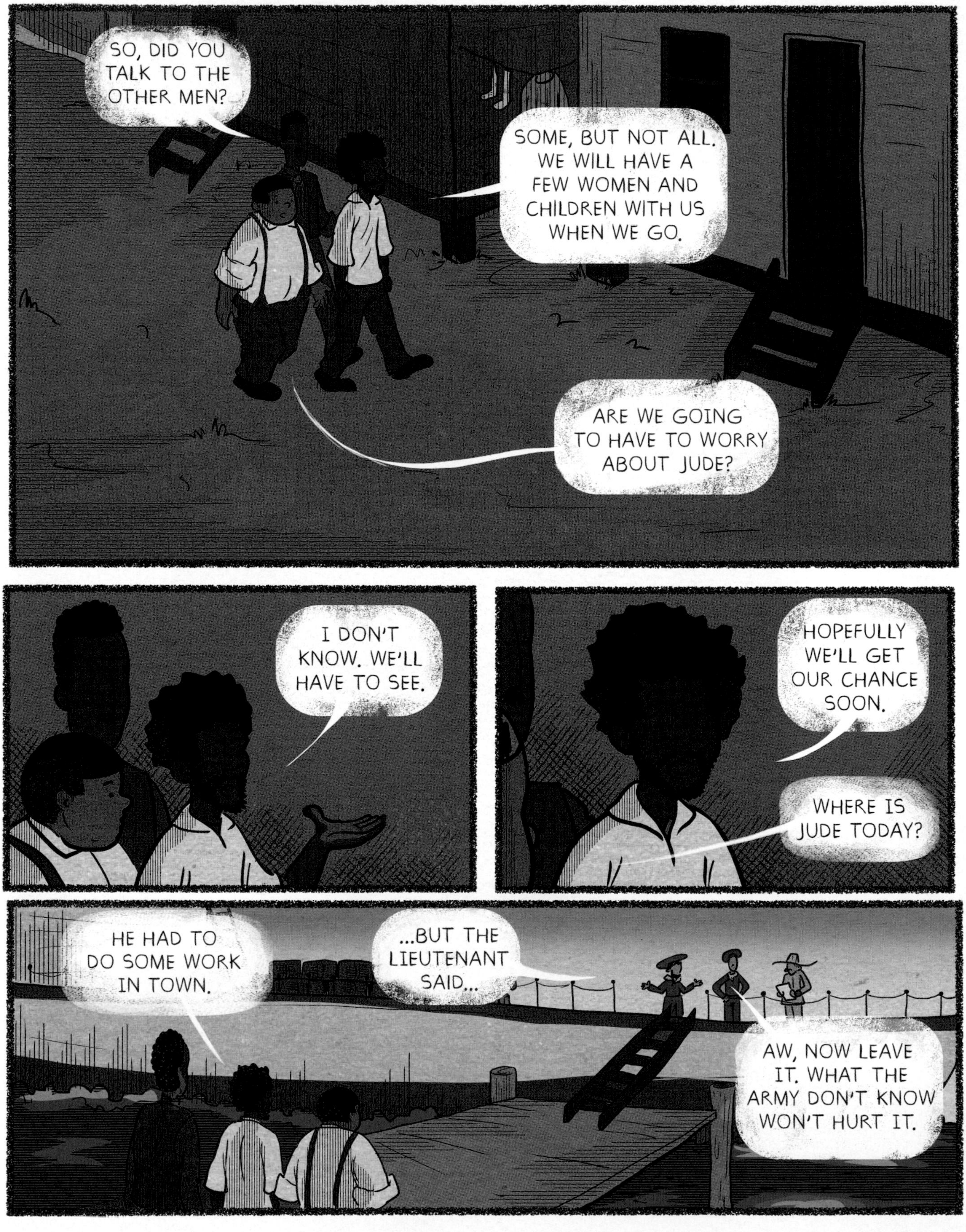
SO, DID YOU TALK TO THE OTHER MEN?
SOME, BUT NOT ALL. WE WILL HAVE A FEW WOMEN AND CHILDREN WITH US WHEN WE GO.
ARE WE GOING TO HAVE TO WORRY ABOUT JUDE?
I DON'T KNOW. WE'LL HAVE TO SEE.
HOPEFULLY WE'LL GET OUR CHANCE SOON.
WHERE IS JUDE TODAY?
HE HAD TO DO SOME WORK IN TOWN.
...BUT THE LIEUTENANT SAID...
AW, NOW LEAVE IT. WHAT THE ARMY DON'T KNOW WON'T HURT IT.

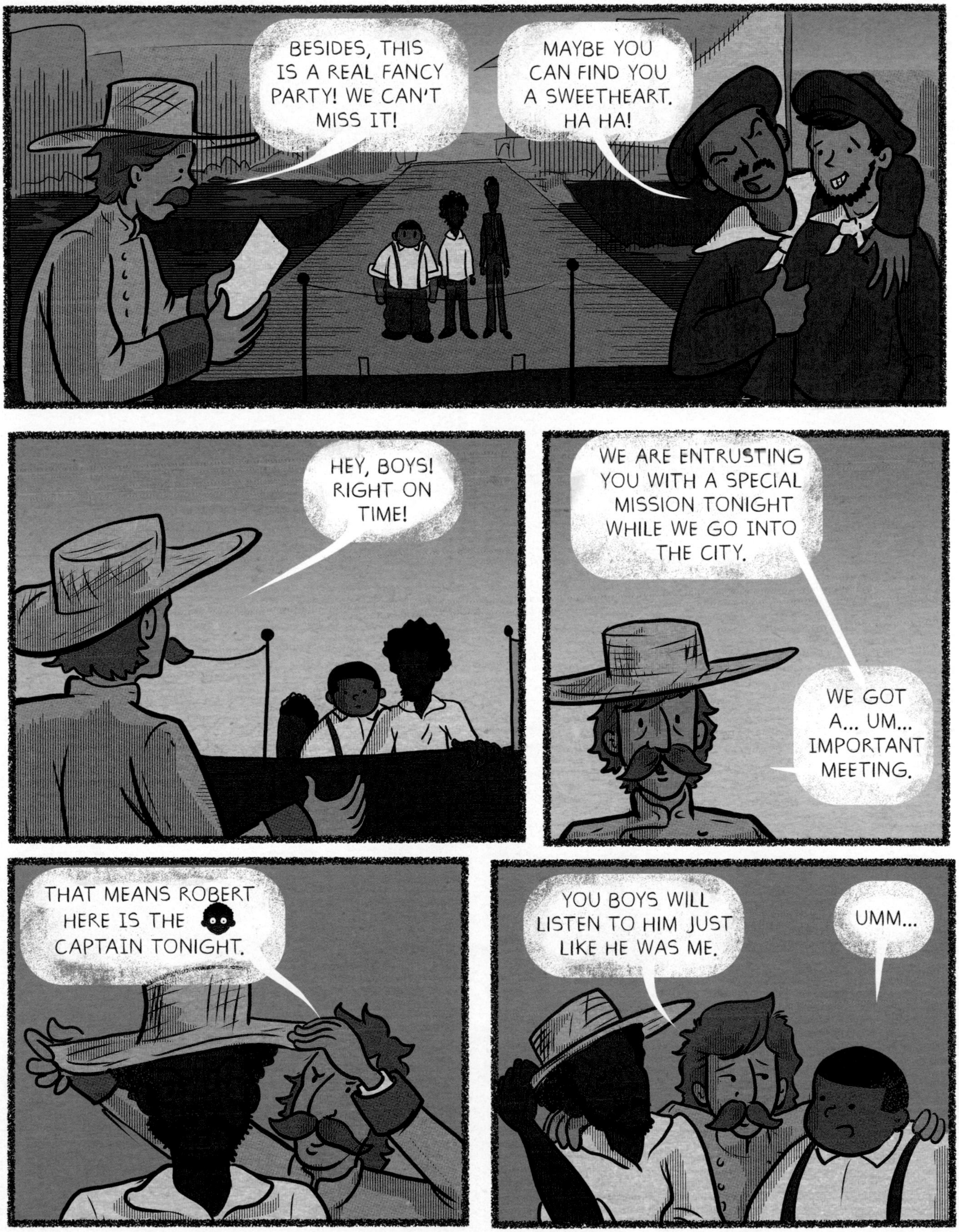
BESIDES, THIS IS A REAL FANCY PARTY! WE CAN'T MISS IT!
MAYBE YOU CAN FIND YOU A SWEETHEART. HA HA!
HEY, BOYS! RIGHT ON TIME!
WE ARE ENTRUSTING YOU WITH A SPECIAL MISSION TONIGHT WHILE WE GO INTO THE CITY.
WE GOT A... UM... IMPORTANT MEETING.
THAT MEANS ROBERT HERE IS THE CAPTAIN TONIGHT.
YOU BOYS WILL LISTEN TO HIM JUST LIKE HE WAS ME.
UMM...

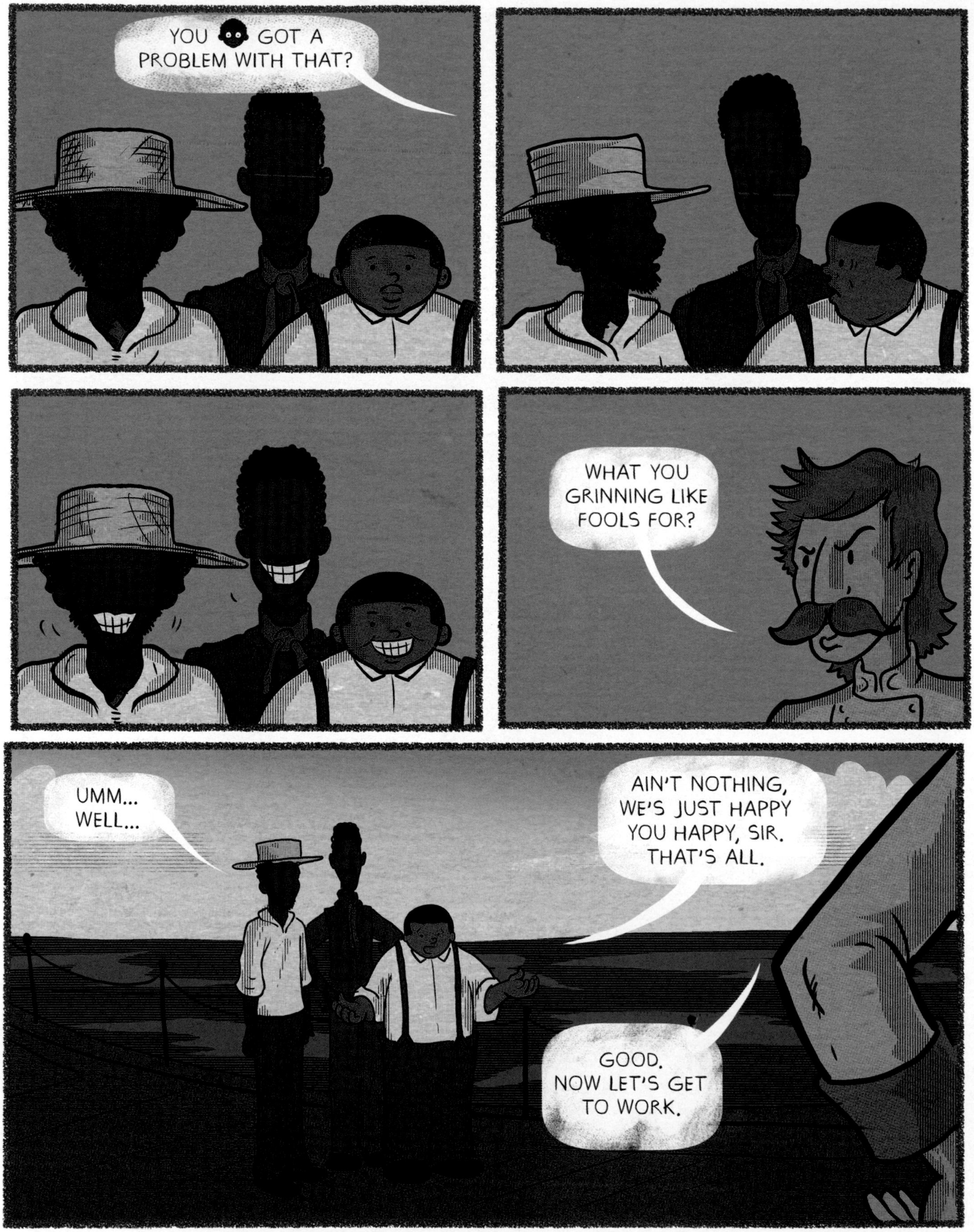
YOU [symbol] GOT A PROBLEM WITH THAT?
WHAT YOU GRINNING LIKE FOOLS FOR?
UMM... WELL...
AIN'T NOTHING, WE'S JUST HAPPY YOU HAPPY, SIR. THAT'S ALL.
GOOD. NOW LET'S GET TO WORK.

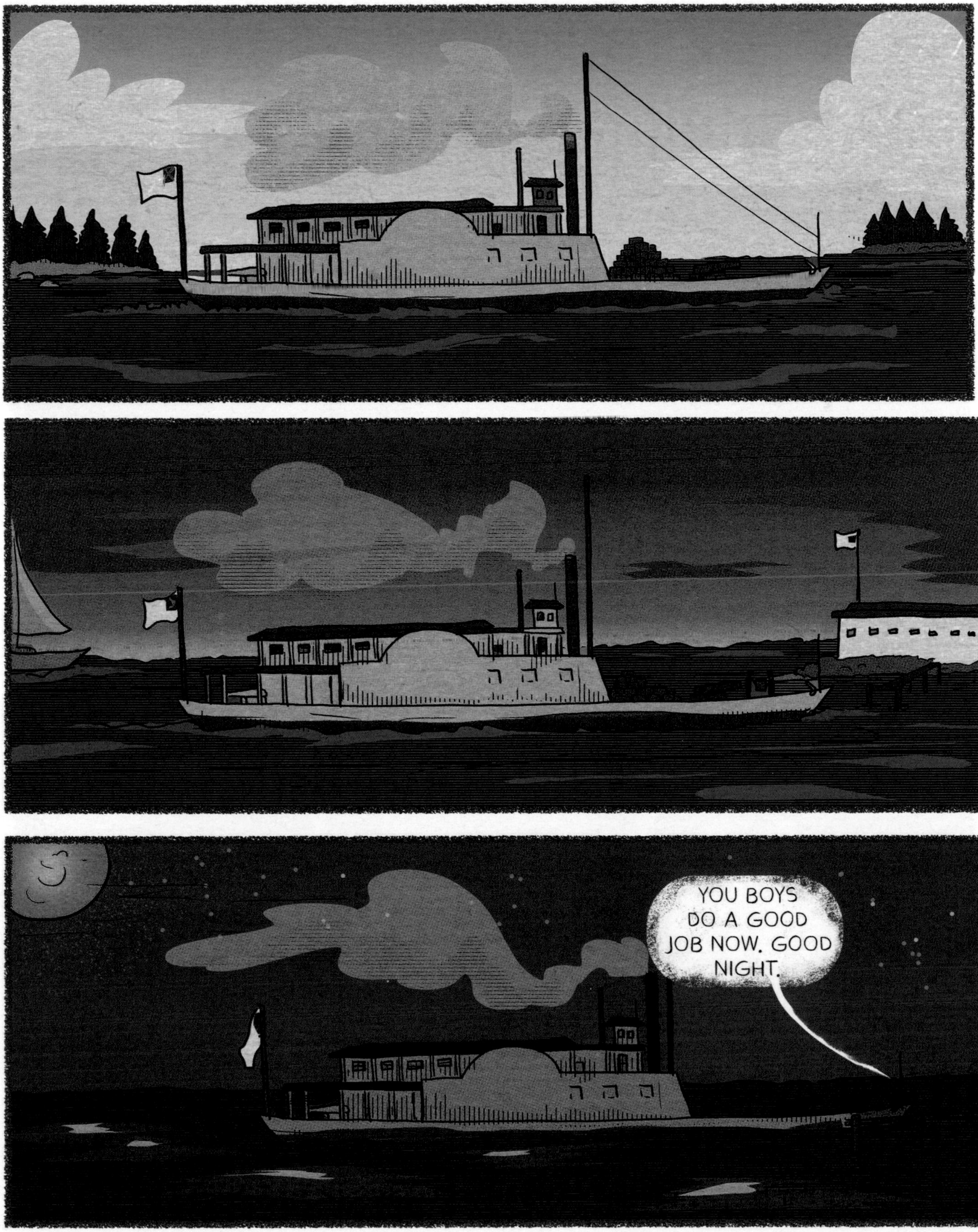
YOU BOYS DO A GOOD JOB NOW. GOOD NIGHT.

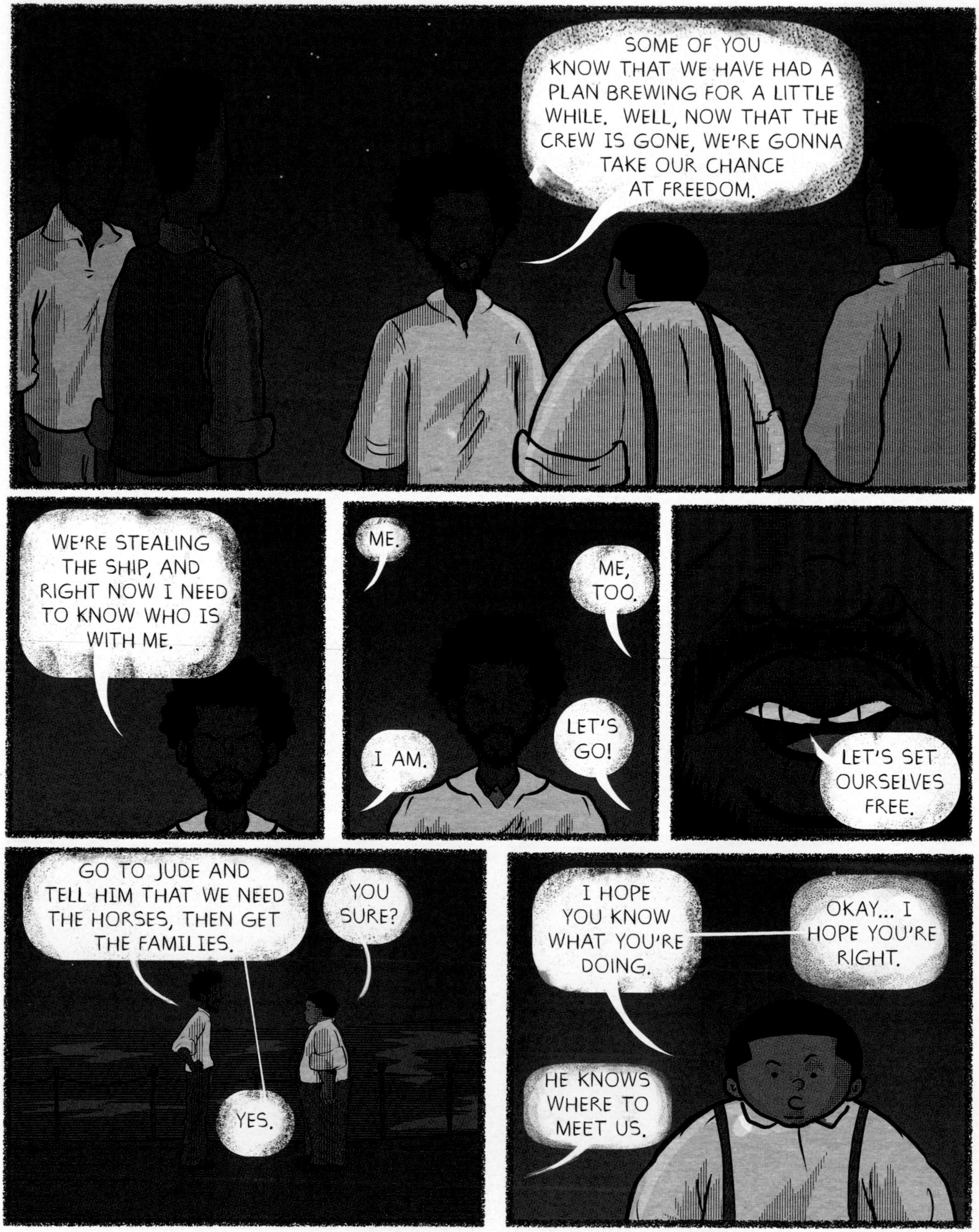
SOME OF YOU KNOW THAT WE HAVE HAD A PLAN BREWING FOR A LITTLE WHILE. WELL, NOW THAT THE CREW IS GONE, WE'RE GONNA TAKE OUR CHANCE AT FREEDOM.
WE'RE STEALING THE SHIP, AND RIGHT NOW I NEED TO KNOW WHO IS WITH ME.
ME.
ME, TOO.
I AM.
LET'S GO!
LET'S SET OURSELVES FREE.
GO TO JUDE AND TELL HIM THAT WE NEED THE HORSES, THEN GET THE FAMILIES.
YOU SURE?
YES.
I HOPE YOU KNOW WHAT YOU'RE DOING.
OKAY... I HOPE YOU'RE RIGHT.
HE KNOWS WHERE TO MEET US.

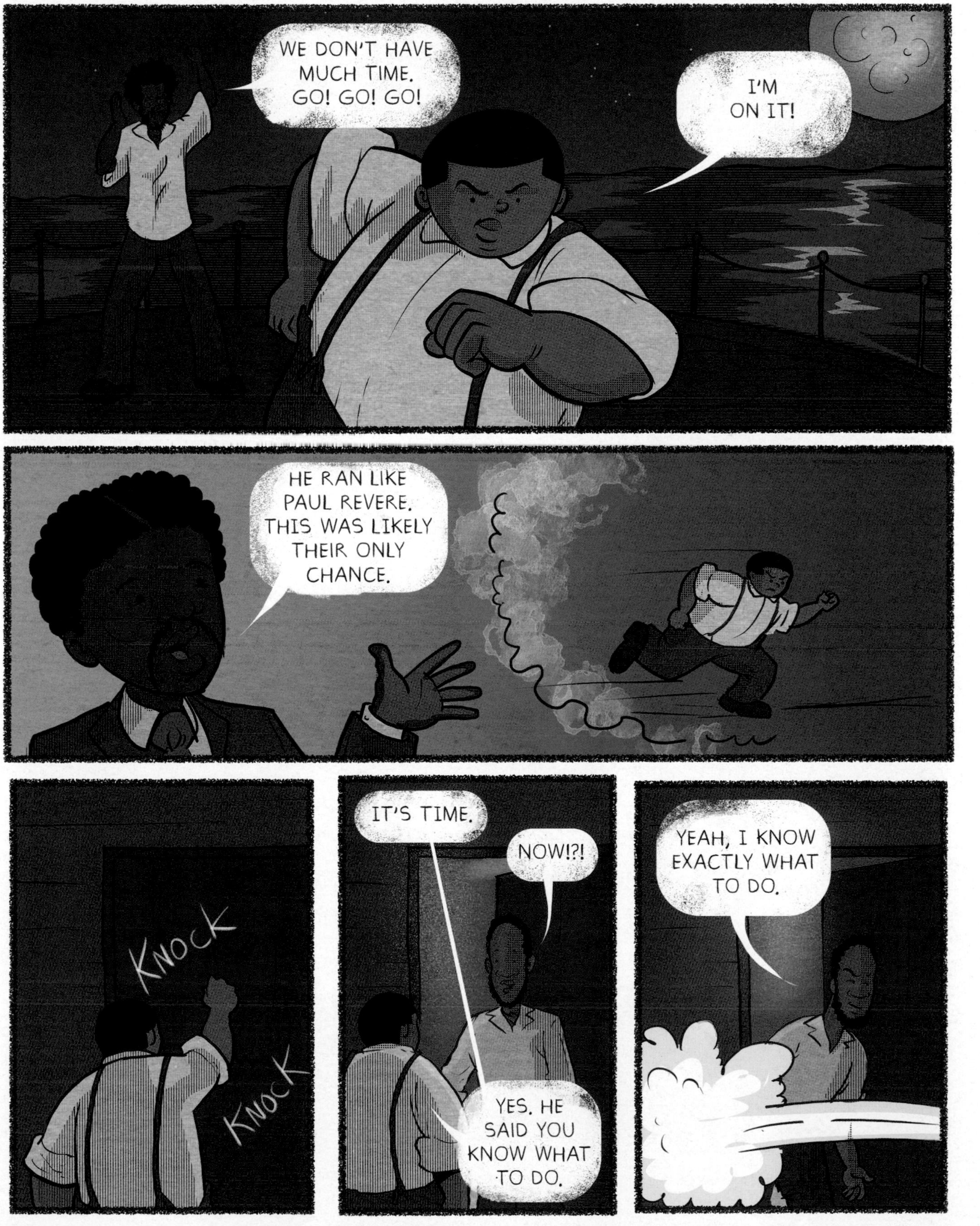
WE DON'T HAVE MUCH TIME. GO! GO! GO!
I'M ON IT!
HE RAN LIKE PAUL REVERE. THIS WAS LIKELY THEIR ONLY CHANCE.
KNOCK
KNOCK
IT'S TIME.
NOW!?!
YES. HE SAID YOU KNOW WHAT TO DO.
YEAH, I KNOW EXACTLY WHAT TO DO.

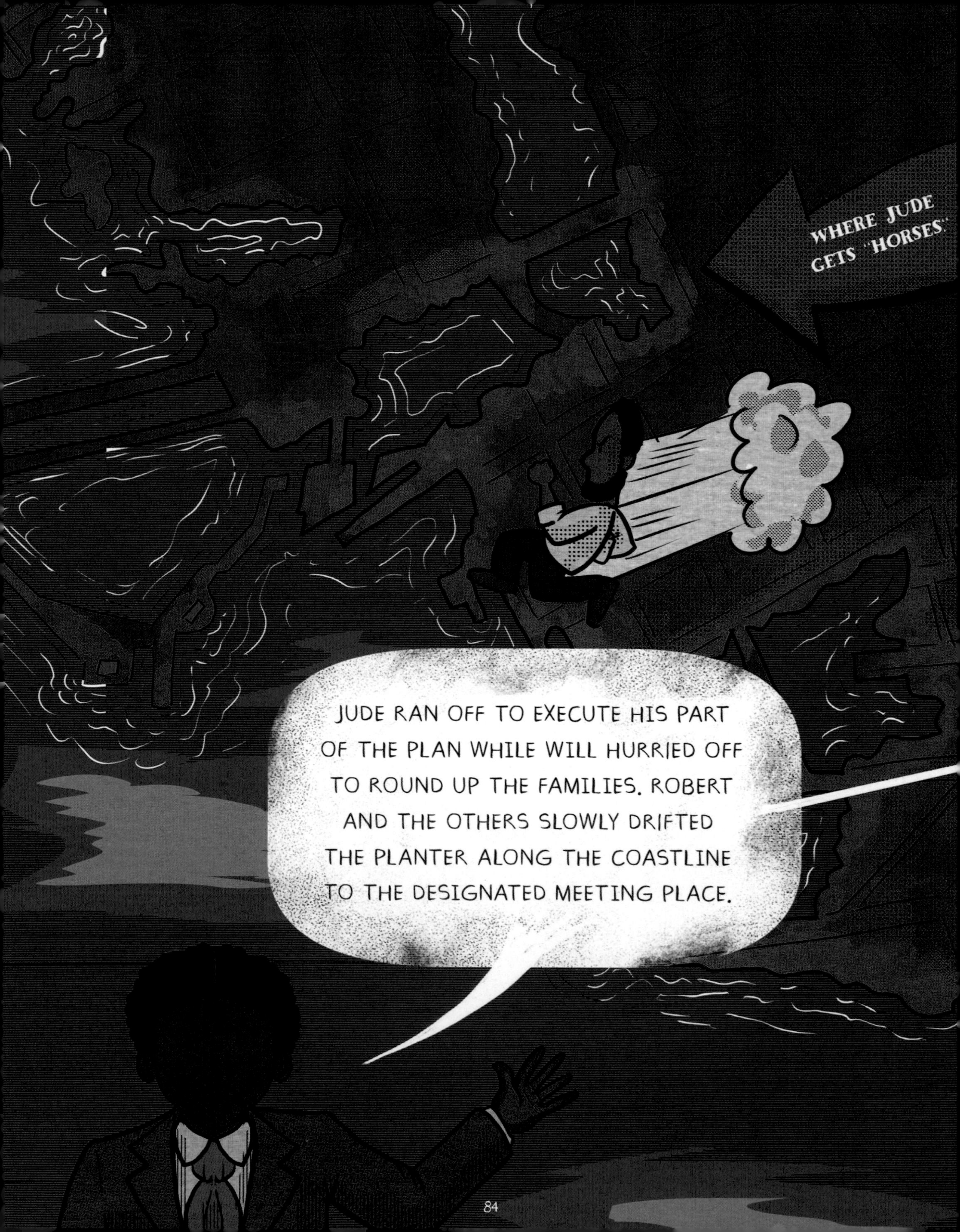
WHERE JUDE GETS "HORSES"
JUDE RAN OFF TO EXECUTE HIS PART OF THE PLAN WHILE WILL HURRIED OFF TO ROUND UP THE FAMILIES. ROBERT AND THE OTHERS SLOWLY DRIFTED THE PLANTER ALONG THE COASTLINE TO THE DESIGNATED MEETING PLACE.

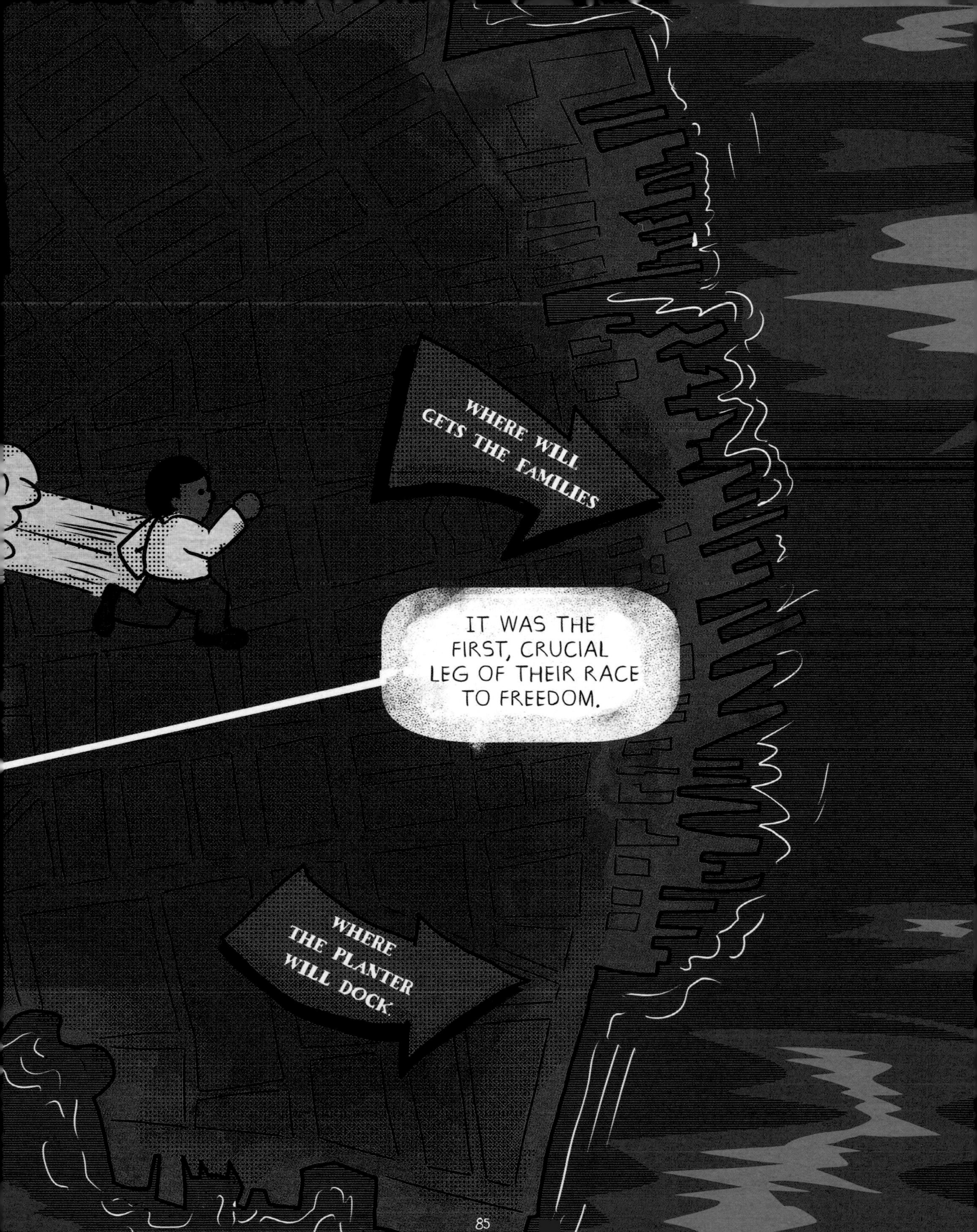
WHERE WILL GETS THE FAMILIES
IT WAS THE FIRST, CRUCIAL LEG OF THEIR RACE TO FREEDOM.
WHERE THE PLANTER WILL DOCK

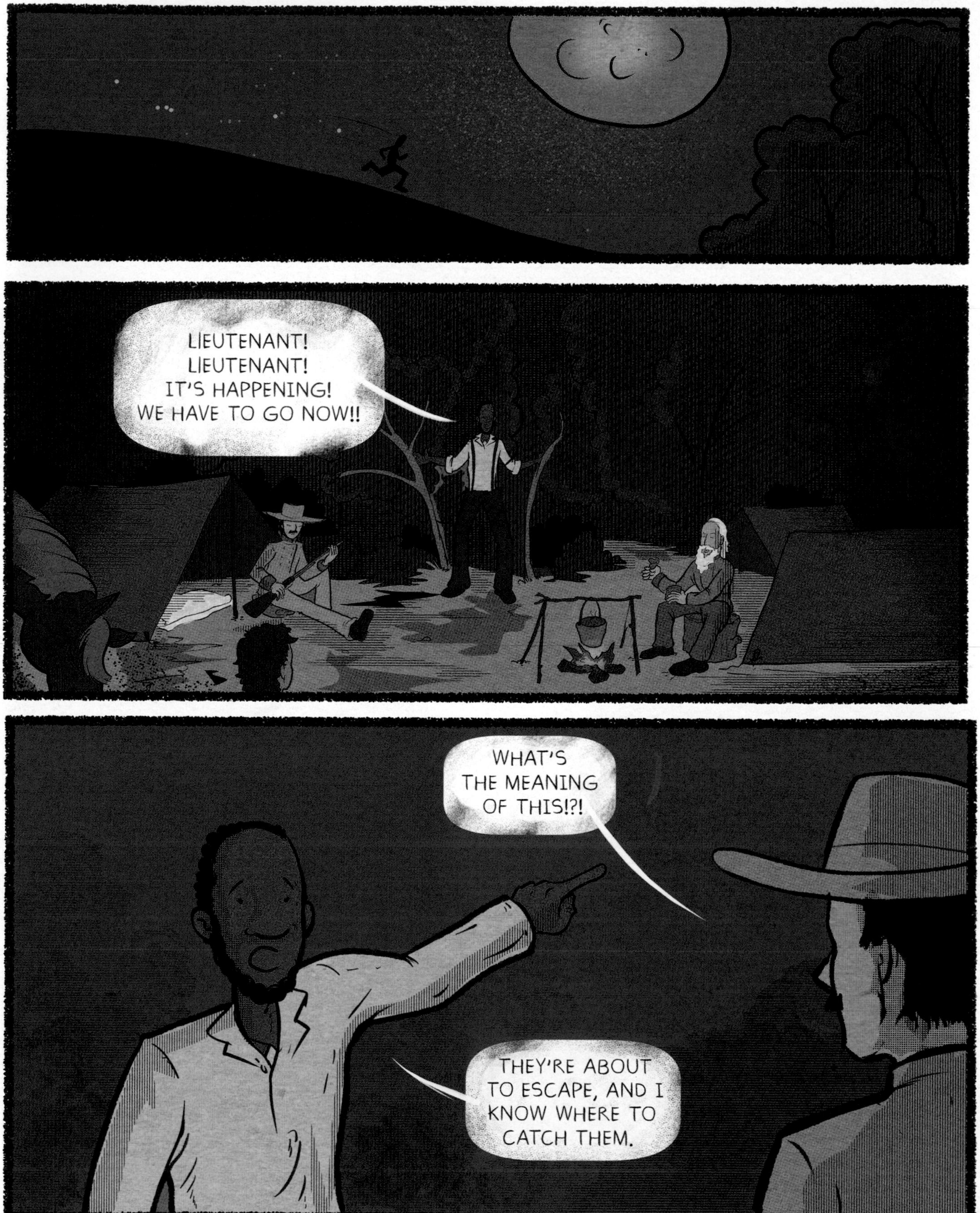
LIEUTENANT! LIEUTENANT! IT'S HAPPENING! WE HAVE TO GO NOW!!
WHAT'S THE MEANING OF THIS!?!
THEY'RE ABOUT TO ESCAPE, AND I KNOW WHERE TO CATCH THEM.

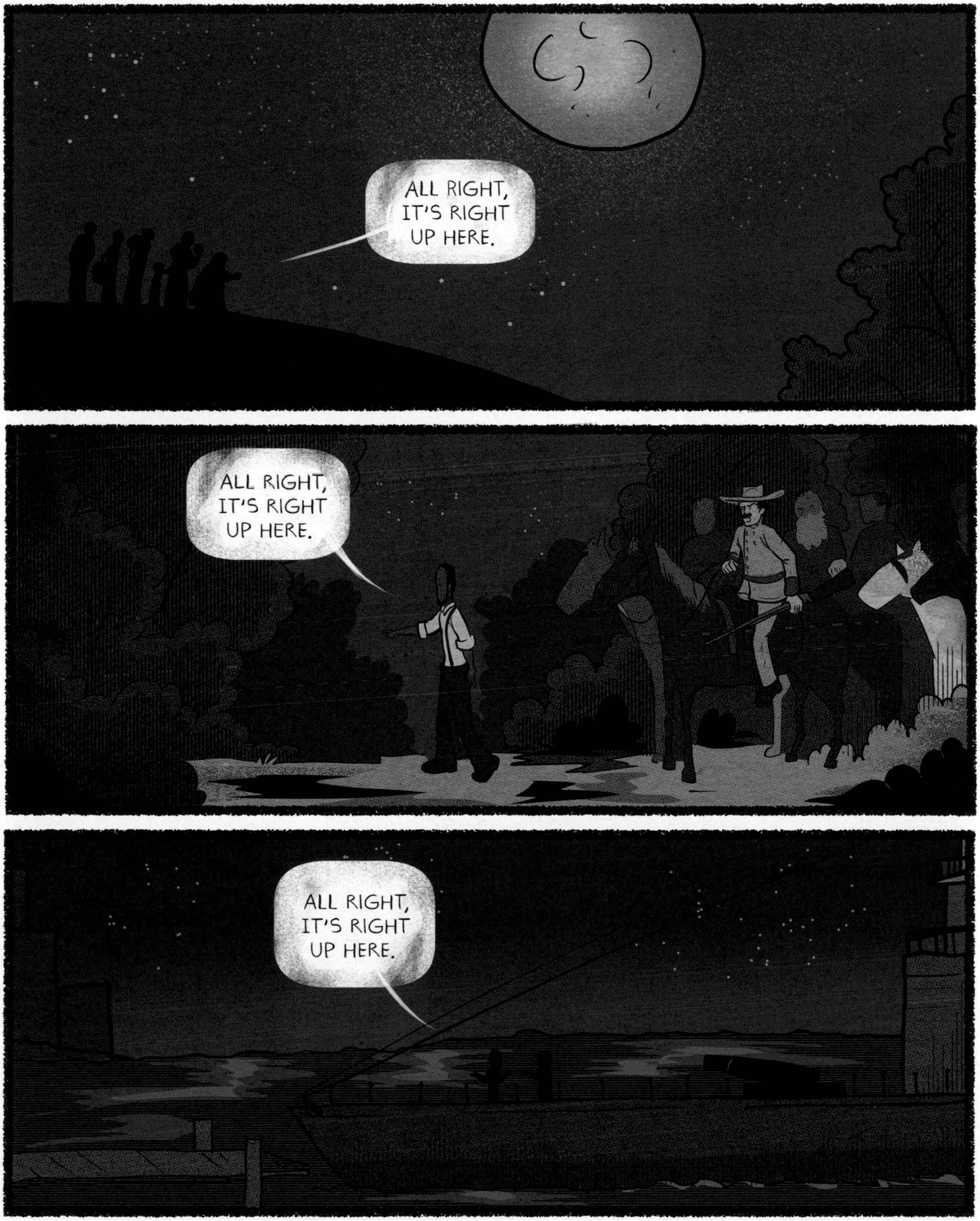
ALL RIGHT, IT'S RIGHT UP HERE.
ALL RIGHT, IT'S RIGHT UP HERE.
ALL RIGHT, IT'S RIGHT UP HERE.

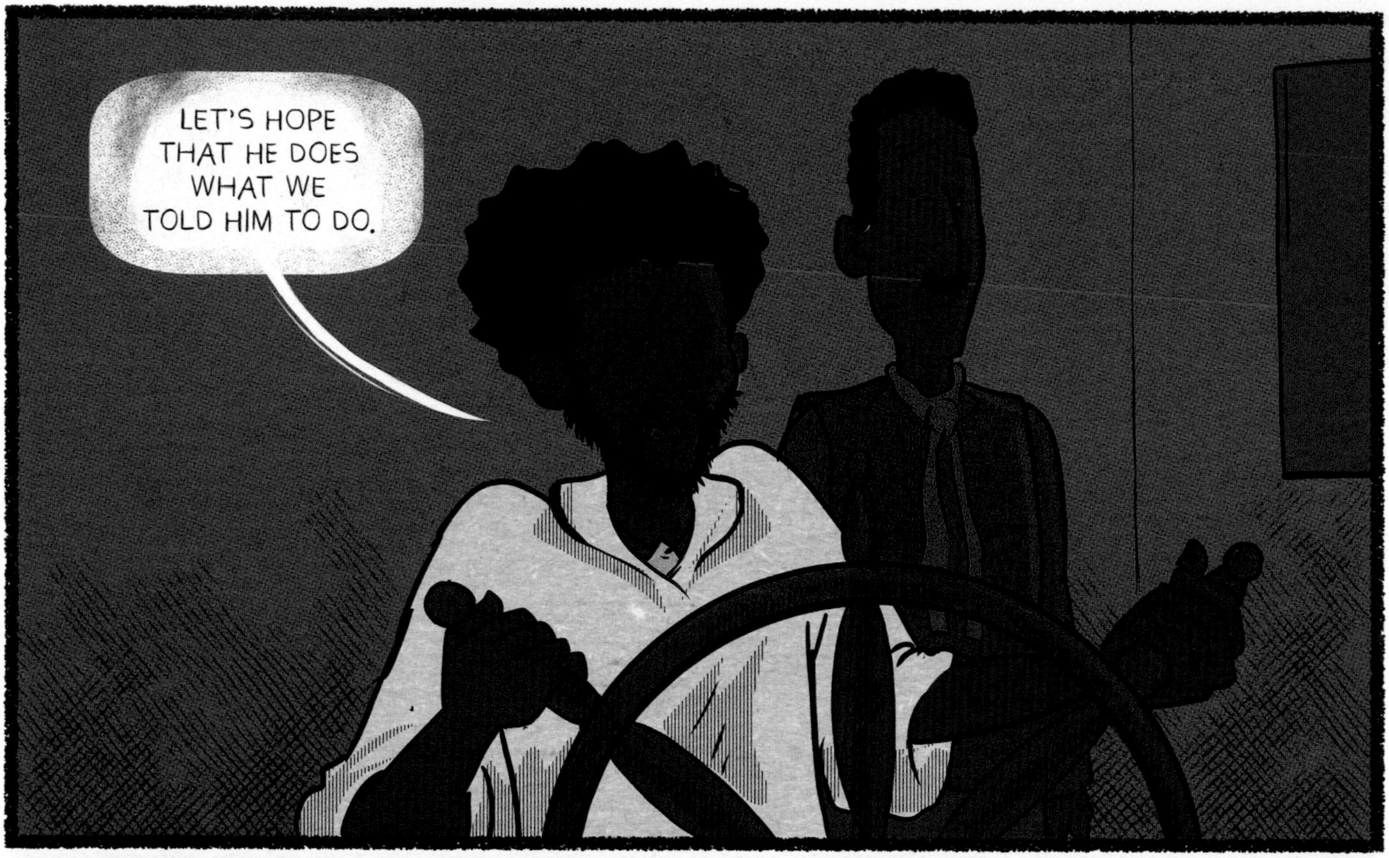
LET'S HOPE THAT HE DOES WHAT WE TOLD HIM TO DO.

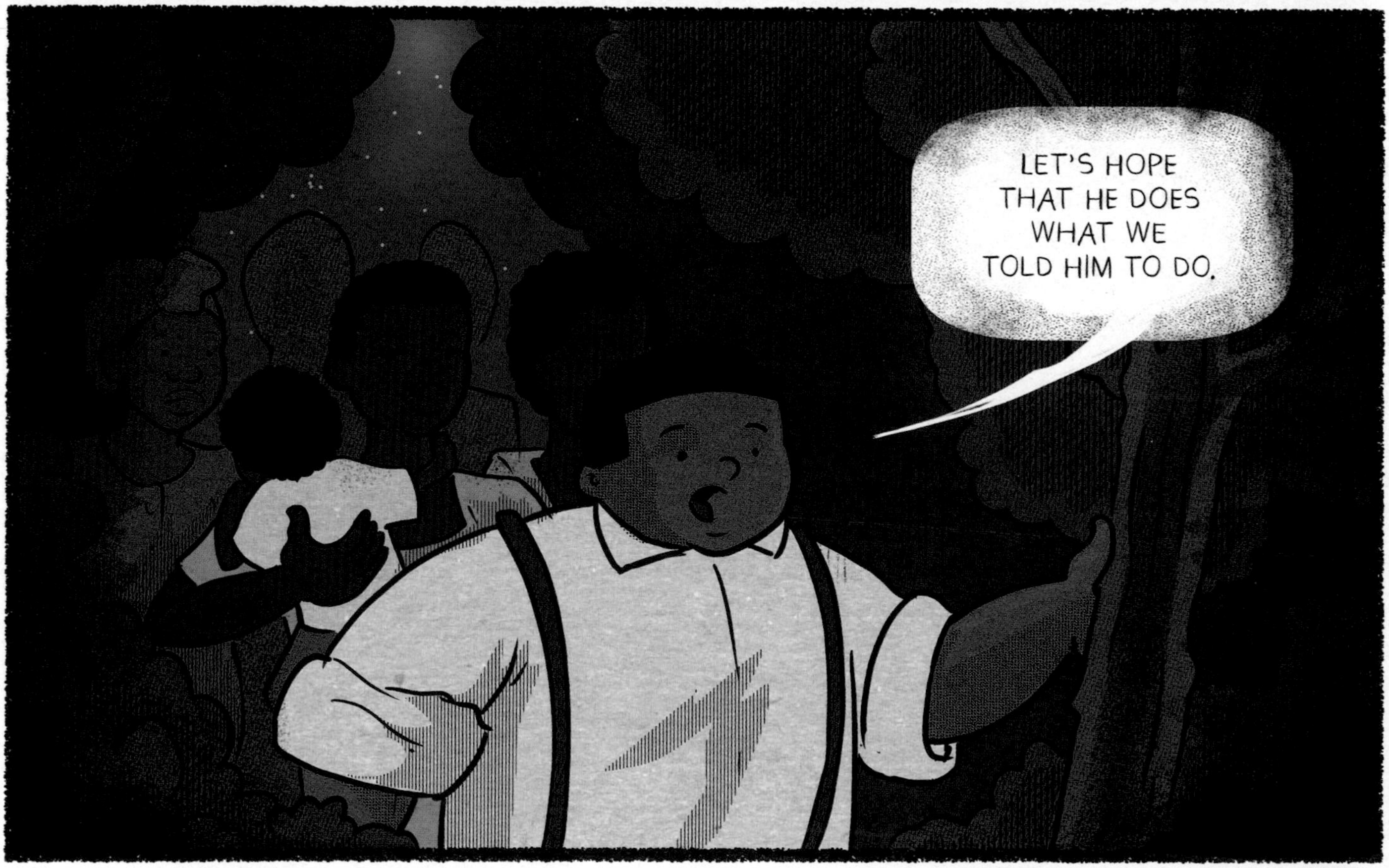
LET'S HOPE THAT HE DOES WHAT WE TOLD HIM TO DO.

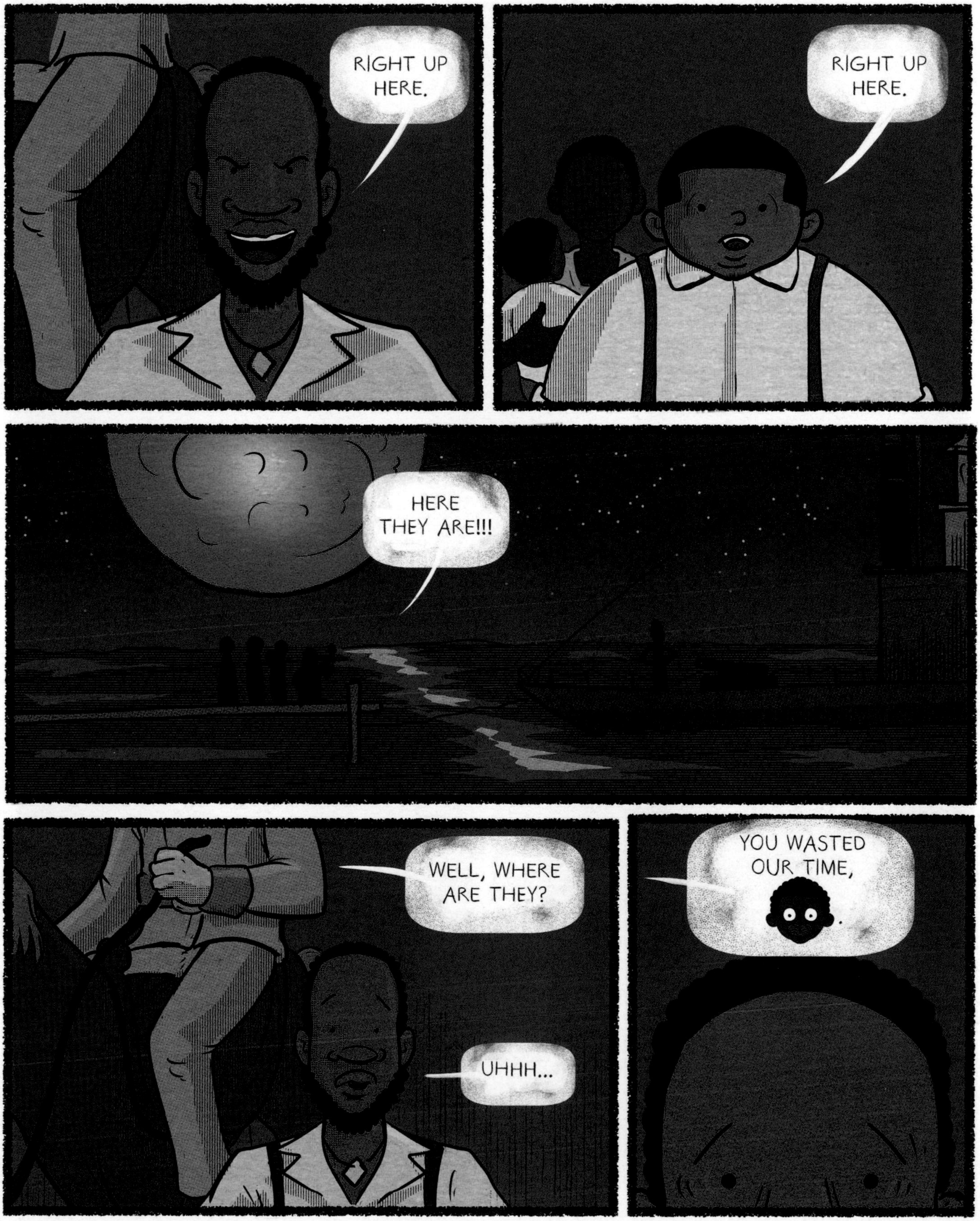
RIGHT UP HERE.
RIGHT UP HERE.
HERE THEY ARE!!!
WELL, WHERE ARE THEY?
UHHH...
YOU WASTED OUR TIME,

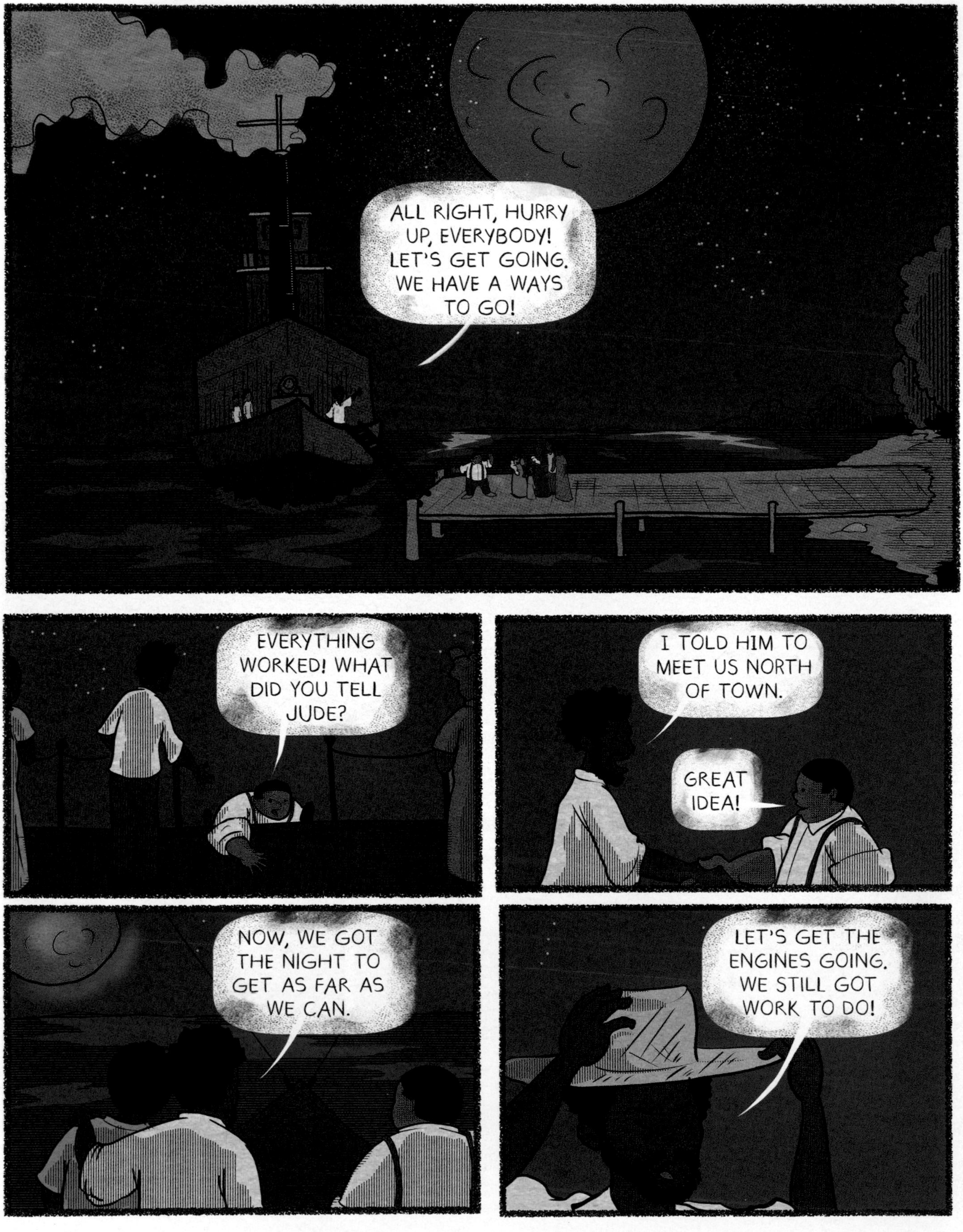
ALL RIGHT, HURRY UP, EVERYBODY! LET'S GET GOING. WE HAVE A WAYS TO GO!
EVERYTHING WORKED! WHAT DID YOU TELL JUDE?
I TOLD HIM TO MEET US NORTH OF TOWN.
GREAT IDEA!
NOW, WE GOT THE NIGHT TO GET AS FAR AS WE CAN.
LET'S GET THE ENGINES GOING. WE STILL GOT WORK TO DO!

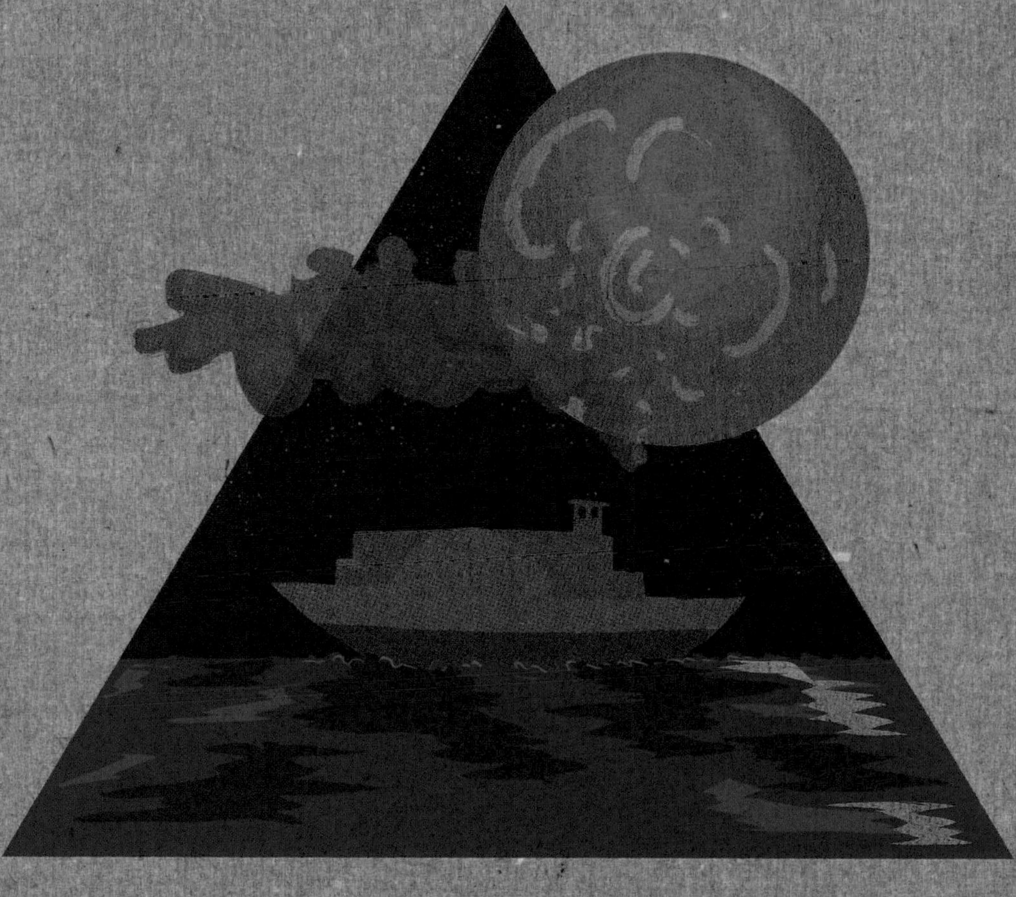

CHAPTER EIGHT

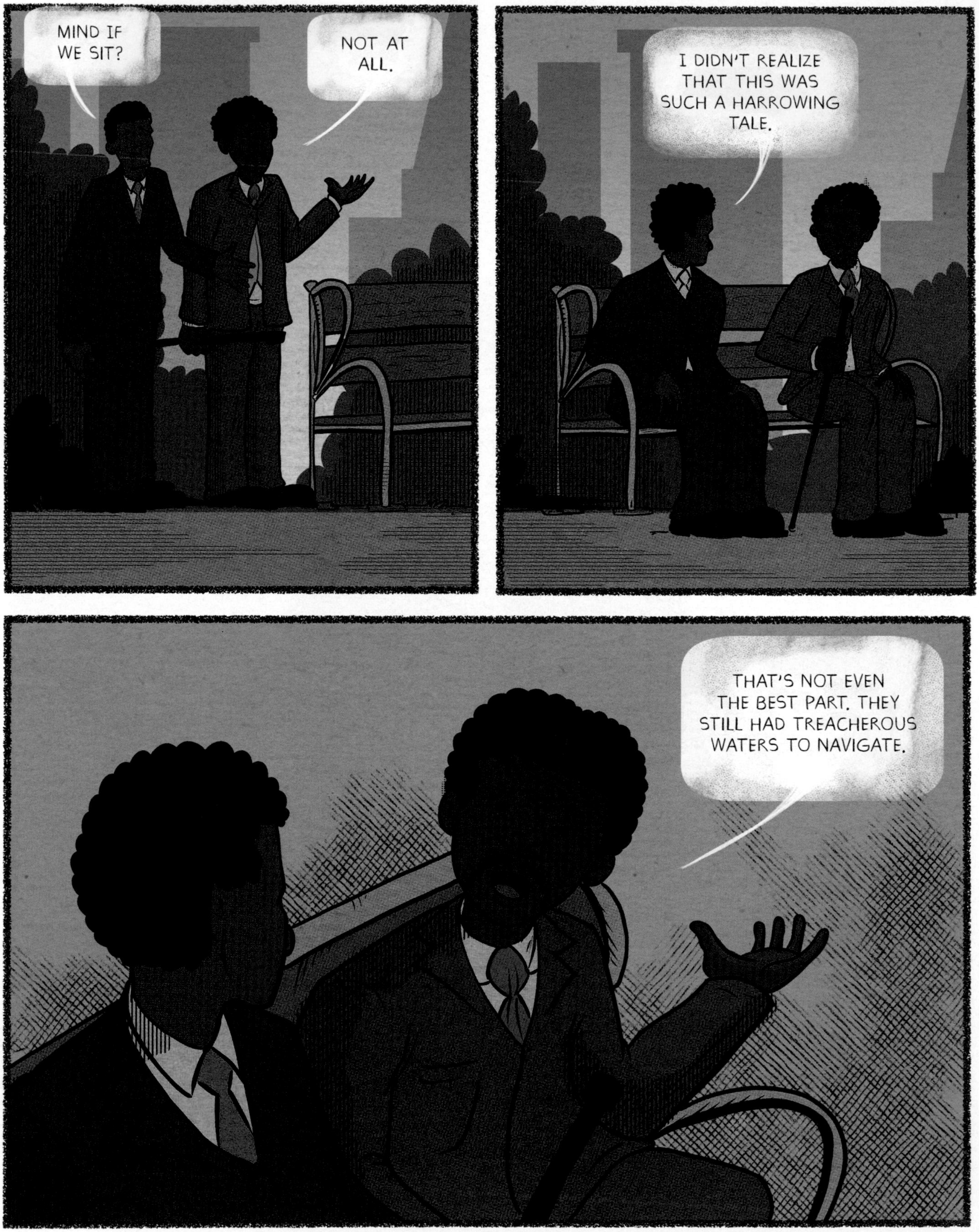
MIND IF WE SIT?
NOT AT ALL.
I DIDN'T REALIZE THAT THIS WAS SUCH A HARROWING TALE.
THAT'S NOT EVEN THE BEST PART. THEY STILL HAD TREACHEROUS WATERS TO NAVIGATE.

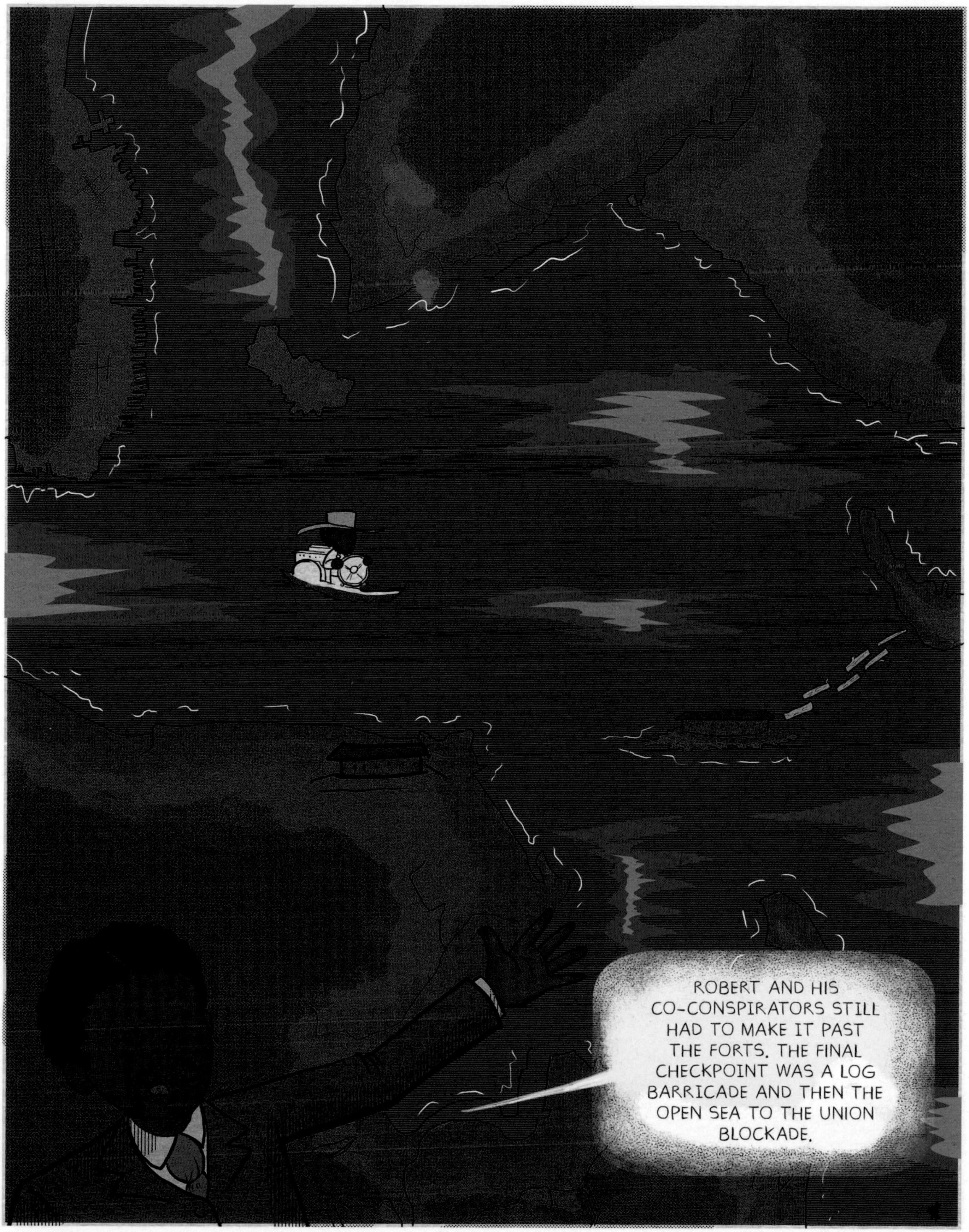
ROBERT AND HIS CO-CONSPIRATORS STILL HAD TO MAKE IT PAST THE FORTS. THE FINAL CHECKPOINT WAS A LOG BARRICADE AND THEN THE OPEN SEA TO THE UNION BLOCKADE.

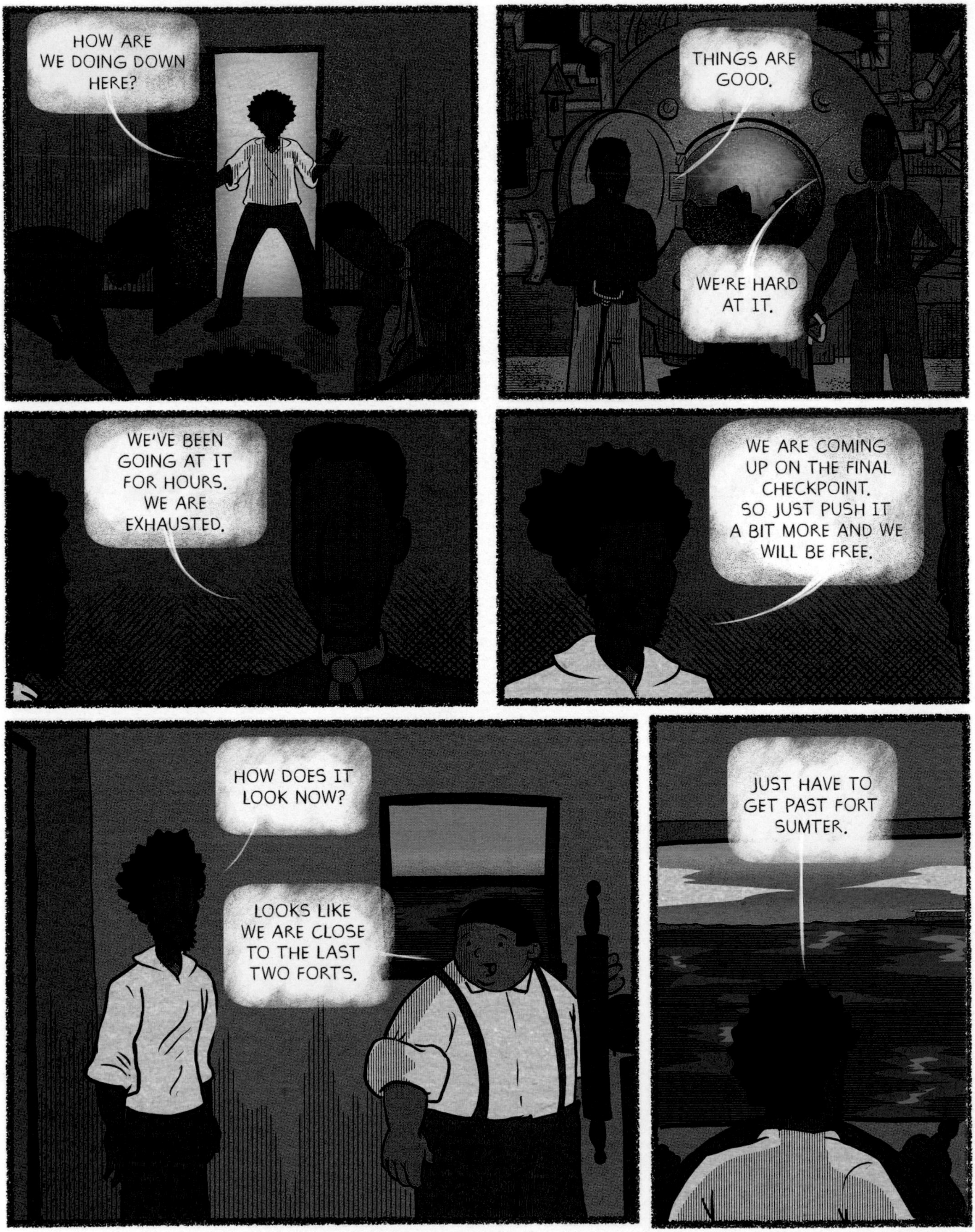
HOW ARE WE DOING DOWN HERE?
THINGS ARE GOOD.
WE'RE HARD AT IT.
WE'VE BEEN GOING AT IT FOR HOURS. WE ARE EXHAUSTED.
WE ARE COMING UP ON THE FINAL CHECKPOINT. SO JUST PUSH IT A BIT MORE AND WE WILL BE FREE.
HOW DOES IT LOOK NOW?
LOOKS LIKE WE ARE CLOSE TO THE LAST TWO FORTS.
JUST HAVE TO GET PAST FORT SUMTER.

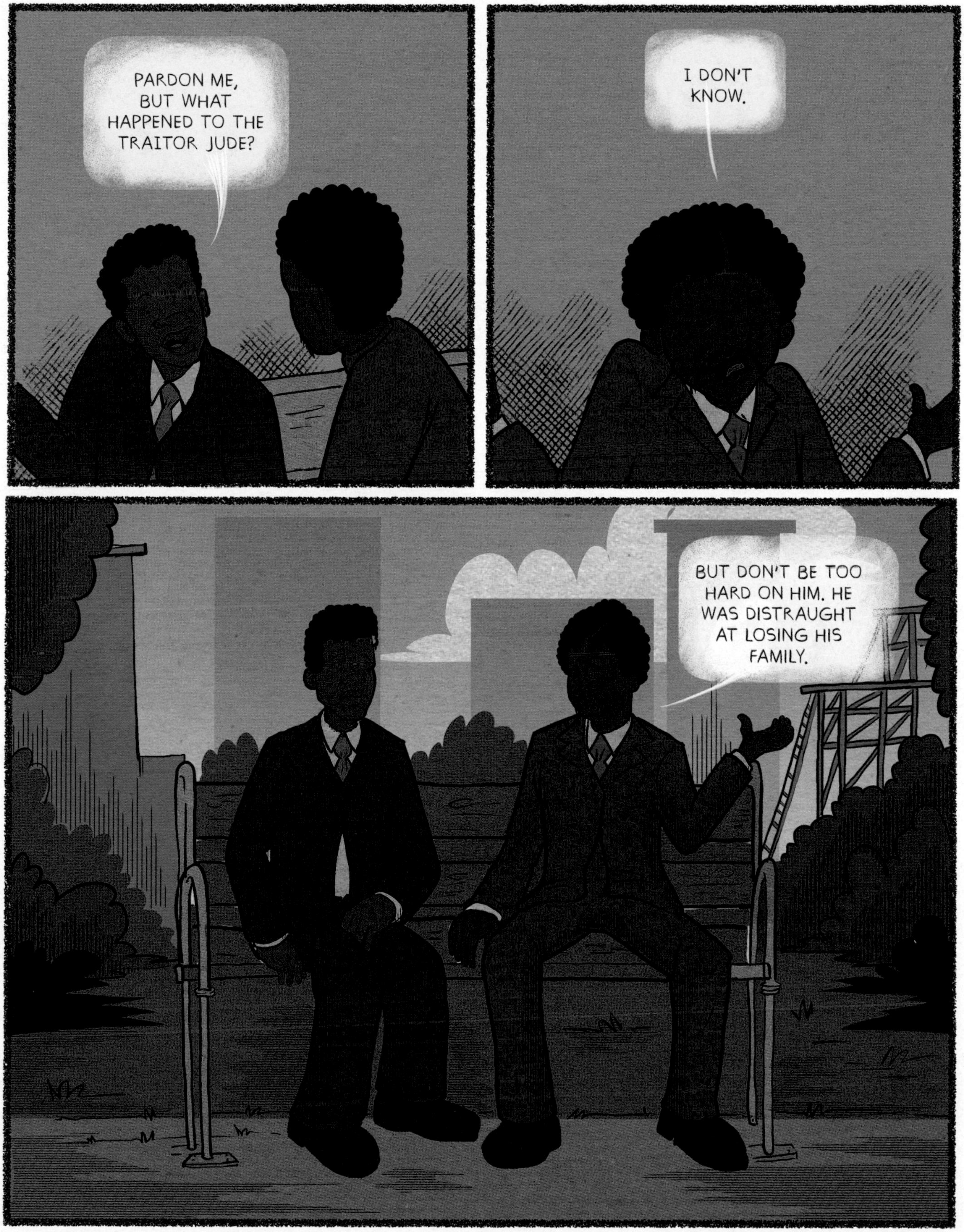
PARDON ME, BUT WHAT HAPPENED TO THE TRAITOR JUDE?
I DON'T KNOW.
BUT DON'T BE TOO HARD ON HIM. HE WAS DISTRAUGHT AT LOSING HIS FAMILY.

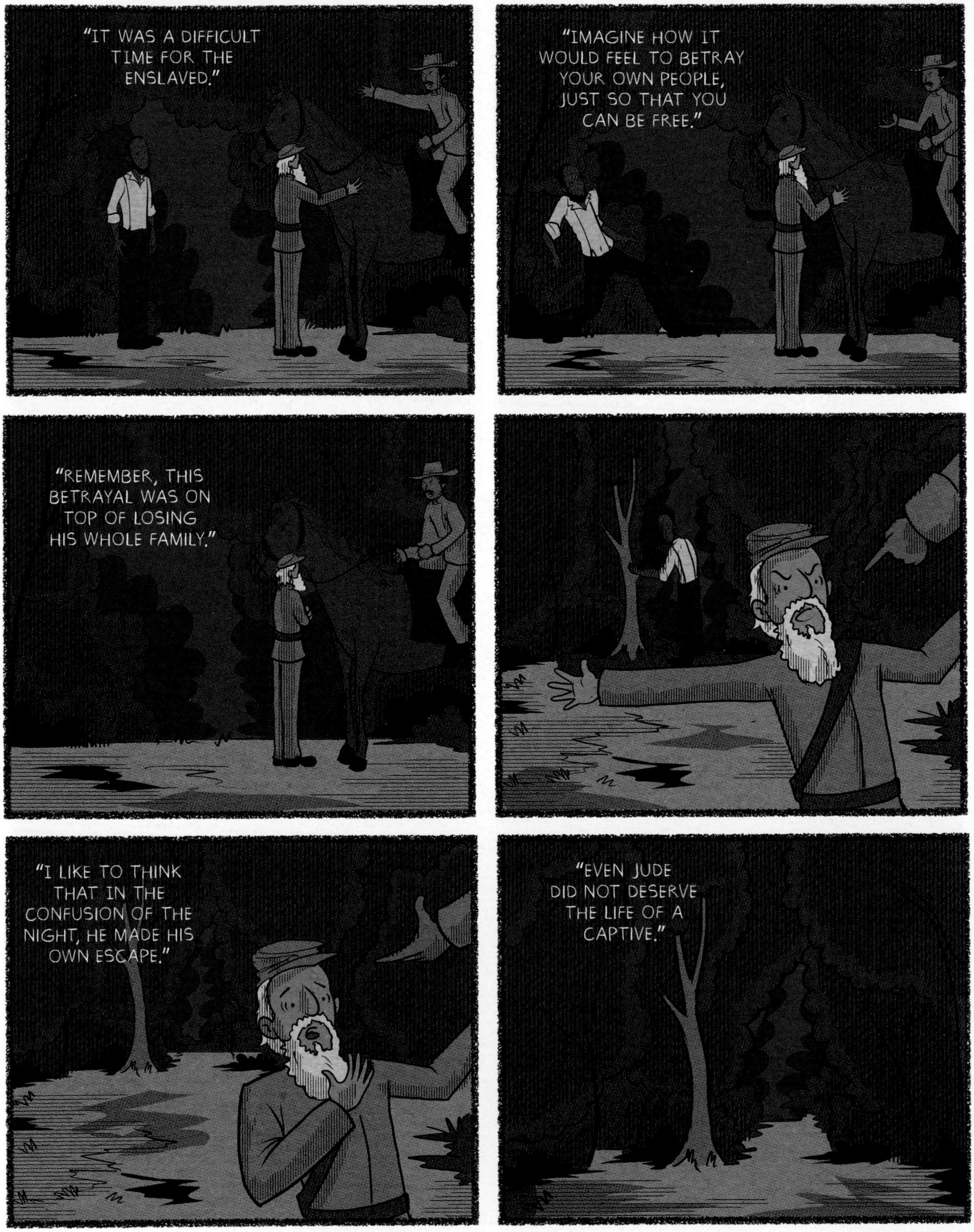
"IT WAS A DIFFICULT TIME FOR THE ENSLAVED."
"IMAGINE HOW IT WOULD FEEL TO BETRAY YOUR OWN PEOPLE, JUST SO THAT YOU CAN BE FREE."
"REMEMBER, THIS BETRAYAL WAS ON TOP OF LOSING HIS WHOLE FAMILY."
"I LIKE TO THINK THAT IN THE CONFUSION OF THE NIGHT, HE MADE HIS OWN ESCAPE."
"EVEN JUDE DID NOT DESERVE THE LIFE OF A CAPTIVE."

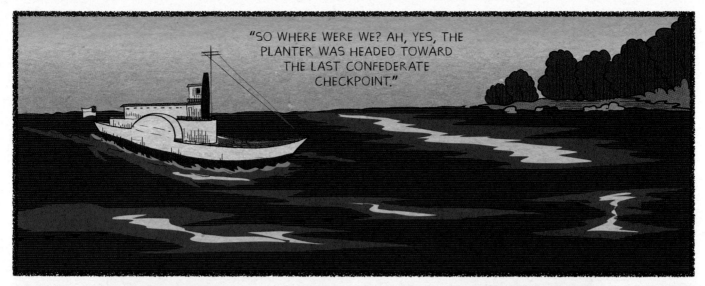

"SO WHERE WERE WE? AH, YES, THE PLANTER WAS HEADED TOWARD THE LAST CONFEDERATE CHECKPOINT."

ALL RIGHT... IT'S TIME.

WHAT SHOULD I DO?

GET EVERYONE HIDDEN DOWN BELOW.

GOT IT.

LET'S GO! LET'S GO! LET'S GO!

"THIS WAS THE MOST PRECARIOUS CROSSING, BECAUSE NOW THEY WERE TRAVELING WHEN IT WAS LIGHT OUT."

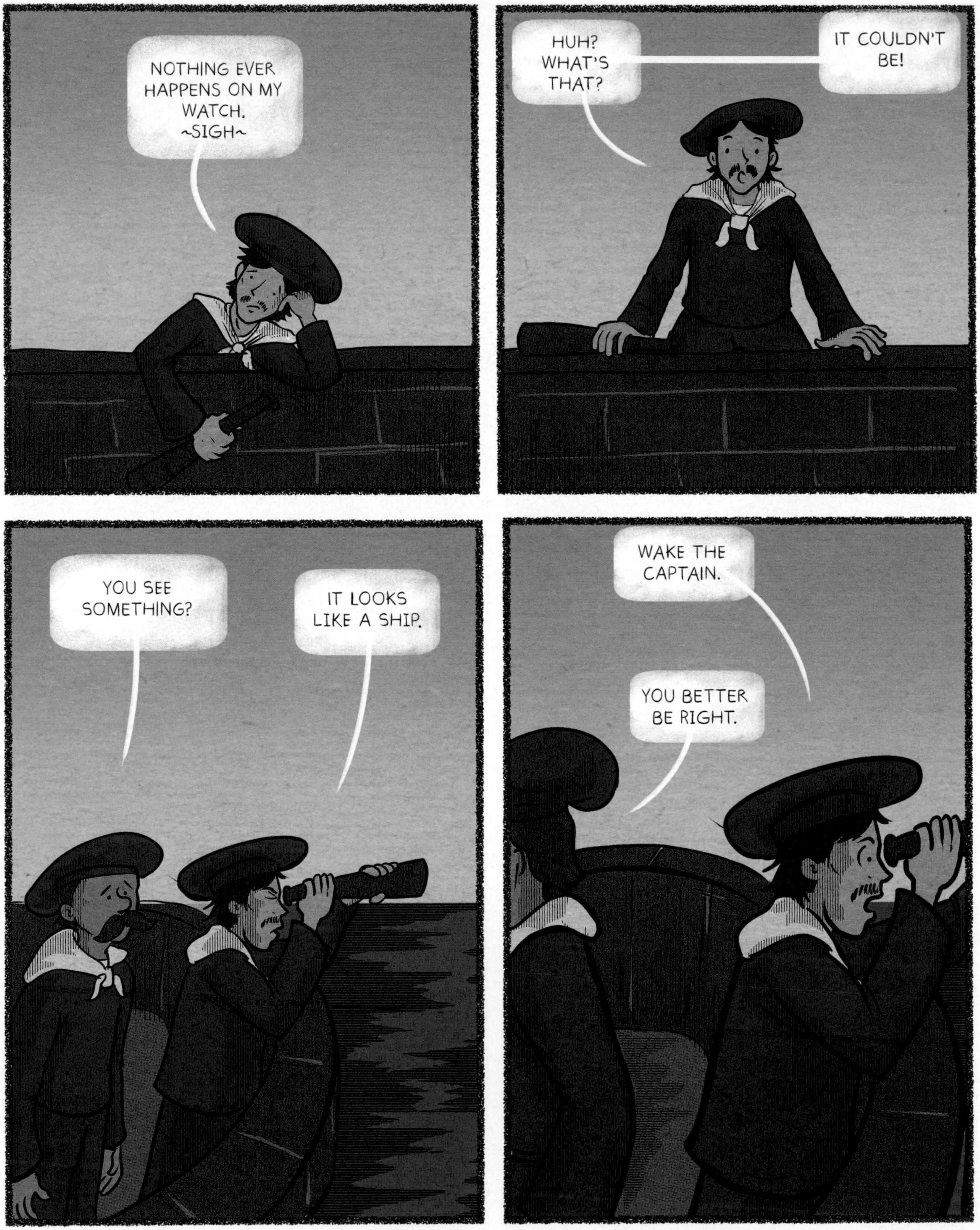
NOTHING EVER HAPPENS ON MY WATCH. ~SIGH~
HUH? WHAT'S THAT?
IT COULDN'T BE!
YOU SEE SOMETHING?
IT LOOKS LIKE A SHIP.
WAKE THE CAPTAIN.
YOU BETTER BE RIGHT.

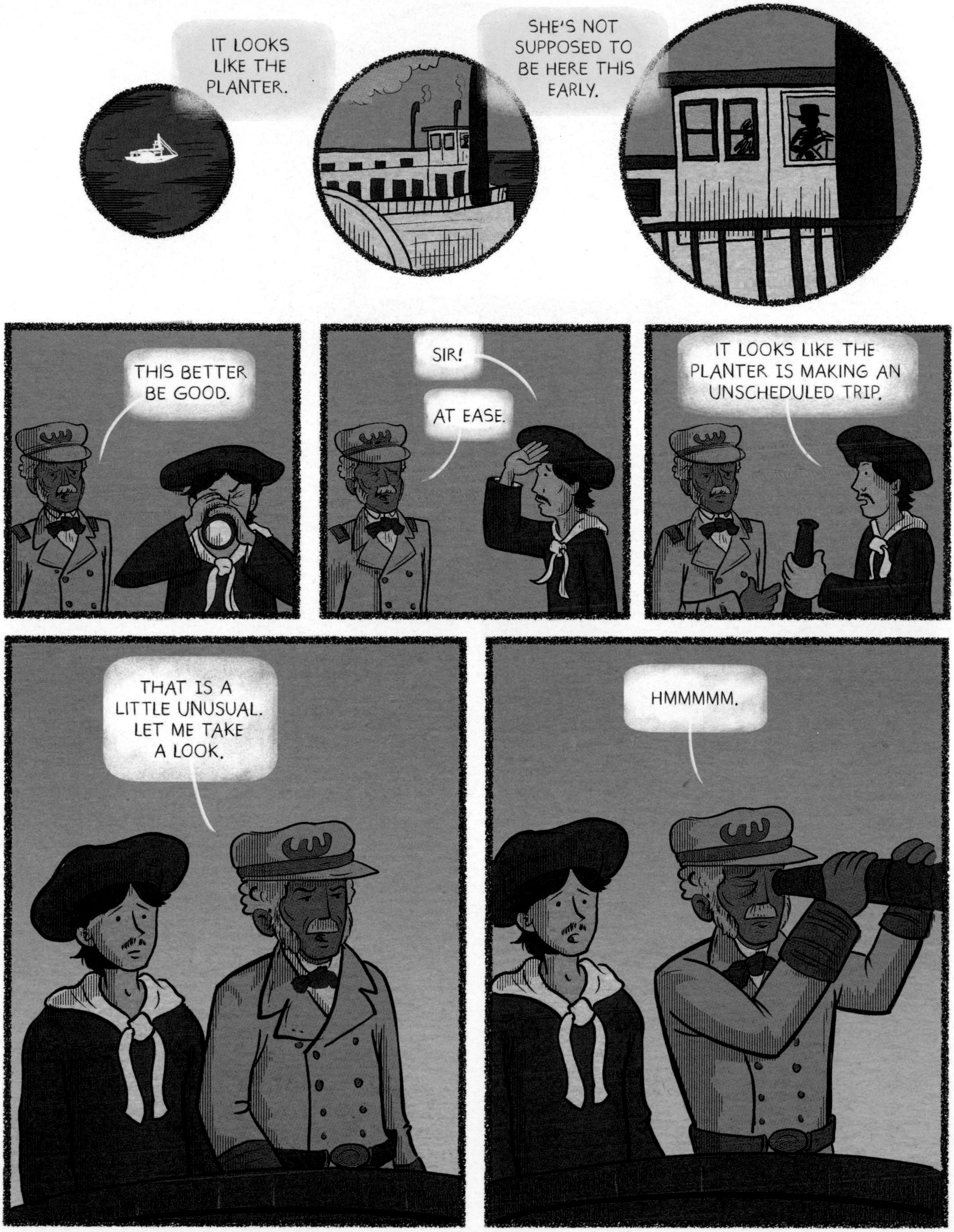

IT LOOKS LIKE THE PLANTER.
SHE'S NOT SUPPOSED TO BE HERE THIS EARLY.
THIS BETTER BE GOOD.
SIR!
AT EASE.
IT LOOKS LIKE THE PLANTER IS MAKING AN UNSCHEDULED TRIP.
THAT IS A LITTLE UNUSUAL. LET ME TAKE A LOOK.
HMMMMM.

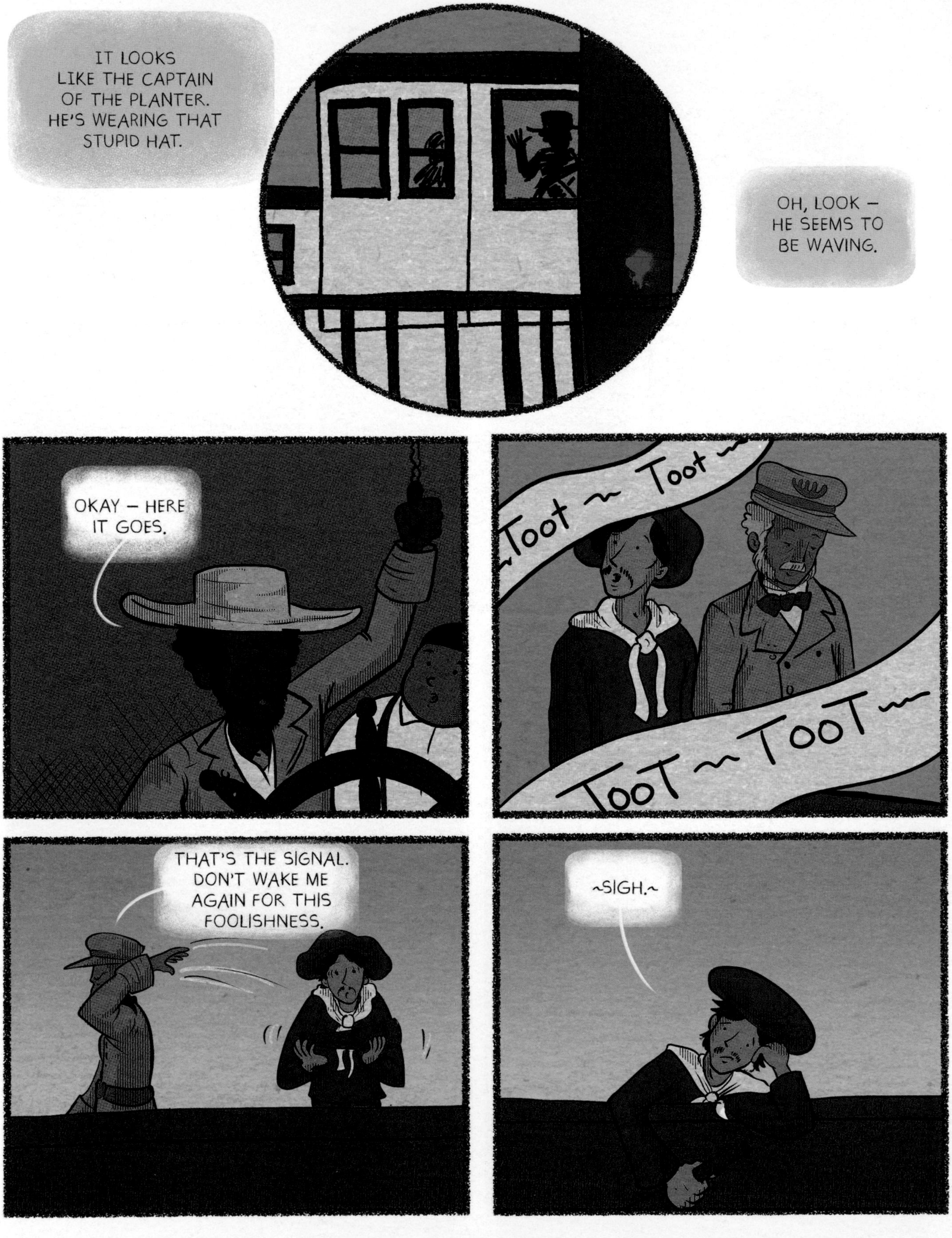
IT LOOKS LIKE THE CAPTAIN OF THE PLANTER. HE'S WEARING THAT STUPID HAT.
OH, LOOK – HE SEEMS TO BE WAVING.
OKAY – HERE IT GOES.
Toot ~ Toot ~
TOOT ~ TOOT ~
THAT'S THE SIGNAL. DON'T WAKE ME AGAIN FOR THIS FOOLISHNESS.
~SIGH.~

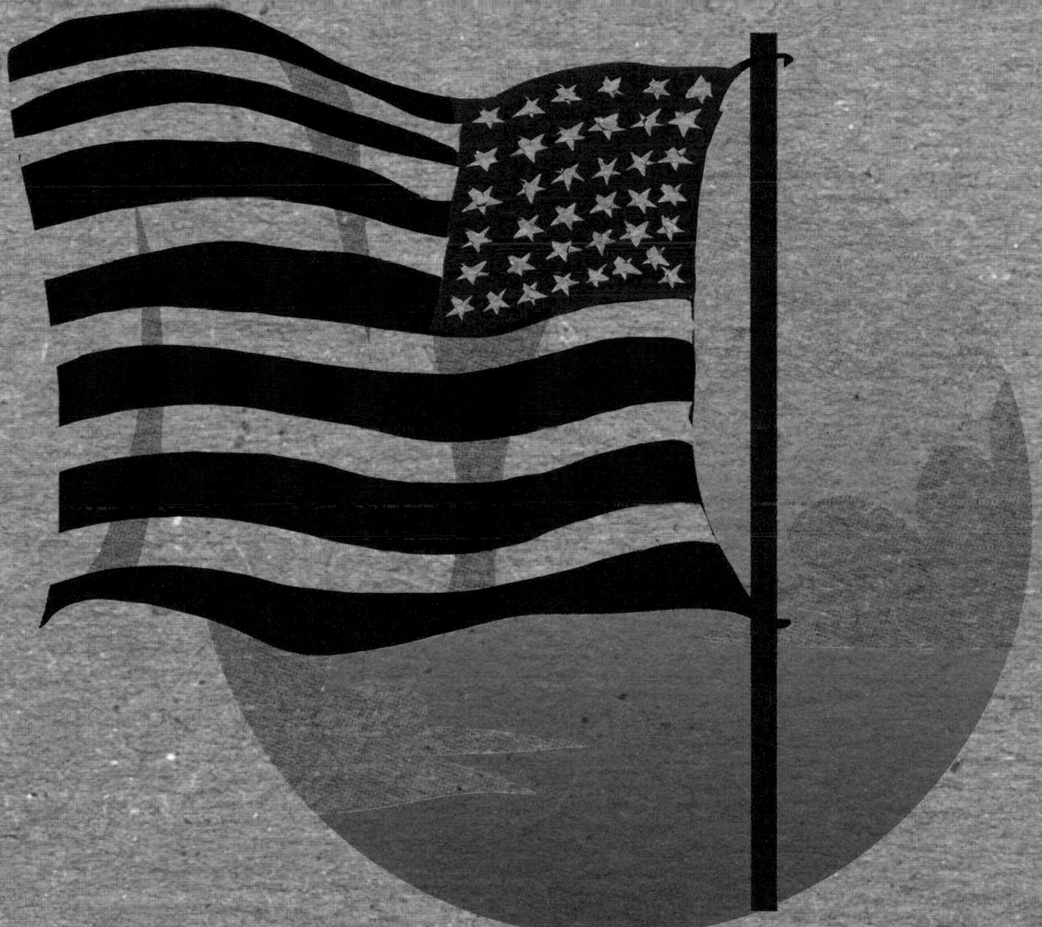

CHAPTER NINE

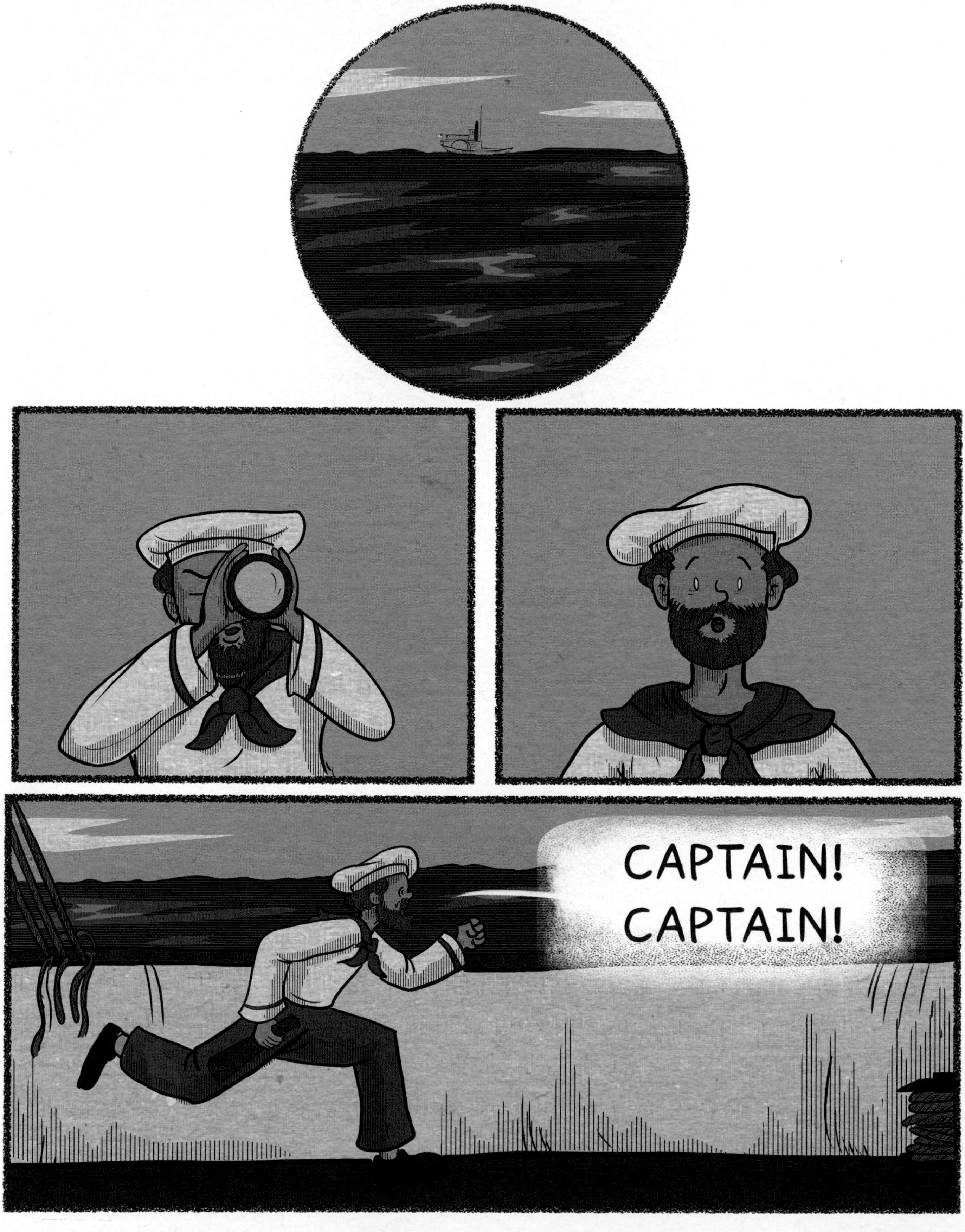
CAPTAIN!
CAPTAIN!

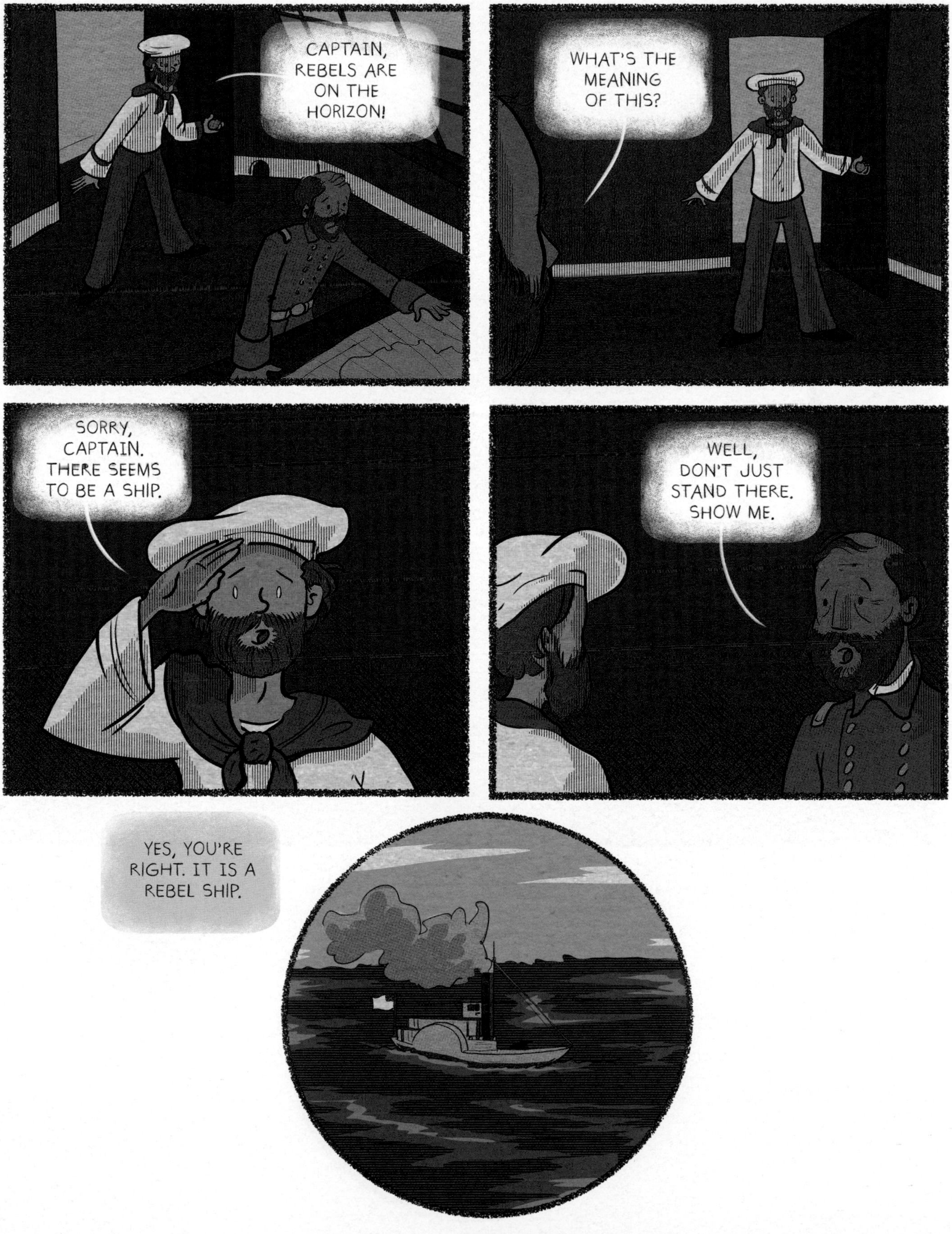
CAPTAIN, REBELS ARE ON THE HORIZON!
WHAT'S THE MEANING OF THIS?
SORRY, CAPTAIN. THERE SEEMS TO BE A SHIP.
WELL, DON'T JUST STAND THERE. SHOW ME.
YES, YOU'RE RIGHT. IT IS A REBEL SHIP.

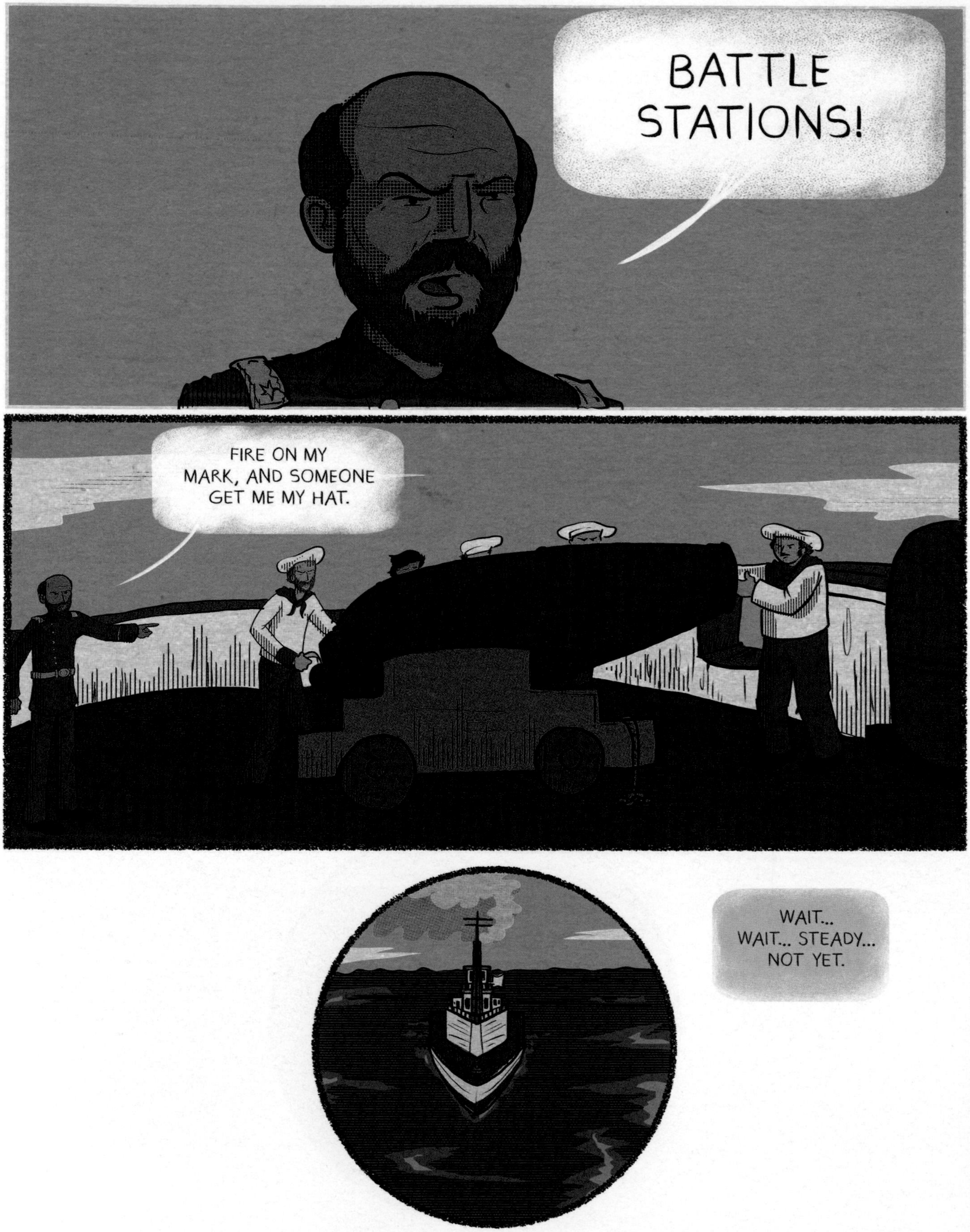
BATTLE STATIONS!
FIRE ON MY MARK, AND SOMEONE GET ME MY HAT.
WAIT... WAIT... STEADY... NOT YET.

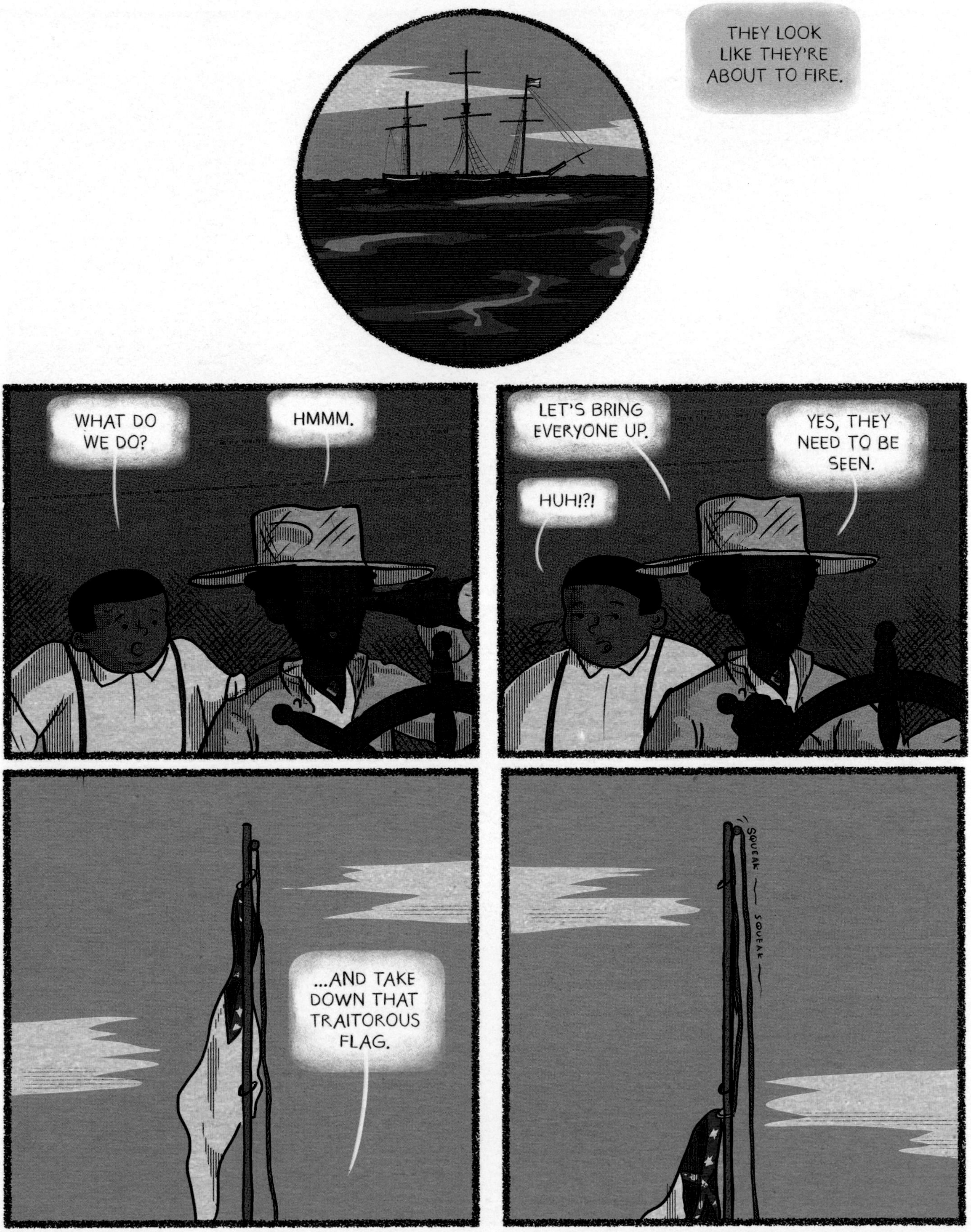
THEY LOOK LIKE THEY'RE ABOUT TO FIRE.
WHAT DO WE DO?
HMMM.
LET'S BRING EVERYONE UP.
HUH!?!
YES, THEY NEED TO BE SEEN.
...AND TAKE DOWN THAT TRAITOROUS FLAG.
SQUEAK — SQUEAK —

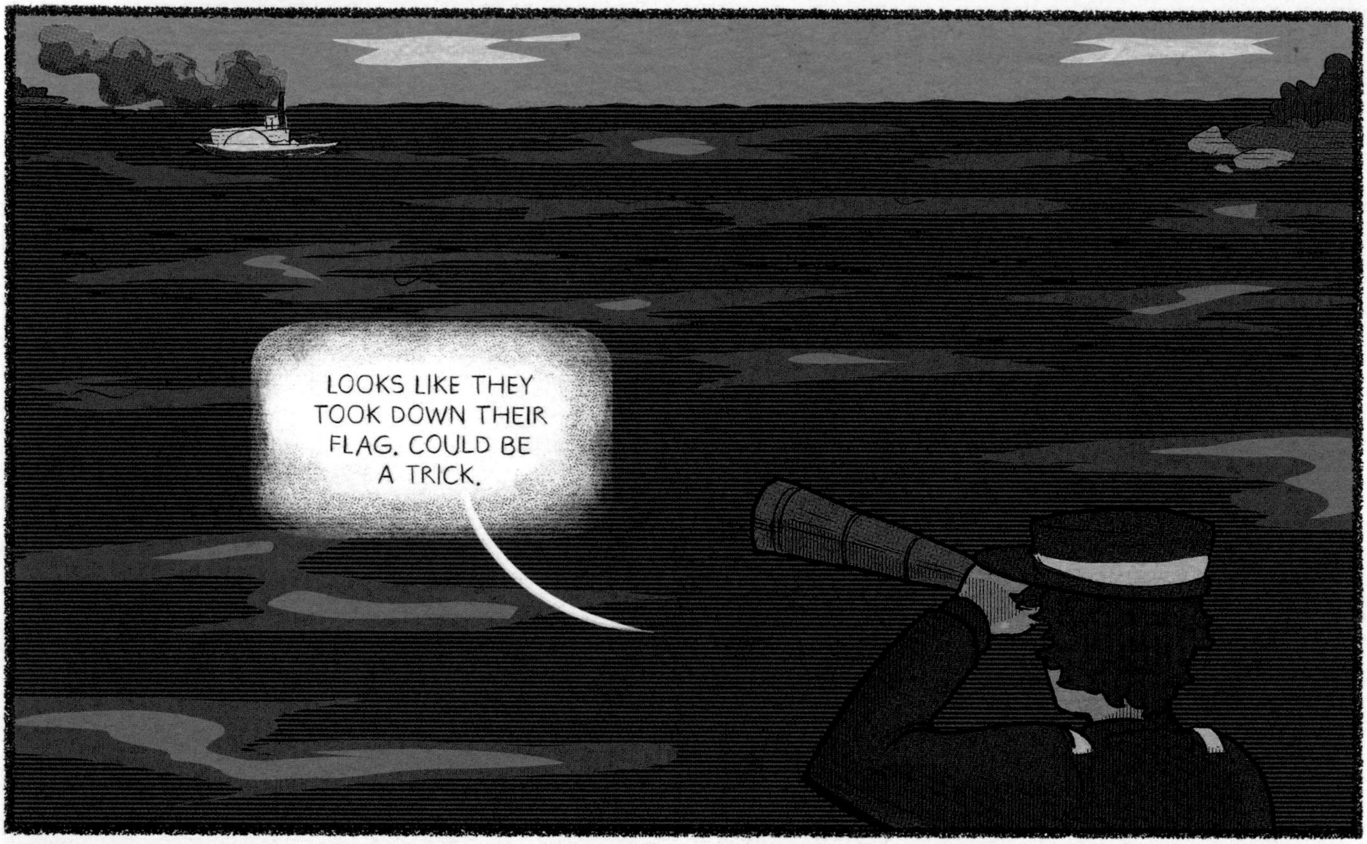
LOOKS LIKE THEY TOOK DOWN THEIR FLAG. COULD BE A TRICK.

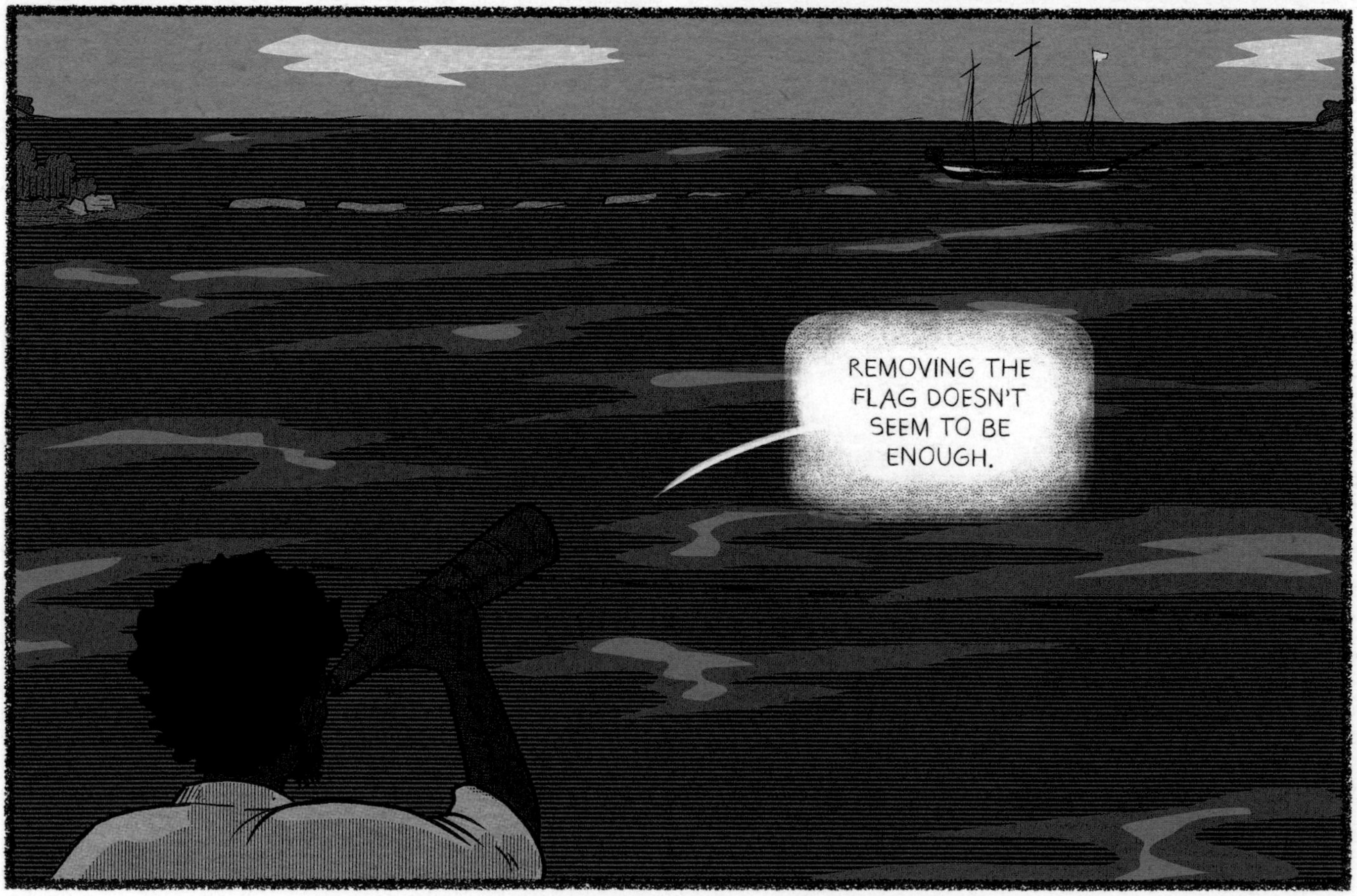
REMOVING THE FLAG DOESN'T SEEM TO BE ENOUGH.

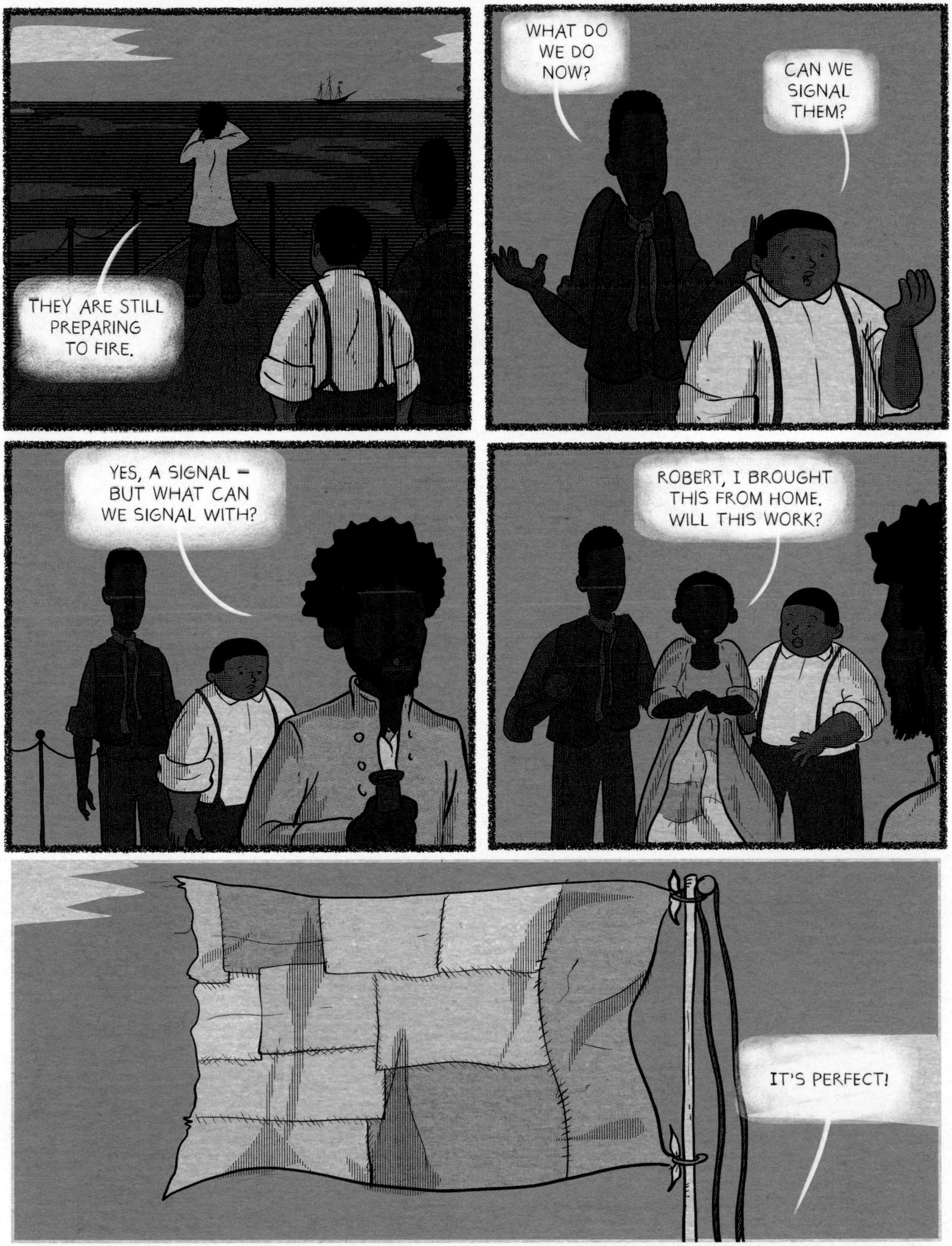
THEY ARE STILL PREPARING TO FIRE.
WHAT DO WE DO NOW?
CAN WE SIGNAL THEM?
YES, A SIGNAL — BUT WHAT CAN WE SIGNAL WITH?
ROBERT, I BROUGHT THIS FROM HOME. WILL THIS WORK?
IT'S PERFECT!

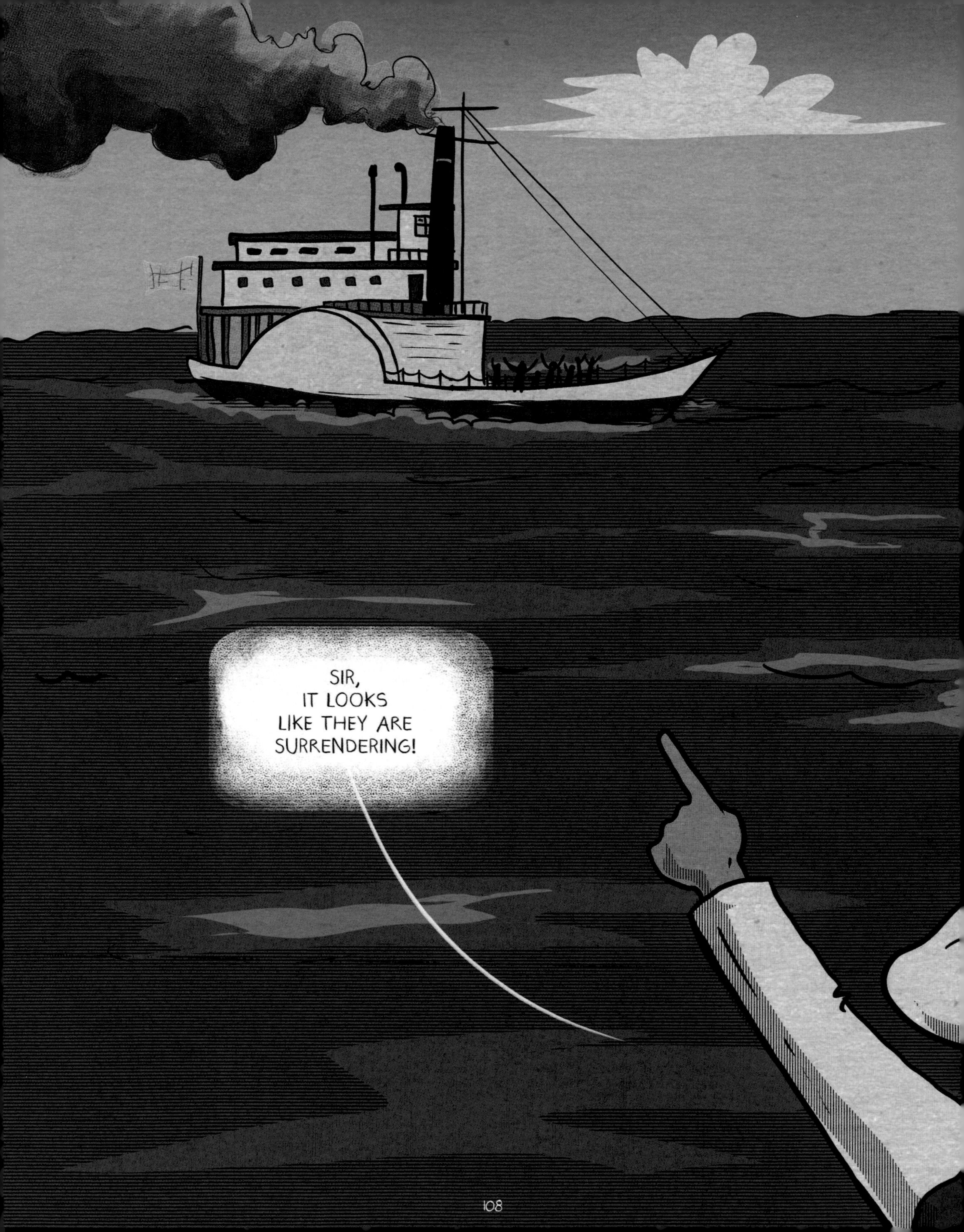
SIR, IT LOOKS LIKE THEY ARE SURRENDERING!

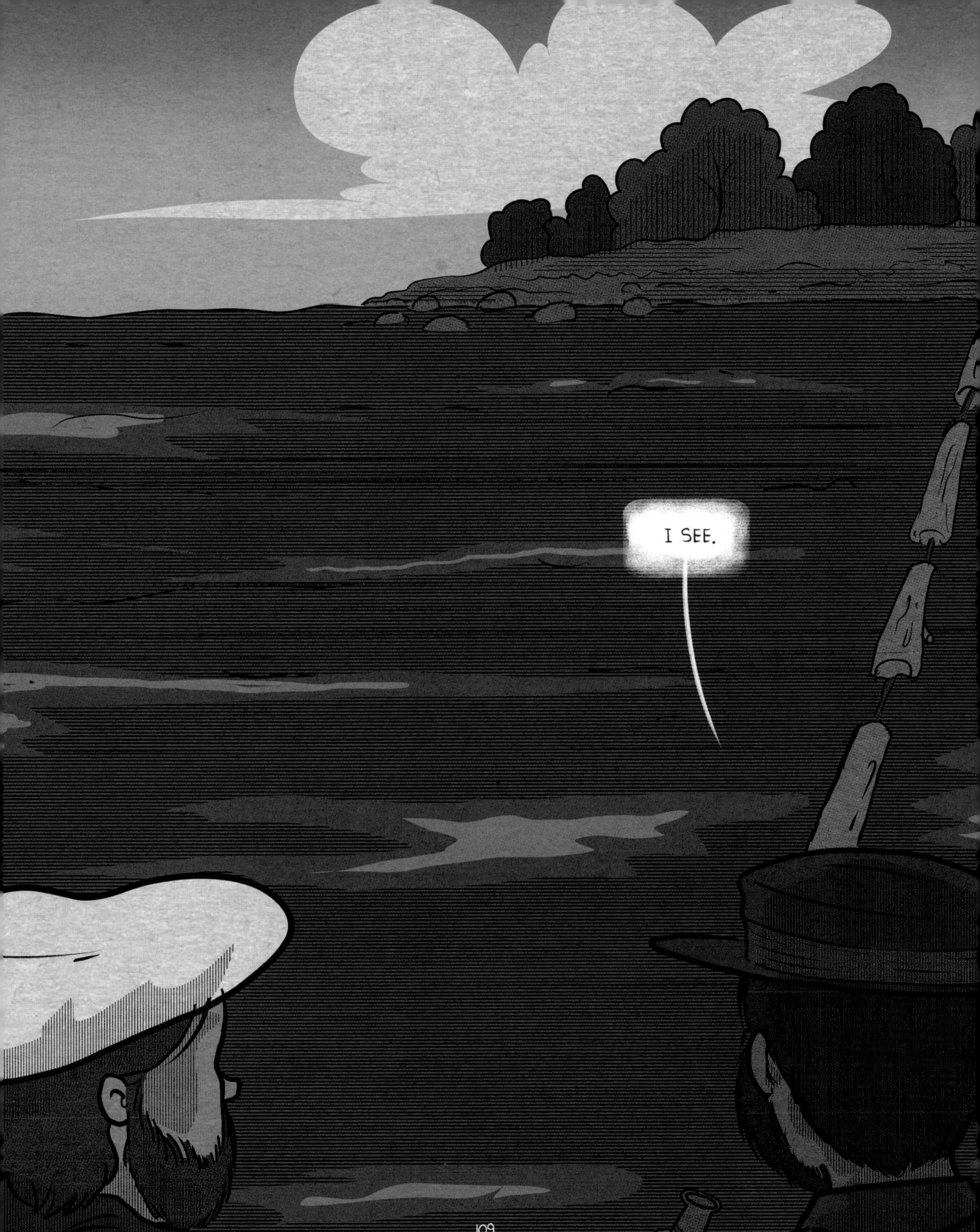
I SEE.

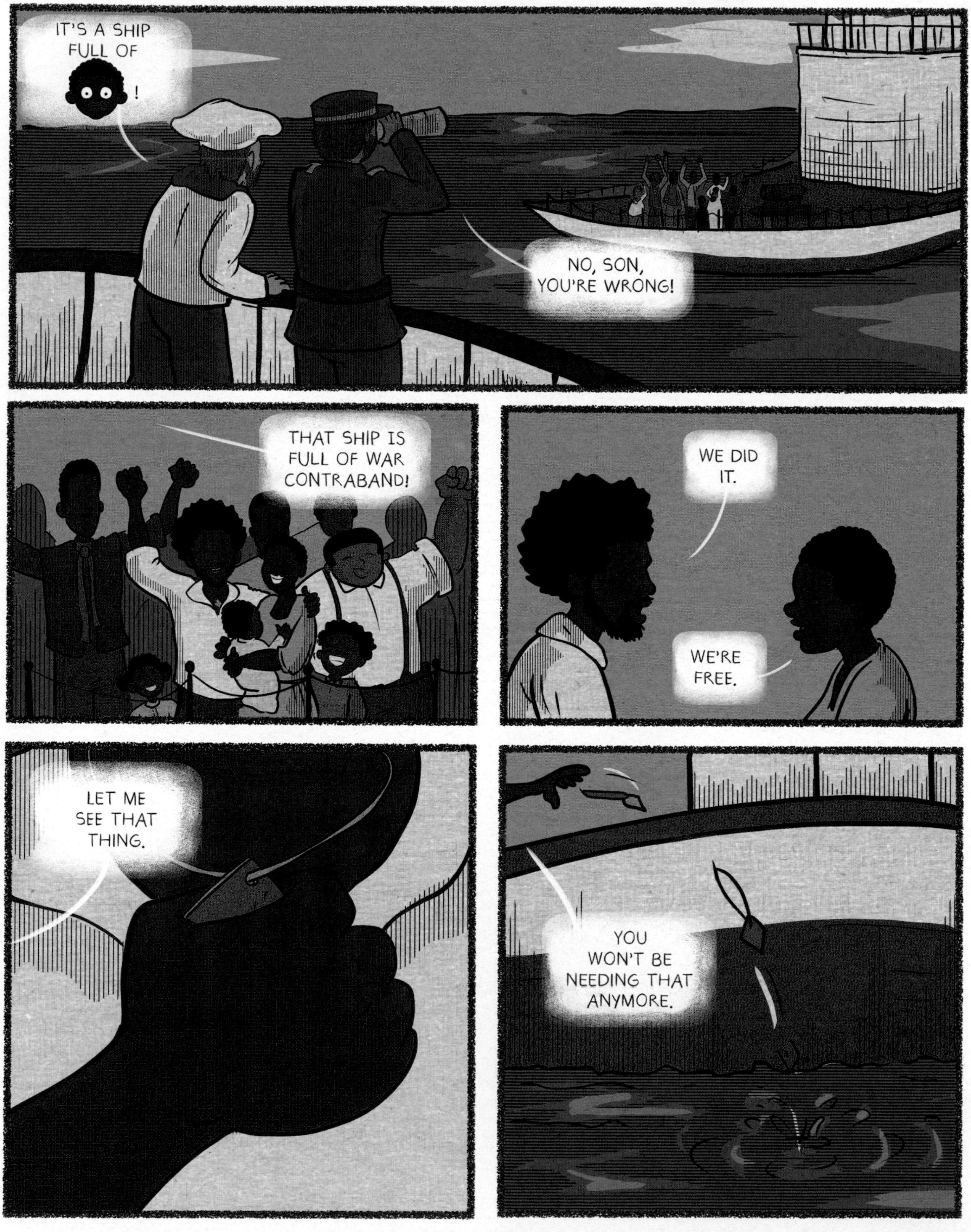
IT'S A SHIP FULL OF !
NO, SON, YOU'RE WRONG!
THAT SHIP IS FULL OF WAR CONTRABAND!
WE DID IT.
WE'RE FREE.
LET ME SEE THAT THING.
YOU WON'T BE NEEDING THAT ANYMORE.

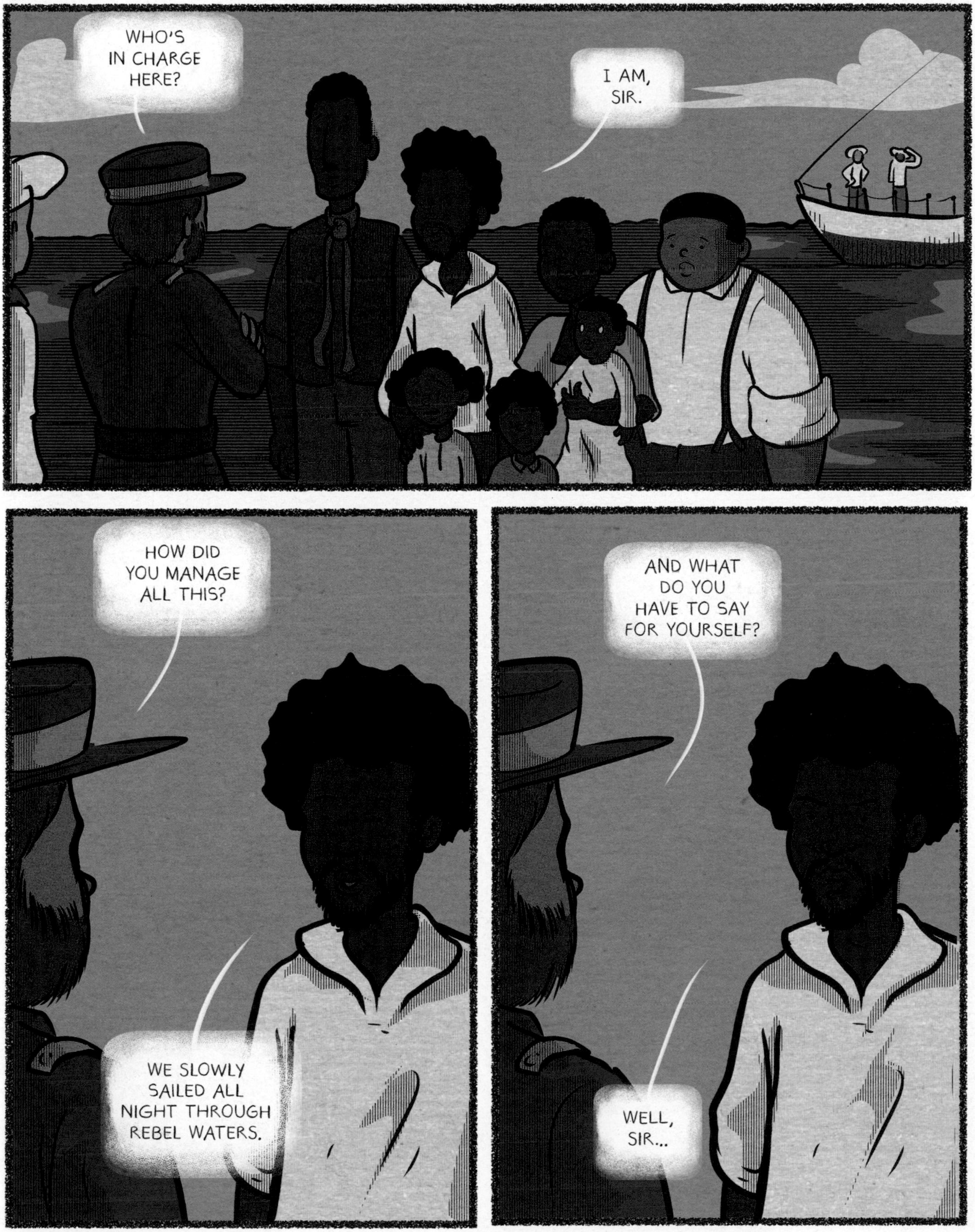
WHO'S IN CHARGE HERE?
I AM, SIR.
HOW DID YOU MANAGE ALL THIS?
WE SLOWLY SAILED ALL NIGHT THROUGH REBEL WATERS.
AND WHAT DO YOU HAVE TO SAY FOR YOURSELF?
WELL, SIR...

I AM DELIVERING THIS WAR MATERIAL. I'M SURE UNCLE ABRAHAM LINCOLN CAN PUT THEM TO GOOD USE!

EPILOGUE

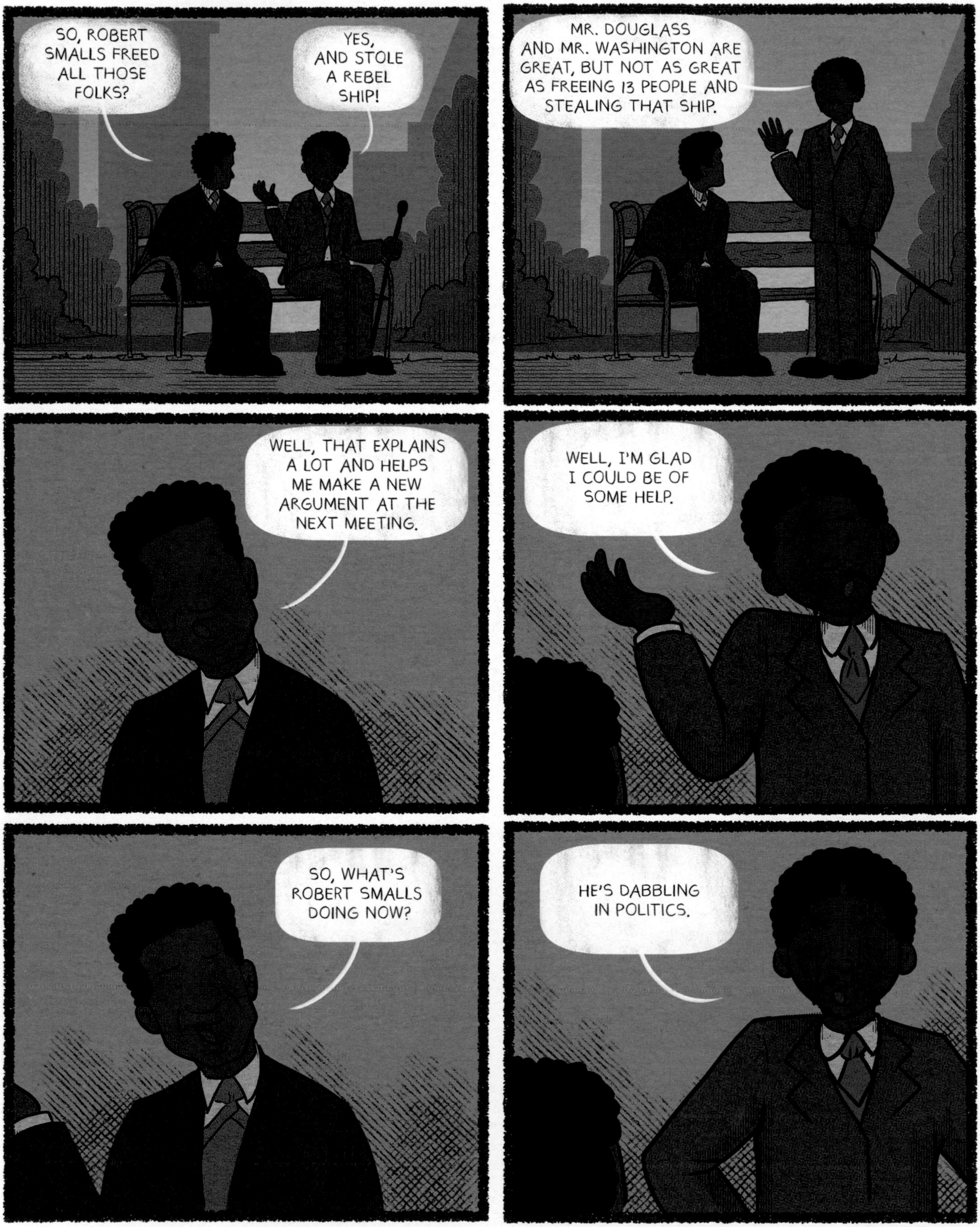
SO, ROBERT SMALLS FREED ALL THOSE FOLKS?
YES, AND STOLE A REBEL SHIP!
MR. DOUGLASS AND MR. WASHINGTON ARE GREAT, BUT NOT AS GREAT AS FREEING 13 PEOPLE AND STEALING THAT SHIP.
WELL, THAT EXPLAINS A LOT AND HELPS ME MAKE A NEW ARGUMENT AT THE NEXT MEETING.
WELL, I'M GLAD I COULD BE OF SOME HELP.
SO, WHAT'S ROBERT SMALLS DOING NOW?
HE'S DABBLING IN POLITICS.

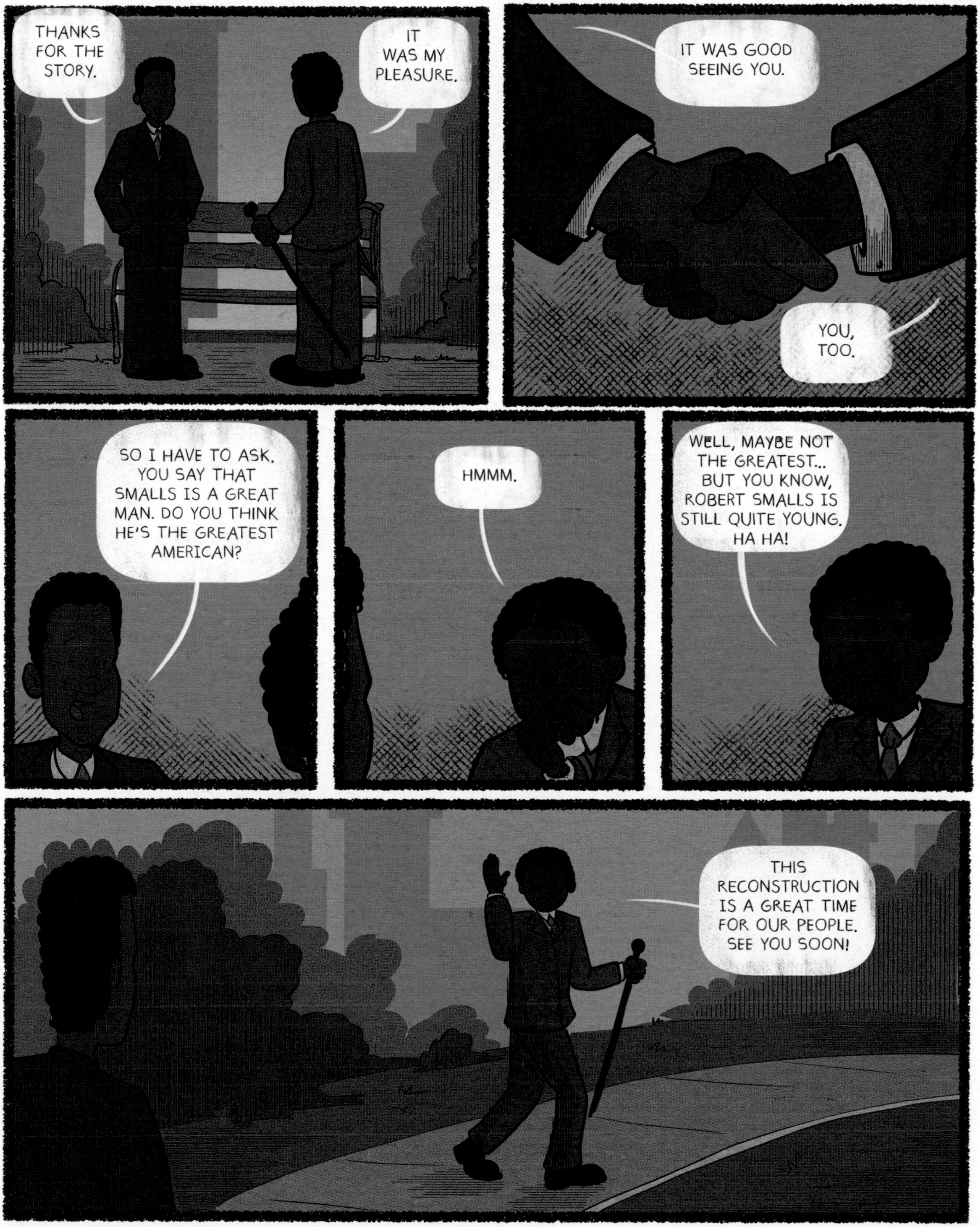
THANKS FOR THE STORY.
IT WAS MY PLEASURE.
IT WAS GOOD SEEING YOU.
YOU, TOO.
SO I HAVE TO ASK. YOU SAY THAT SMALLS IS A GREAT MAN. DO YOU THINK HE'S THE GREATEST AMERICAN?
HMMM.
WELL, MAYBE NOT THE GREATEST... BUT YOU KNOW, ROBERT SMALLS IS STILL QUITE YOUNG. HA HA!
THIS RECONSTRUCTION IS A GREAT TIME FOR OUR PEOPLE. SEE YOU SOON!

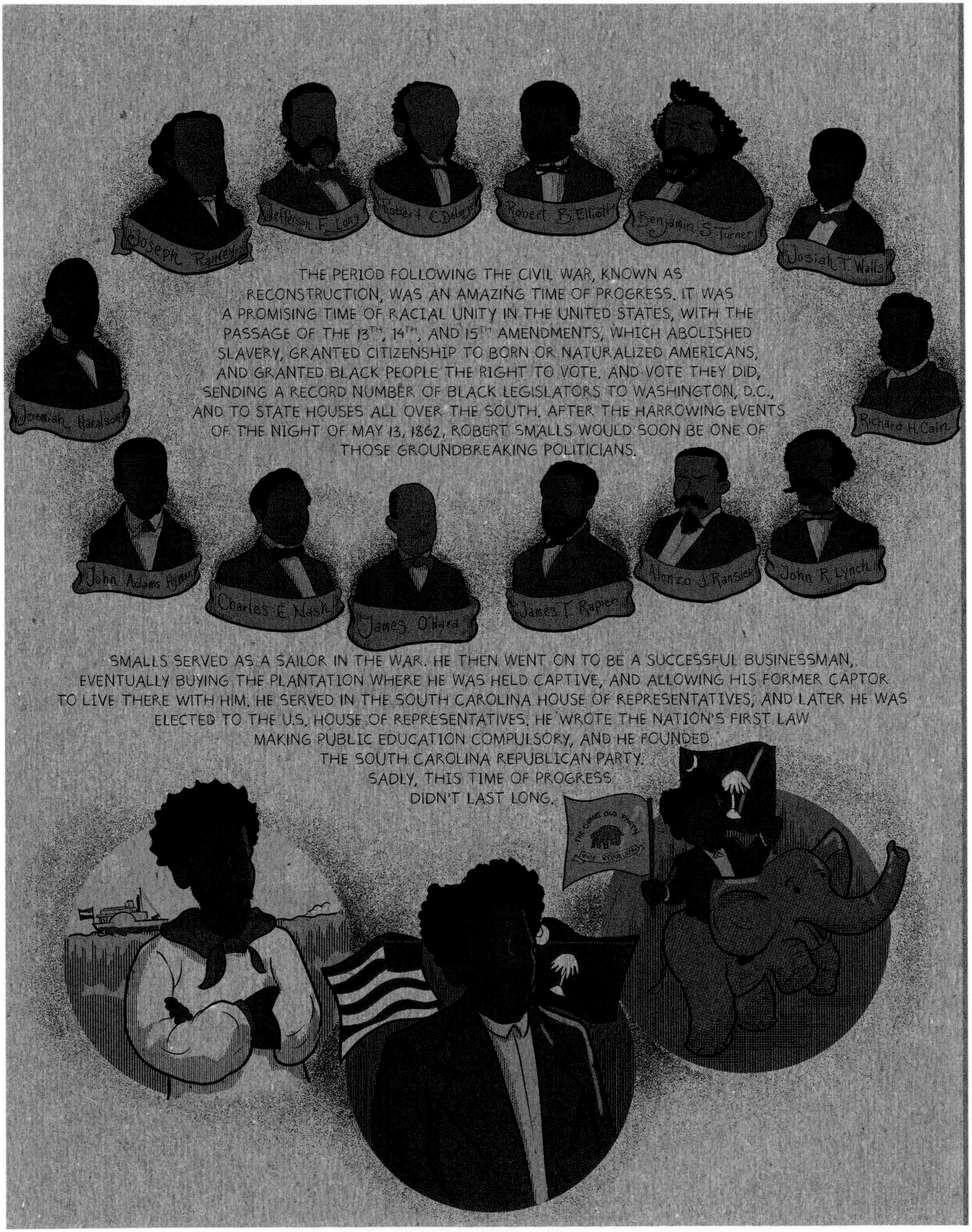
Joseph Rainey
Jefferson F. Long
Robert C. DeLarge
Robert B. Elliott
Benjamin S. Turner
Josiah T. Walls
THE PERIOD FOLLOWING THE CIVIL WAR, KNOWN AS RECONSTRUCTION, WAS AN AMAZING TIME OF PROGRESS. IT WAS A PROMISING TIME OF RACIAL UNITY IN THE UNITED STATES, WITH THE PASSAGE OF THE 13TH, 14TH, AND 15TH AMENDMENTS, WHICH ABOLISHED SLAVERY, GRANTED CITIZENSHIP TO BORN OR NATURALIZED AMERICANS, AND GRANTED BLACK PEOPLE THE RIGHT TO VOTE. AND VOTE THEY DID, SENDING A RECORD NUMBER OF BLACK LEGISLATORS TO WASHINGTON, D.C., AND TO STATE HOUSES ALL OVER THE SOUTH. AFTER THE HARROWING EVENTS OF THE NIGHT OF MAY 13, 1862, ROBERT SMALLS WOULD SOON BE ONE OF THOSE GROUNDBREAKING POLITICIANS.
Jeremiah Haralson
Richard H. Cain
John Adams Hyman
Charles E. Nash
James O'Hara
James T. Rapier
Alonzo J. Ransier
John R. Lynch
SMALLS SERVED AS A SAILOR IN THE WAR. HE THEN WENT ON TO BE A SUCCESSFUL BUSINESSMAN, EVENTUALLY BUYING THE PLANTATION WHERE HE WAS HELD CAPTIVE, AND ALLOWING HIS FORMER CAPTOR TO LIVE THERE WITH HIM. HE SERVED IN THE SOUTH CAROLINA HOUSE OF REPRESENTATIVES, AND LATER HE WAS ELECTED TO THE U.S. HOUSE OF REPRESENTATIVES. HE WROTE THE NATION'S FIRST LAW MAKING PUBLIC EDUCATION COMPULSORY, AND HE FOUNDED THE SOUTH CAROLINA REPUBLICAN PARTY.
SADLY, THIS TIME OF PROGRESS DIDN'T LAST LONG.

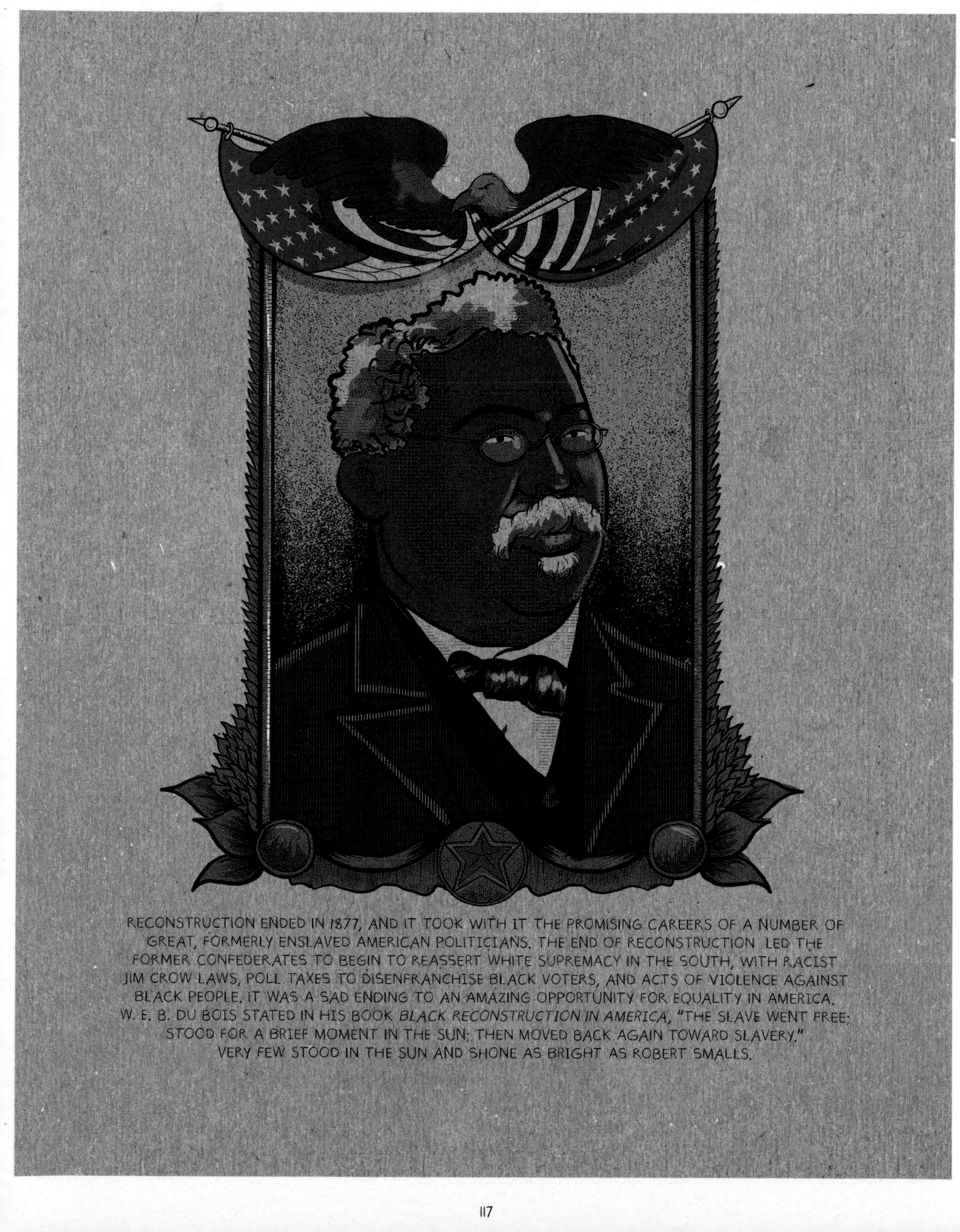

RECONSTRUCTION ENDED IN 1877, AND IT TOOK WITH IT THE PROMISING CAREERS OF A NUMBER OF GREAT, FORMERLY ENSLAVED AMERICAN POLITICIANS. THE END OF RECONSTRUCTION LED THE FORMER CONFEDERATES TO BEGIN TO REASSERT WHITE SUPREMACY IN THE SOUTH, WITH RACIST JIM CROW LAWS, POLL TAXES TO DISENFRANCHISE BLACK VOTERS, AND ACTS OF VIOLENCE AGAINST BLACK PEOPLE. IT WAS A SAD ENDING TO AN AMAZING OPPORTUNITY FOR EQUALITY IN AMERICA. W. E. B. DU BOIS STATED IN HIS BOOK *BLACK RECONSTRUCTION IN AMERICA*, "THE SLAVE WENT FREE; STOOD FOR A BRIEF MOMENT IN THE SUN; THEN MOVED BACK AGAIN TOWARD SLAVERY." VERY FEW STOOD IN THE SUN AND SHONE AS BRIGHT AS ROBERT SMALLS.

Bibliography

"Civil War USS Planter Gunboat Information." www.learningabe.info/Uss_Planter_Gunboat_info.htm. (August 10, 2020).

"Congressman Smalls of South Carolina." *Washington Chronicle*, August 1, 1876.

Edward, William, et al. *Black Reconstruction in America: An Essay toward a History of the Part Which Black Folk Played in the Attempt to Reconstruct Democracy in America, 1860–1880*. Oxford: Oxford University Press, 2007.

Evans, Marshall. *The Wheelman: How the Slave Robert Smalls Stole a Warship and Became King*. Spartanburg, South Carolina: Land's Ford Publishing, 2015.

Gallagher, Gary W, and Nolan, Alan T. *The Myth of the Lost Cause and Civil War History*. Bloomington Indiana University Press, 2010.

Gates, Jr., Henry Louis. "The African Americans: Many Rivers to Cross." www.pbs.org/wnet/african-americans-many-rivers-to-cross/history/which-slave-sailed-himself-to-freedom/. November 6, 2013.

Gates, Jr., Henry Louis. "Robert Smalls, from Escaped Slave to House of Representatives" | *African American History Blog*.

Levith, Will. "The Incredible Story of Robert Smalls, and His Flight to Freedom." *InsideHook*, www.insidehook.com/article/history/enslaved-man-stole-confederate-ship-sailed-freedom. June 7, 2017.

Lineberry, Cate. *Be Free or Die: The Amazing Story of Robert Smalls' Escape from Slavery to Union Hero*. New York: St. Martin's Press, 2017.

Lineberry, Cate. "The Thrilling Tale of How Robert Smalls Seized a Confederate Ship and Sailed It to Freedom." *Smithsonian*, Smithsonian.com, June 13, 2017.

Moore, Michael B. "The Audacity of Robert Smalls | TEDxStMarksSchool." youtu.be/w6T7ksyhUkw. November 6, 2015.

"Robert Smalls House." Discoversouthcarolina.com, discoversouthcarolina.com/products/3544. (August 10, 2020).

Rowland, Tim. "It's not your grandfather's Civil War: the National Park Service used the sesquicentennial to shed new light on an old story." *America's Civil War*, vol. 28, no. 2, May 2015, p. 42+.

"SMALLS, Robert | US House of Representatives: History, Art & Archives." @USHouseHistory, 2020, history.house.gov/People/Detail/21764.

"The Steamer 'Planter' and Her Captor," *Harper's Weekly*, vol. 6, pp. 372, 14 June 1862 (Courtesy of Library of Congress).

Stodghill, Ron. "In Charleston, Coming to Terms With the Past." *International New York Times*, November 15, 2016. SPN. SP24, https://link.gale.com/apps/doc/A470802680/SPN.SP24?u=mlin_b_bpublic&sid=SPN.SP24&x.

Thomas-Lester, Avis. "Civil War Hero Robert Smalls Seized the Opportunity to Be Free." *Washington Post*, March 2, 2012.

Praise for Joel Christian Gill

"Joel Christian Gill is a modern-day graphic griot. His mastery of visual storytelling coupled with his tireless research make him one of the most important artist/scholars working today."

— John Jennings, Eisner-nominated comics scholar and award-winning graphic novelist, in praise for the *Tales of the Talented Tenth* series

"Joel Christian Gill gives Robert Smalls the adventure genre treatment that he deserves. We need so much more of what Gill consistently delivers."

— Rebecca Wanzo, author of *The Content of Our Caricature: African American Comic Art and Political Belonging*

"Gill's graphic novel series is a tool with which to discuss African Americans, social justice, and a shared history."

— *The Philadelphia Tribune*

"Still more thoughtful reflections come from Joel Christian Gill's graphic novel *Strange Fruit: Uncelebrated Narratives from Black History*, which unpacks its power through drawings and pointed text that chronicle the trials and triumphs of black Americans who struggled against prejudice more than a century ago. At a moment when racial inequities have ignited this nation, Mr. Gill offers direction for the road ahead from the road behind."

— *The New York Times*

"By the time I finished reading *Strange Fruit*, I thought, let the comic-book sellers have their mythic superheroes; through Joel Gill, we can have our own. But, instead of flying around in capes or spinning webs, the superheroes in *Strange Fruit* are extraordinary-ordinary black folks making - 'a way out of no way.' The difference: they really lived."

— Dr. Henry Louis Gates Jr.

Alphonse Fletcher University Professor, Harvard University

"Gill's book [*Strange Fruit*] fills a definite void in America's painfully white history books, but on top of that, it's just a really good read. Gill doesn't sugarcoat — not everyone gets a happy ending — but the book is visually witty, engaging, and well researched. History truly comes to life under Gill's skillful hand."

— *Foreword Reviews*

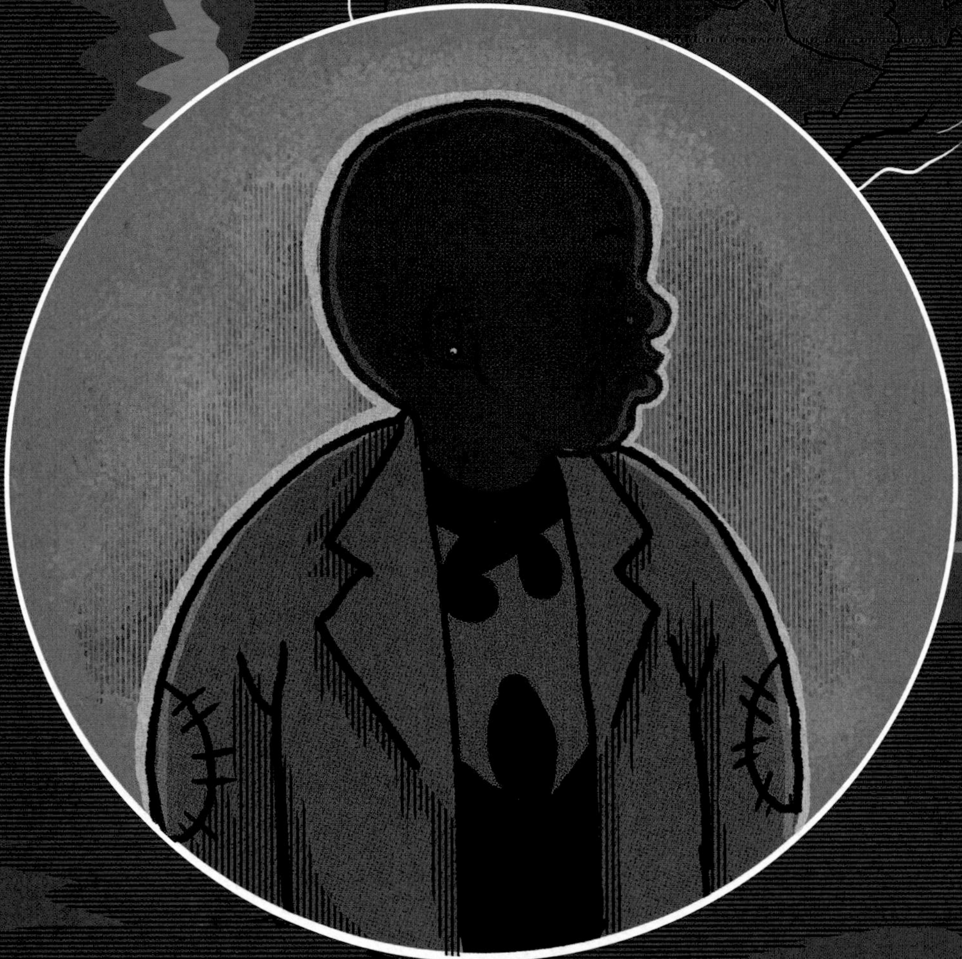

Joel Christian Gill is a cartoonist, historian, and Associate Professor of Illustration at Massachusetts College of Art and Design. He wrote the words and drew the pictures in the series *Strange Fruit* and *Tales of The Talented Tenth*. His latest work is a memoir chronicling how children deal with abuse and trauma: *Fights: One Boy's Triumph Over Violence*. He is currently adapting into a graphic novel the 2016 National Book Award-winning *Stamped from the Beginning: a Definitive History of Racist Ideas in America* by Professor Ibram X. Kendi. Gill has dedicated his life to creating stories to build connections with readers through empathy, compassion, and ultimately humanity. He received his MFA from Boston University and his BA from Roanoke College.

Visit his website at joelchristiangill.wordpress.com or connect with him on Twitter (@jcg007). Gill believes that 28 days are not enough when it comes to Black History. Join the discussion on social media by following Joel's #28DaysAreNotEnough, his call-to-action about Black History.